BX

D0845027

PSYCHOTHERAPY

THE LISTENING VOICE

Rogers and Erickson

Richard A. Leva, Ph.D.

Associate Professor of Psychology
Fredonia State University College
Fredonia, New York

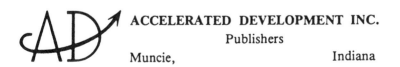

ACCELERATED DEVELOPMENT INC.
Publishers
Muncie,   Indiana

Library of Congress Number: 87-70346

International Standard Book Number: 0-915202-68-9

Technical Development: Virginia Cooper
Tanya Dalton
Marguerite Mader
Sheila Sheward

For additional copies order from

ACCELERATED DEVELOPMENT Inc., PUBLISHERS
3400 Kilgore Avenue, Muncie, IN 47304
(317) 284-7511

DEDICATION

To Abel, Guiseppe, Carl, Milton, Marcel, and Gianfranco without whom this Italian's renaissance could not have happened, and to Judy, Tracy, and Anthony.

PREFACE

When Milton Erickson died in 1980, he took with him one of the most fertile minds to study human behavior in the history of psychotherapy. Erickson's insights into how people think, change, grow, and pattern their lives have become landmarks in the field of individual and family psychotherapy.

He was the foremost hypnotherapist in the 20th century, and his contributions to this field were enormous. The popularity of his methods and ideas in psychotherapy and hypnosis is demonstrated by the attendance of over 2,000 therapists from all over the world at both the 1980 and 1984 International Congresses of Ericksonian Psychotherapy.

Fortunately, Erickson's death did not put an end to the dissemination and development of his ideas. In the last twenty years of his life, he held many teaching seminars throughout the country and in his home, and a number of therapists studied intensely with him. Among these (all of whom have written important works about Erickson and his ideas alone or in collaboration with Erickson) were Ernest Rossi, Jeffery Zeig, and Sidney Rosen, to name just a few.

We are quite fortunate not only to have the legacy of Erickson's own work, which is quite extensive, but many books written by his disciples which deal with the vast array of Ericksonian innovations. These include his use of stories, metaphors, language, hypnosis, and family therapy plus specific approaches to alcoholism, obesity, schizophrenia, and smoking. Such a vast amount of writings about this one therapist can be overwhelming to someone who has an interest in the work of Milton Erickson and wishes to begin to learn Erickson's methods and incorporate them into his/her own therapeutic relationships.

My introduction to Milton Erickson's work goes back to 1970. I was a graduate student in counseling psychology at the University of Utah, and a fellow graduate student loaned me a copy of Haley's *Strategies of Psychotherapy* which describes some of Erickson's work. I was fascinated with Erickson's audacity and skill, but I dismissed the approach as unlearnable and saw his therapeutic success due mainly to Erickson's personality rather than to anything else. My first impression of Erickson (without seeing any photographs of him) was that of a tall distinguished-looking man, well dressed with graying temples and operating out of a plush New York office. While Erickson was distinguished in appearance, he was a man confined to a wheelchair, and his Pheonix office was more homey than plush.

I did try to incorporate some of Erickson's ideas in my own training at that time. This would come about when I would discuss the approach with my friend. Out of these discussions came one attempt at trying to "get the client to play the therapist's game," and in my opinion it failed miserably.

What disappoints me most about that time was that I was so close to Phoenix, and Erickson, though past his prime as a therapist, was engaged in his teaching seminars of which I was unaware.

I really did not begin to study Erickson's work again for another ten years. Around 1979, I was reintroduced to Erickson by a reference to Bandler and Grinder's *neurolinguistic programming* which is based largely upon Erickson's linguistic patterns.

With this beginning, I became aware of the vast literature of Erickson and his followers. Perhaps the timing was better now as I began to see the enormous potential in Erickson's work. I had been a counselor-educator for about ten years at that point and could see the importance of Erickson's ideas, not only in counseling but in human interaction and education.

Since that reintroduction to Erickson's work, I have emersed myself in Erickson's writings and those of his followers; and I have visited the Milton Erickson Foundation in Phoenix and attended several workshops. Throughout these experiences, I have gradually incorporated Erickson's ideas into my own counseling and teaching—but this has not been easy. Faced with the vast body of literature and dozens of training programs, where does one begin?

Most therapists unfamiliar with Erickson are hooked on at least finding out more about him after they have read or heard even one story of his unusual interactions with clients. After some initial information, if they want to learn more, the vast amount of literature can be confusing. This book focuses on Erickson's basic ideas so a therapist can learn them and work them into an already existing counseling style. However, new therapists can also benefit from this work because of the integration of

Erickson's work with Carl Rogers' person-centered approach, which is the basis for a very large percentage of the graduate training programs. Although I introduce some new ideas for counselors, the synthesis of Erickson and Rogers is probably the most important part of this work.

Erickson himself remarked about these similarities and recently two other therapists (Daniel Araoz and Hugh Gunnison) have called attention to this. Rogerian concepts for therapy are indispensible. My own feeling is that many who study Erickson forget that before successful interactions can be made, a foundation for therapy must be built. Rogers gave us the foundation, and Erickson allows the construction.

ACKNOWLEDGEMENTS

As a Rogerian I have always understood the importance of understanding and support. This book is indebted to the following people who gave both to me. First to my wife Judy. In addition to her helpful comments, she spent many hours typing and editing. The whole process was made easier because of her.

Joe Hollis' comments and editing were very helpful. In 1985, Dean David Hess and Dr. Tom Rywick of Fredonia State College gave needed encouragement by supporting my sabbatical which gave me time to research, read, and start the book.

I would also like to thank all those who gave permission to me to use their material including Daniel Araoz, Ernest Rossi, James Wilk, Ronald Havens, and William Huff. Jeff Zeig's comments about the manuscript were helpful.

Although my children's contributions are not in the professional area both of them, Tracy and Anthony, made important contributions to this book by being who they are.

Finally, to all my students whose insights, interest, questions, and ideas, provided much needed stimulation with special thanks to Susan Goulding for reading parts of the manuscript and giving valuable comments.

CONTENTS

SECTION I   PHILOSOPHY FOR CHANGE

1   WHY ERICKSON? OR ERICKSON AS MYTH 9

2   THE NATURE OF MAN AND THE GOAL OF COUNSELING 19

SECTION II READINGS IN ERICKSONIAN AND ROGERIAN THERAPY

9 TWO LEVEL COMMUNICATION AND THE MICRODYNAMICS OF TRANCE AND SUGGESTION
by Milton H. Erickson, M.D., and Ernest L. Rossi, Ph.D 137

INTRODUCTION TO CHAPTER 10 165

10 TRADITIONAL DELUSIONS VERSUS ERICKSONIAN REALITIES
by Ronald A. Havens, Ph.D. 167

SECTION III TECHNIQUES FOR CHANGE

13 BASIC FACILITATIVE SKILLS—TRANCE-ACTIONS 199

14 LAYERS OF COUNSELING: ESTABLISHING THE CORE CONDITIONS 215

17 THE USE OF SELF-REFERENCE IN ERICKSONIAN THERAPY 263

18 SELF-REFERENCE AND THE IMMEDIACY OF THE THERAPEUTIC RELATIONSHIP 277

INDEX 281
ABOUT THE AUTHOR 295

LIST OF FIGURES

LIST OF TABLES

TWO EXEMPLARY LIVES

Carl Rogers, Ph.D.

Milton H. Erickson, M.D.

TWO EXEMPLARY LIVES

February 6, 1987

Carl Rogers, Ph.D.

I have just received word that Carl Rogers has died of a heart attack in California. He was 85. So both Rogers and Erickson now are dead, but what a legacy they leave and what lives they led.

Rogers' life was indeed productive right up to the end. I last saw him one year ago in December 1985 at the "Evolution of Psychotherapy Conference" in Phoenix, Arizona organized by the Milton H. Erickson Foundation. At 84 years old, he was as active at the conference as colleagues much younger. He gave live demonstrations, workshops, and lectures. He spoke tirelessly to students and signed autographs.

Touching was the five minute standing ovation he was given by therapists from all over the world before his first presentation at that conference. But even more impressive was the story he told us of how, only recently, a difficult patient made him question his own value and worth to an extent that he himself needed understanding. Here was a man we all followed, admired, and revered; and he was risking all this by showing us his humanness and vulnerability. Was there a lesson in his story? Was he showing us how much he cared for us by giving us his trust?

Rogers did have special qualities. Without speaking to him personally you felt his warmth and caring. He was like that understanding parent or grandfather we all need. I have an audio tape which was made by Rogers that I use in my class every semester. Students listen to it and then write a two-page reaction to it. Every semester at least a half dozen or more students comment on the warmth that comes through the audio tape.

His professional life and contributions were enormous. His *New York Times* obituary points out that he is only second to Freud in his impact on psychotherapy. It may be when all is said and done that his impact will exceed Freud's. If Freud is seen as psychotherapy's Galileo, Rogers is its Newton. Moreover, while much of Freud's ideas have never been subjected to scientific scrutiny, Rogers pioneered in researching therapy, and his outcome studies set forth a model still followed today.

He was born in 1902 in Illinois and received his Doctorate in psychology in 1931 from Columbia University. His first position was as Director of a child guidance clinic in Rochester, N.Y. Following the publication of his first book, *Clinical Treatment of the Problem Child,* he was Professor of Psychology at Ohio State University. His next book, *Counseling and Psychotherapy,* introduced more fully his then radical approach to treatment—radical because of his departure from the psychoanalytic approach which then was dominant in the field. His classic book, *Client-centered Therapy,* fully articulated his position and was published while he was Professor of Psychology at the University of Chicago. From there he went to the University of Wisconsin, and then later he formed the Center of Study of the Person at La Jolla, California.

Although Rogers maintained an everchanging growth oriented outlook, his basic ideas of warmth, genuineness, and understanding to create a therapeutic climate necessary for clients remained unchanged.

Milton H. Erickson, M.D.

Erickson's life had the fullness of Rogers, but it was not until the latter part of his life that he began to receive recognition. Erickson, while he was alive, did not enjoy the acceptance and status of his ideas as did Rogers. His ideas, nevertheless, are now at the cutting edge of psychotherapy, and while Rogers may be seen as psychotherapy's Newton, Erickson may be regarded as the field's Einstein. Rogers gave us the foundation with which to build our ideas of what is necessary in the psychotherapeutic relationship. Erickson took us beyond this into the vast inner space of the human unconscious.

Erickson practiced what he preached. He had contracted polio as a child, and at fifty-one he suffered what was probably post-polio syndrome. After his first bout with polio, he relearned to walk. In pain, because of his physical problems, he learned to ease the discomfort through self-hypnosis. These examples show that when Erickson taught people to use their own resources, he knew what he was talking about—he was there himself.

Erickson was born in 1901 and reared in Wisconsin farm country. In 1928, Erickson graduated from the University of Wisconsin and did a psychiatric internship in a Colorado hospital. This was followed by psychiatric positions in Rhode Island and Worcester State Hospital (1929-34). His first paper on hypnosis was published in 1932. From 1934 to 1948, he served as Director of Psychiatric Research at Wayne County General Hospital in Michigan, and during these years he conducted many experimental studies dealing with the nature of hypnosis.

In 1948, he took the position as Clinical Director at Arizona State Hospital, and after a second bout with polio he began his long "second" career as teacher, lecturer, therapist, and consultant.

During this next period, Erickson collaborated with others in teaching and publishing his ideas of hypnosis. Jay Haley edited his works and published a book titled *Uncommon Therapy: The Psychiatric Techniques of Milton Erickson.* In the 1970s he collaborated with others, the most important of those were Ernest Rossi and Jeffrey Zeig who published works elucidating his now-famous utilization approach to hypnosis and psychotherapy.

His last years were spent as the "Sage" of Phoenix seeing patients, and perhaps more importantly holding seminars out of which came many of his disciples who continue his work today (Erickson, 1983). He, like Rogers, worked practically up to the day he died, and he had been scheduled to appear at the first Ericksonian Conference in his honor in 1980.

Both men stressed throughout their lives the importance of being yourself—not imitating them but finding your own way. I hope I have followed their advice by combining their ideas in this book in my own way.

REFERENCES

Erickson, M.H. (1983). *Healing in hypnosis,* edited by E. Rossi, M. Ryan, and F. Sharp. New York: Irvington.

Haley, J. (1973). *Uncommon therapy, the psychiatric techniques of Milton H. Erickson, M.D.* W.W. Norton: New York, London.

Rogers, C. (1939). *Clinical treatment of the problem child.* Boston, MA: Houghton Mifflin.

Rogers, C. (1942). *Counseling and psychology: Newer concepts in practice.* Boston, MA: Houghton Mifflin.

SECTION I

PHILOSOPHY FOR CHANGE

INTRODUCTION TO SECTION I

The older I get, the more tolerant I have become especially of the beliefs and perceptions of others. I do not change my beliefs or perceptions easily but, while I may not see it your way, I now take time to see how you may have arrived at where you are.

This section deals, in part, with belief systems since, after all, what we believe certainly affects our behavior and feelings. Also views on the nature of man, new views of the unconscious, and a philosophy for change are included. Thus, this section contains chapters for the philosophical foundation of counseling and the chapters that follow.

Perhaps as this whole book is, this section is a mosiac. A work of intricate and broad ideas—together, I hope they make a picture that says much to each who views it.

Erickson in transition
(Drawing by the author)

CHAPTER 1

WHY ERICKSON
OR ERICKSON AS MYTH

Since Erickson's death the increase in the popularity of his work is quite remarkable. In 1985 an Ericksonian conference in Italy was widely attended even though the major presenters were English-speaking and the majority of the audience was Italian-speaking. A large number of new Ericksonian institutes can be found not only in the United States but in Europe, South America, Asia, and Australia. Countless books are written about him, regional workshops are held, and meetings at the International Congress bearing his name usually attracts 2,000 therapists.

Why such interest and late acceptance of a man whose work was not widely accepted during his life, even though he published numerous articles and books himself? And why interest in a man who shunned the theoretical and never really developed anything resembling a theory but rather taught in vague concepts (e.g., "You know more than you think you know")? Perhaps this beginning chapter will help explain this.

In spite of all I have read by him and about him, and see and hear of him on video and audio tapes, Erickson sometimes is still a confusing picture. Yet, I am now accustomed to seeing him as an almost constant point of departure or reference. Perhaps, in spite of his lack of theory, much is in his work to be learned, and in a way that I think he himself was trying to convey but never really communicated. What has helped me clarify for myself Erickson's role in my life have been the writings of

Gianfranco Baruchello and Henry Martin (1983, 1985). The collaboration of these two artists has resulted in two works (*How to Imagine* and *Why Duchamp*) which have had a profound effect upon how I work and see the world and also seem to have helped me to answer the above questions about Milton Erickson. Milton Erickson was the first person who began to change my thinking about five years ago, and now Baruchello's writings about the artist, Marcel Duchamp, and how Duchamp affected his thinking bears striking similarity to my study of Milton Erickson. While reading Baruchello's account of Duchamp, I was struck by the strong similarities between these two independent thinkers. The thoughts in this chapter are inspired by and draw from the two works mentioned above, and these thoughts draw a great deal from the strong parallels found between Duchamp's influence in art and Erickson's influence in psychotherapy. The basic issues in this chapter are how we can use Erickson, and what strengths does he give us.

The Confusion in Counseling and Psychotherapy and the Need for Myth

This combination of ideas from Erickson, Duchamp, and Baruchello has been an alchemy that has resulted in a newer higher form of personal awareness. The problem with the study of Erickson at this point for many is to decide whether he was just a great therapist and nothing more, a great teacher and nothing more, or will he be seen as an illusion or myth. Erickson should go down in history as a great therapist. But, can someone simply be remembered as a great therapist? Freud is not remembered only as a great therapist. This is because whether or not he was a great therapist is unimportant to his legacy. On the other hand, Freud as an illusion or myth is quite another thing.

A myth is a traditional or legendary story which contains beliefs which attempt to explain basic truths. Or, put another way, it can be a belief or subject of belief whose truth is accepted uncritically. At this point, Erickson's life and his work and its present acceptance by therapists worldwide fit the description of myth.

Erickson's Myth

That his teachings are accepted without criticism is quite striking. In all the published literature about Erickson since his death, one cannot ignore the fact that virtually no experiments have been done which evaluate any of his concepts or ideas. This is not the case for example for Rogerian ideas which have been supported by many studies. Also only a handful of papers have reviewed studies done in other areas (e.g., unconscious reading, subliminal perception) where results can be taken as support for some of Erickson's concepts.

Yet, how can we explain this vast uncritical following. When Erickson began to work, the first cracks in the walls of uncritical acceptance of Freud were beginning to appear. But those who replaced Freud (behaviorists) went to such extreme control and over-simplification that they left too many unanswered questions. Seeing this, Erickson seems to have decided to go his own way.

But the breakdown of psychotherapy, which begain in the 1930s and '40s and seemed to plateau in the '60s and '70s, seems to have culminated in the '80s. The 1985 Evolution of Psychotherapy Conferences sponsored by the Milton Erickson Foundation in Phoenix merely reinforced what we already knew—modern psychotherapy, after Freud, is in disarray. The title of one article by a national wireservice covering the conference was "The Twilight of Psychotherapy." National magazines reporting on the conference focused on the confusion of conflicting therapies and theories.

At such a time, at the end of a breakdown, is when myths and new beliefs are needed. Erickson's own personal history unfolds as a myth. What gives solid foundation to the myth are two things: Erickson's own triumph over personal illness, and the countless stories by those who worked with him which support and carry on the myth.

He lived on a farm in the Midwest, and his family is described as traditional. In his early history, he is described as "that wily American farmboy who had enough mischieviousness to outfox tragic personal illness and become a genius in healing and hypnosis" (Erickson, Rossi, Ryan, & Sharp, 1983). In the same paragraph his parents are described as pioneering, and Milton's birthplace is a three-sided log cabin—two images steeped in American mythology.

Erickson was afflicted with polio—not once, but twice (at 17 and 51). As a 17-year-old his case was so severe that he was not expected to survive. He heard the doctor announce to his mother that there was no hope for survival; and as he looked out the window to see the sunset, he had the determination to live to see one more sunrise.

While on crutches one summer, he took a canoe trip alone which began before college and ended "a robust young man with a new sense of confidence, pride, and personal independence."

These are the foundations of myth.

As a professional, especially in his later years, he conducted teaching seminars with many professionals. From these seminars and from the many people who attended them come stories which are rife with his powers of perception, use of language, and wit.

Necessity of Myth

Baruchello talks about myths in a positive way. "A myth is something alive and it has to live in the consciousness of a great many people—...and if it doesn't it's nothing, it's dead and exists as having been only a passing illusion" (Baruchello & Martin, 1985, p. 32). Milton Erickson's greatest contribution may be that he indeed does live in the consciousness of many people. The fact that I study him and am now sitting and writing of him is proof enough. So he is more than a great therapist, and he is more than just a passing illusion.

Myth is seen in this context as a positive source of energy. As Rollo May pointed out in his lectures at the Evolution of Psychotherapy Conference, all of us function by a hierarchy of myths and cultures collapse when their myths are no longer functional. Perhaps Erickson saw the need for a myth. His use of stories and metaphor attest to this, but he also saw that no longer were any myths available. Rollo May sees this lack of myths as a prevailing cause of some of the ills in our society. So perhaps Erickson began to make a myth of his own. This would be characteristic of him.

Now Erickson's myth is filling the void at this time of confusion. The titles of some of the books about him which give evidence to his mythology are, *My Voice Will Go With You: The Teaching Tales of Milton Erickson* (Rosen, 1982), and *Practical Magic* (Lankton, 1980). The feeling I have about him as myth is that he made the choice to be separate as an example. Like the artist Marcel Duchamp, Erickson used his life as a teaching tool, and what he wanted us to do, like Duchamp, was to create our own world, not to copy him but to invent our own universe. So, you then learn how you can use Erickson to create a world of your own—a world which runs alongside his. We create our own worlds anyway. The world can never really be known as it is (see Chapter 3). Our senses report to us what they think is out there. But even if they were one hundred percent accurate in their reporting, and they are not, their signals are still interpreted by our brains; and our brain, of course, is to a large degree made up of impressions and ideas of how we think the world *should be* (Baruchello & Martin, 1985).

Erickson reawakens us to what the great minds knew hundreds of years ago—that the world in which we live is largely our own invention. Erickson saw that the key to understanding people was simply to find out how they put the world together.

So theory is not where we will find Erickson's message to us (see Chapter 10). How he lived his life and how we can live ours is what really counts.

Erickson and Creative Thinking

While Carl Rogers, the fatherly figure, gave us the humanistic foundation to build upon, Erickson is the one who frees us from constraints and straight-jacket-thinking and pulls us to more creative lives and dealings with our clients.

The many existing ideas and theories about what constitutes therapy can cause anxieties and doubts about what one is doing. While this doubt can have its positive effects, it can also force people into fortresses of theory which give security but shuns exploration of new ideas.

The skill which therapists have to learn is how to live with this confusion. This world of confusion and complexity is what Erickson seems to have opened up. He opens it up and gives us the courage to do as he did—to undertake a journey with our clients. He helps us live with the contradictions and tells us that we too can take experimental journeys.

Yes, Erickson did avoid theory and explanations of what he did. He did seem vague and unresponsive at times, and this is part of the myth. But, he never seemed to need an excuse for what he did, and this is vastly important. For while some of his interventions appear audacious and even absurd, they are never capricious. Perhaps, our own insecurities are what compel us to know the why and how, but Erickson never seemed to demean his therapy with psychological explanations. Rather the key to Erickson is the realization that he was continually reminding us in all he did of what the mind can learn about itself when it learns that one of the things it can do is be totally arbitrary (Baruchello & Martin, 1985).

Being Independent

I wanted first to be another Rogers and then to be another Erickson. But the challenge isn't to be another Erickson or another Rogers but to be independent, especially in thinking. As I am a colleague and peer with other psychologists and teachers, so I want to be a peer with Erickson and Rogers. But this has nothing to do with adopting their styles. I don't have Rogers' warmth and genuineness, and I don't possess Erickson's perception and wit. I understand some Ericksonian followers have gone so far as to imitate the master to the extent that they act and speak like him. This is a mistake. They miss the importance of being a peer rather than a mere imitation. To be their peers is to do what you do honestly and to adopt a way of living with rules by which you have decided to live. Be yourself, isn't this what they have been telling us all along? But, you can adopt them as partners. When you do this, you realize that it's not technique that matters but to be an artist in your life and work. In my case, I have adopted three partners: Milton Erickson, Marcel Duchamp, and Carl Rogers. You begin to look at people in a different way than you have been; and when you do, you begin to attach new meanings and insights. This gives you a new outlook with renewed energy (Baruchello & Martin, 1985). Baruchello eloquently described this process and the pioneering spirit of Marcel Duchamp in the following passage.

Duchamp was the first great volunteer in the experiment of living and dealing with contradiction like those people who make a living and profession putting out fires in oil wells. I mean, there is always somebody who describes to you and does things that are practically unimaginable for everybody else. Maybe the people who put out fires in oil wells do it for money, but there are always those audacious types of individuals who do things out of solitude, or, originality, or because of some other kind of bizarreness, and they express themselves in ways that don't have the comfort or the approval of anyone but themselves. And that's the sort of person I think Duchamp as having been. (Baruchello & Martin, 1985, p. 103).

And that's the sort of person I think of Erickson as having been.

This book is a culmination of the study of Milton Erickson, Carl Rogers, and Marcel Duchamp. The chapters all lead to the ultimate goal in answer to the question, *"How can I be more effective as a therapist, as an artist, in relating to other humans."* One of the ways is to begin to see one's interactions as artistic creations.

Infusing Counseling with Art

What you initially discover through an Ericksonian way of thinking, and Rogers thought his way too, is to deny the need for a set theory in dealing with clients. Both have stressed the need to treat each client as unique. This is hard to do because theory, no matter how irrelevant, gives us security and the illusion of success. But it's how you live as a therapist, how you do therapy that is important. Could it be anything else? Certainly not theory. Ruesch (1961) said, "Self realization can be encouraged if the therapist has a profound knowledge not of therapeutic formulations but of people and their personal experience." The question is to learn how to extract benefits from experiences and also teach clients this. To do so is an artistic approach.

The word art could easily be replaced by the word psychotherapy in the following passage from Baruchello and Martin's "How to Imagine":

> When people say that something is art what they probably mean is nobody is being amused by it. That's really such an empty way of looking at things. People are blind to all metaphors that are really fundamental to art. But a process of growth, or a procedure of survival, a procedure of perception, a procedure that also offers some sort of remedial to psychic suffering and that's involved in the physical nutrition of the body as well, this kind of experience is at one and the same time very, very complex and extremely simple, and complex and physically simple, it's a question of things you hear, and smells you smell, of things you see and your sense of rhythm of you breathing, all of this has an extremely powerful pertinence to art. (1983, p. 145)

Baruchello went on to explain that what he was attempting to find is an interior "search for power." This metaphor works also for psychotherapy as it does for art:

> Art is a question of reappropriating yourself, of making a restitution. I'm searching out something that everybody feels a need to have; I'm simply looking for things that can give me energy and motivation. I'm trying to fill myself with so much force. So much interior power that my way of looking at things will become inevitably stronger and stronger and even more completely articulated. (1983, p. 147)

Isn't this what Erickson and Rogers extracted from their clients? Let me try to clarify. Therapy is not anything you want it to be, but I'm trying to advocate that psychotherapy, as well as living itself, needs to be infused with the artist's perceptions. Most therapists (especially behaviorists) would disagree, but taking psychotherapy from science to art is an advance. "In the world of categories, the category of art is the higher category with respect to science" (Baruchello & Martin, 1983).

The problem we run into as psychotherapists is that we are still scientists, and because of this we are always being reductive. Scientists always reduce something to something else. We are always reducing our clients to something else. It's time the divisions in our field admit that none have the final truth. I refer again to the extreme divergence of ideas evident at the Evolution of Psychotherapy Conference.

Baruchello and Martin (1985) asked us to consider that science has failed in many of its promises and that it's a necessity to use an artistic viewpoint in approaching our problems.

> At the very least, an artist running an oil refinery might be counted on to make it smell a little less awful, and it wouldn't be allowed to be such a hazard for the health of the people who work in it. An artist would probably run it to make it produce a little less. (Baruchello & Martin, 1983, p. 152)

By incorporating our field into art, we would be asking ourselves a whole different set of questions, and we would see ourselves in a much different way. This is part of Erickson's legacy.

We adopt the idea that we are going to operate at a new and different level of consciousness, and you look for what is human in endeavors. Baruchello and Martin (1983) believed that, "Art is the only form of activity through which man can manifest himself as a real individual." And I would add to this that art is the only way to infuse our profession with ways to lead our clients to be individuals.

Look at this whole thing from another perspective which after all is the major emphasis of this book. What Duchamp, Erickson, and Rogers have done is to take us to a new level of awareness. They help us see the relationship between things—that everything relates at some level. By enlisting them as partners, they give us a sense of freedom and perhaps even the confidence that allows us to be ourselves and to try things.

REFERENCES

Baruchello, G., & Martin, H. (1983). *How to imagine.* New Paltz, NY: Documentext—McPherson & Company.

Baruchello, G., & Martin, H. (1985). *Why Duchamp.* New Paltz, NY: Documentext—McPherson & Company.

Erickson, M., Rossi, E., Ryan, M., & Sharp, F. (Eds.). (1983). *Healing in hypnosis* (Vol. 1). New York: Irvington Publishers.

Lankton, S. (1980). *Practical Magic.* Cupertino, CA: Meta Publications.

Rosen, S. (Ed.). (1982). *My voice will go with you: The teaching tales of Milton Erickson, M.D.* New York: W.W. Norton.

Ruesch, J. (1961). *Therapeutic communications,* p. 290. New York: W.W. Norton.

CHAPTER 2

THE NATURE OF MAN AND THE GOAL OF COUNSELING

While dozens of different models of counseling and psychotherapy have been developed over the past fifty years, these models generally adhere to one of three basic philosophies with respect to the nature of man. A philosophy of man's nature (something we all carry with us but may not be able to state explicitly) dictates in many ways our perceptions of how emotional and psychological difficulties develop, and how to help people if they come to us because of personal problems.

While Erickson never explicitly stated his philosophy, one can clearly deduct from his writing that his ideas were very similar to Rogers' (See Chapter 12) and both were fundamentally humanistic. We can more clearly see Erickson's and Rogers' philosophy if we contrast them with the other two major schools—the Freudians and behaviorists. A brief overview of Freud should also help us because Erickson freely used the concept of the unconscious in his work, and his view of the unconscious (as well as Rogers') was so radically different from Freud's. In addition, this chapter introduces a concept not usually found in Ericksonian literature—a global goal of counseling.

---

[1]This text takes the position that no difference exists between counseling and psychotherapy and that either word refers to the same process.

Psychoanalytic Viewpoint

The psychoanalytic view of the nature of man is, of course, mostly represented by Sigmund Freud (1856-1939). Freud's, and the behaviorist's, view of human nature is deterministic. That is, both views carry with them the idea that all behavior is determined by forces which are either external or internal to the person but are essentially away from his/her control.

From the psychoanalytic viewpoint, behavior is determined by internal forces which are largely unconscious. These forces consist of instincts and biological drives with which we are born and motivations we develop through relationships in childhood and interactions with significant others.

Personality

The psychoanalytic view of personality is complex. It consists of three parts: id (the biological component), ego (the psychological component) and superego (the sociological-psychological component). These three components work as a unit and behavior is a result of interaction of the three.

Id is the unconscious part of the personality, and it is what we inherit when we are born. It is unconscious and remains so always and consists at birth of drives toward sex and aggression. It has been referred to as a seething cauldron of energy that constantly seeks expression. However, because of environmental and societal constraints, release of these drives cannot be expressed at any and every moment, so another part of the personality must develop with the role of delaying expression and gratification of the id's energies within societal guidelines. This results in development of the ego. Ego is the conscious part of the personality concerned with thinking and the rational part of the personality. It also gives us a personal sense of ourselves and is involved in planning and remembering.

The superego is the final key part of the personality system. It is the result of growth and learning which largely reflects the morals, values, ethics, and taboos of the society. Superego can be understood as what we refer to as conscience. It works through the ego and strives to do the same as ego, mainly to hold the id and its drives in check.

Freud's View of the Unconscious

Perhaps Freud's greatest contribution was his "discovery" of the unconscious. For Freud, all behavior originated in the unconscious and was a result of either internal pressures of expression of a drive (hunger, sex) or the result of childhood interactions with significant others (parents) which later results in adult behaviors (going to school to please Mommy).

Freud's view of the unconscious was extreme and expressed the view that *all* behavior was determined and the result of unconscious drives and patterns. Therefore, according to this view, we can never know why we do what we do. We will compare Freud's concept of the unconscious with Erickson's extensively in Chapter 4. But for now, suffice to say that Freud's vision of it was negative. The pressures emanating from it were always in its primitive and base interests and for self gratification.

Psychological Maladjustment. Difficulties arise when the ego is unable to handle pressure from the id for gratification or unresolved conflicts or memories are threatening to push into conscious awareness. Finding what has been repressed and what conflicts reside in the unconscious is the key for therapy.

Behaviorist View

While the psychoanalytic model points toward internal determinants of behavior, the behavioral model is just as deterministic, but it points toward external determinants of behavior.

Freud's psychoanalysis dominated psychological thought early in the 20th Century, but behaviorism became a chief rival in the 1930s and 1940s and remains a dominant force in psychology.

The behaviorist's perspective is organized around the central theme of learning in human behavior. Behaviorists also have emphasized scientific research to obtain data.

The beginning of behaviorism starts actually in Russia when Ivan Pavlov (1844-1936), a Russian physiologist, discovered the *conditioned reflex*. He demonstrated that a dog could be conditioned to salivate to a neutral stimulus (bell) after the stimulus had been regularly accompanied by food. This *classical conditioning model* was developed to its fullest by

American psychologist, J.B. Watson (1878-1958), who is considered the father of American behaviorism.

Watson emphasized the role of learning in the development of behavior and he felt it was the key to understanding how people act as they do. So important was learning in the development of behavior that Watson said he could take a healthy child and make him/her whatever the parent wanted by utilizing behaviorist principles.

Watson's approach dominated psychology in the 30s and 40s and placed heavy emphasis on the role of external factors in the development of human behavior.

While Watson was studying the conditioned reflex, other psychologists in the behaviorist school were discovering other human learning principles. The chief investigator was B.F. Skinner (b. 1904). Skinner found that in addition to the conditioned reflex, behavior was also a result of the consequences it produced. That is a behavior that was rewarded (reinforced) tended to be repeated, while a behavior that was not followed by a reinforcer or was punished, tended to decrease or was not likely to be repeated.

Skinner labeled this type of learning instrumental or operant conditioning. His name for this type of learning was chosen to emphasize that behavior was learned through a series of acts or operations on the environment and whether these behaviors continued or not was a function of the consequences of the behaviors.

Psychological Maladjustment. Difficulties arise when people have learned behaviors which are not in their best interests. Since all behavior is learned then, seeking causes in the unconscious for difficulties is unnecessary. Replacing old unwanted behaviors with new productive ones through a system of rewards and punishment is how readjustment takes place.

Humanistic View

Humanistic psychology is the term given to the "3rd force" in psychological thought in contrast to the psychoanalytic and behavioral views.

Although not recognized as a school until the 1960s, humanistic psychology actually has its roots in the 1930s and can be traced to the writings of Gordon Allport (1887-1971) and Abraham Maslow (1908-1970). Unlike other schools of psychology, humanistic psychology advocates an attitude or orientation for psychology as a whole.

Humanistic psychology grew largely as a reaction against the predominance of the psychoanalytic and behavioral schools views that human beings responded to and were shaped by various determining tendencies that impinged upon them from within and without.

As we have seen, the psychoanalytic view sees the importance of biological drives within the organism as determining behavior while the behaviorists emphasize the role of reinforcers as externally controlling behavior. Because the humanistic position is the one adhered to in this book, a description of the three principles in the humanistic position is presented in the following paragraphs.

1. Importance of Experience. Humanistic psychology is strongly phenomenological or experiential. The starting point is conscious experience.

According to this position, conscious experience provides important data for the psychologist. For a large part, the extreme behaviorists had ruled out conscious or subjective experience as something worthy of study. According to the humanistic view, each person has a right to his/her unique feelings and point of view. The humanist tries to retain an empathetic view and maintains that ''reality'' is a subjective experience.

2. Drive Towards Growth. Theorists such as Rogers, Allport, Maslow, and Erickson saw the essential motivation in man as drive toward unity, growth, and wholeness. Maslow has labeled this drive as self actualization. Allport described it as becoming. Man is never complete but always in a process of utilizing potentials and becoming more and more whole. This has vast implications for therapy.

3. Freedom. While acknowledging that man has limits, humanistic psychology insists that human beings retain an essential freedom and autonomy.

This view also holds that people can at the very least attempt to transcend limits. That is, they can choose their attitudes toward limits and conditions imposed upon them.

Psychological Maladjustment. While man's essential drive is toward growth and development, this may be thwarted by societal demands and cultural proscriptions. Often a group's goals can be different from an individuals (e.g., a person's creativity may be thwarted in large organization). Moreover, we are constantly bombarded with messages that compete with our internal ones and in fact may go against our drive towards growth (e.g., accumulate materials rather than satisfy needs for warmth, love, truth, beauty).

When the natural drive toward self-actualization is thwarted, we have frustration and maladjustment ensues.

FREEDOM, SELF ACTUALIZATION, AND THE GOAL OF COUNSELING

Let us look more closely at the fundamental issue of freedom versus determinism. Is a person free to do as he/she chooses, or is one's life determined and merely a pawn in the hand of fate? This is a philosophical issue and one that does not seem likely to be resolved in the near future. But the issue is important for anyone who is involved in the counseling profession.

Behaviorists see individuals as not being free. One only has to see the title of one of Skinner's texts to realize his position. In "Beyond Freedom and Dignity" (1971), he argued that it is time we realized we are controlled by external stimuli so that we can start to use these controls for a better world. To Skinner and many behaviorists, freedom is an illusion.

The psychoanalytic view is quite similar except that the control was not external but internal. Freud was quite explicit on this. He offered little hope of freedom from our unconscious instincts. The only hope we did have, according to him, was to gain some control of our unconscious through understanding as a result of psychoanalysis.

Without doubt both positions offer some degree of "truth," the question is, do we have any choice in our behaviors? And, if the truth is that we have no choice, why bother with therapy; or for that matter, why bother at all? This brings to mind a response by one of my students in a seminar on humanistic psychology. We were discussing Eric Fromm's book, *You Shall be as Gods* (1977). One concept with which we were dealing was the existence of an afterlife and the idea of glory or punishment after death depending on how one lived. This student felt that people had to believe that a God exists, and that God would punish us for our transgressions. Otherwise, why would people not do just as they pleased?

For her to find that some people in the seminar, in fact, did not believe in a God or any sort of afterlife but felt as humans they had a responsibility to act in a way as human as possible was a relevation. Internally they felt it was wrong to do certain things. This seems to imply choice, and with choice comes freedom. I choose to act in a way that is consistent with my values. I choose not to hurt others not for fear of punishment but because it is inconsistent with *my* values.

Western Jurisprudence as a Philosophy of Freedom

One has only to look at our court system to see that we operate on the principle of personal freedom. When a court sentences a person to a 10-year jail term for drugs and/or robbery to obtain drugs, it does so on the basis of this person's freedom not to have chosen the life and behaviors he/she did. Not much of external socio-economic factors are taken into consideration. To the court, very little or any difference is made if the person was born of a broken home and in a slum with little chance of education.

Nor are the person's unconscious drives considered or little attention would be given to his/her internal state unless he/she was seen to be psychotic. Our court system clearly sees an individual as free to choose between wrong and right.

Humanistic Existential Philosophy of Freedom

But even the evidence for freedom is not as compelling as the humanistic-existential philosphy by such writers as Frankl, Allport, Maslow, May, and Fromm who in varying ways see individuals as creatures of at least limited choice who can, in a given circumstance, choose among alternatives to act in a way that could be beneficial to self and perhaps to others.

I think Allport's (1955) view best expresses the humanistic philosophy of man's freedom. Allport presented two different examples of one's freedom as shown through choice. For example, he talked about freedom depending on the possession of multiple possibilities for behavior—the more possible behaviors you have in a situation, the more choice.

Also convincing is his argument of one being reflective in that he/she can think about behaviors before one acts.

> Centering attention upon an impulse often brings with it a strong desire to perform the impulsive act. "The evil I would not, that I do." This law of "reversed effort" is familiar to us all. And, at this level, freedom often seems to be a cruel illusion. But, when I stop cracking my knuckles and become momentarily reflective, asking myself whether, "on the whole," this is the course of action I want to take, the picture is changed. The very act of asking, "on the whole" brings with it a lessened strain and opens new pathways of decision. (Allport, 1955, p. 85)

One cannot ignore the reflective part of people when considering the issue of freedom. If I have an alternative of just two choices, and both of them are negative, this still implies choice. This philosophy is developed very well by Victor Frankl.

Frankl and Freedom

Vicktor Frankl spent World War II in a Nazi concentration camp. This brutal experience had a profound influence on him, and from these experiences, he developed his concepts of *Logotherapy.*

Frankl's discovery is that people are free, free to choose how they will live no matter what the circumstances.

One cannot imagine a more horrible condition of living than in a concentration camp. All humanness is gone; people are treated like animals. All is chaos; no humanistic rules exist. A behavior punished today may be rewarded tomorrow. How does one live under these conditions?

For Frankl, the key was that even in these brutal circumstances one had a choice—to live like a human being or live like an animal. A person always has a choice to rise above the circumstance in which he/she finds self.

Frankl uses the term *self-transcendence* to describe this behavior of which he thinks all people are capable: to transcend or go beyond the constraints of the situation. To transcend even our own confining thoughts and limitations.

Other humanistic theorists describe this ability in different ways. Maslow talked about *self-actualization*. Fromm saw it as transcending our present status and becoming more fully human. Essentially, however, they have said that to be human is to have choice and within this we are offered the ultimate choice to grow and develop.

Drive Towards Self-Actualization

Frankl's experiences pointed towards the ability of one to transcend the most extraordinary circumstances and to reach levels of psychological compassion and empathy that go far beyond ordinary daily functioning. And his writings (1963) teach us that individuals have within themselves the capacity to transcend his environment. Frankl, like Abraham Maslow and Rogers, see one's basic drive as a drive toward growth. A number of terms have been used (e.g., self-actualization, self-realization), but they all point to the same drive.

According to Rogers (1961):

Whether one calls it a growth tendency, a drive toward self-actualization, or a forward-moving directional tendency, it is the mainspring of life, and is, in the last analysis, the tendency upon which all psychotherapy depends. It is the urge which is evident in all organic and human life—to expand, extend, become autonomous, develop, mature—the tendency to express and activate all the capacities of the organism, to the extent that such activation enhances the organism or the self. This tendency may become deeply buried under layer after layer of encrusted psychological defenses; it may be hidden behind elaborate facades which deny its existence; but it is my belief that it exists in every individual, and awaits only the proper conditions to be released and expressed. (p. 35)

Such a view gives us the key to what should be the global goal of counseling. This view, when contrasted with the deterministic and negative view of human nature, tells us that not only do we have some freedom of choice, but that within each of us are the potentials to make us all high-functioning, productive human beings.

Goal of Counseling:
Self-Actualization

Patterson (1974), in his excellent work on relationship therapy, proposed that the ultimate goal of counseling is self-actualization. While counselors, of course, help clients deal with short-term immediate goals such as getting rid of phobias, dealing with emotional disturbances, getting an education, ultimately the counselor's role is to help clients begin to reach their full potential—to be all they are capable of becoming—self-actualization.

The goal of counselors then is to help people unlock this unconscious potential. Such a goal is preferred because it does not try to fit people into societal pigeonholes. Rogers, as well as Erickson, is noted for acceptance of this view, and Erickson also tried to point this out to clients in his sessions: "When you stop to think about it, nobody does know his capacities" (Erickson & Rossi, 1976). "It is very charming, the capacity we have if we'll only learn to use the other areas of our brain" (Taped lectures ASCH, 1965).

Rogers has supported such a view all his life. In *On Becoming a Person* (1961) his ideas of the fully functioning person are very similar to the self-actualizing description of Maslow. As for the role of the counselor, Rogers saw the developing of the relationship to provide clients with atmospheres to discover within themselves the capacity to use the relationship for growth. He wrote, "Whether one calls it a growth tendency, a drive towards self-actualization or a forward moving directional energy, it is the mainspring of life, and is, in the last analysis the tendency upon which all psychotherapy depends" (p. 35).

But what is this illusive term? What is a self-actualizing person? The clearest statement of this was made by Maslow, and this was due to his study of self-actualizing people (Maslow, 1970). In an intensive study, Maslow found fourteen characteristics which distinguished self-actualizing people from the normal population. While they did not possess all fourteen characteristics, they had a large portion of them.

Characteristics of Self-Actualizing People

1. *More efficient perception of reality and more comfortable relations with it.* While we can never know completely ac-

curately the world (see Chapter 3), self-actualizing people seem to have a more efficient perception of the physical world and of human interactions. The latter includes their ability to see others as they are, and they are able to detect insincerity and phoniness.

2. *Acceptance of self, others, and nature.* While not being ego-centered, they accept self and others as they are. Recognizing an imperfect world, self-actualizing people accept the imperfections in themselves and others and also in nature as part of life.

3. *Spontaneity in inner life, thoughts, and impulses.* In this sense, they are free. They feel a freedom to be spontaneous—to be whatever it is they are or are feeling at each moment. Moreover, their behavior is natural—they do not strain for effect; they are not actors to an audience or pretentious.

4. *Problem centering: Interest in problems outside themselves, have some mission in life; some task to fill.* All of Maslow's self-actualizing people had this characteristic. They all had a goal which was external. It is a mission in life.

5. *Quality of detachment, need for privacy.* Interestingly, many of his self-actualizing people did not like analysis. Parts of them were private. They also liked to be alone which implies they were comfortable with themselves.

6. *Autonomy, independence of culture and environment.* These people are not *inter*directed, they are *inner* directed. They are not dependent on the culture but dependent on themselves. They have a sense of being their own boss.

7. *Continued freshness of appreciation.* The world can be a spectacular place; the beauty of a sunset remains fresh and different to self-actualizing people.

8. *Enjoyment of peak experiences.* These experiences can help to open up horizons. It is sometimes called the mystic or oceanic experience. Maslow described it as occurring to athletes in the heat of battle where things slow down and the

person has the feeling of unlimited control and potential. The higher the degree of psychological health, the more frequent these experiences occur.

9. *Gemeinschafts gefuhl.* This is a deep sympathy and identification for mankind as a whole.

10. *Deep and profound interpersonal relations.* Self-actualizing people seem more capable of love and more capable of obliterating the ego boundaries. The love is for not what the other person can give (deficiency love) but love for the quality of the other person.

11. *Democratic character structure.* Self-actualizing people respect everyone regardless of race, color, religion, or education.

12. *Discrimination between ends and means.* They have good ethics. They focus on ends rather than means. They seem to know what's right and wrong, and in this they are inner-directed—they follow an inner voice as to what is correct behavior.

13. *Unhostile sense of humor.* Humor is an important part of insight. Laughing at oneself or seeing the humor in our plight can be therapeutic. Self-actualizing people use humor in a creative fashion—it's not humor at the expense of someone.

14. *Creativeness.* Self-actualizing people are creative. They are inventive. It doesn't have to be a painting...but being creative with one's life as a model for others would be an act of creativity.

These fourteen characteristics are realities for some. For many of use they are unrealized potentials that reside within. They are the unconscious human capacities referred to by Rogers and Erickson. These potentials are characteristically human. And while we are unique and different as individuals underneath, if you were to strip away the differences (personality traits and cultural characteristics), you would find we are all very similar. At the core, we would find the fourteen characteristics described by Maslow.

The counselor's role is to help the client reach his/her human potential as a self-actualizing person.

REFERENCES

Allport, G. (1955). *Becoming.* New Haven: Yale University Press, 85-86.

Erickson, M.H., & Rossi, E. (1976). Two level communication and the microdynamics of trance and suggestion. *American Journal of Clinical Hypnosis, 18*(3), 153-171.

Frankl, V. (1963). *Man's search for meaning.* New York: Washington Square Press.

Fromm, E. (1977). *You shall be as gods: A radical interpretation of the Old Testament and its tradition.* New York: Fawcett Book Group.

Maslow, A. (1970). *Motivation and personality, 2nd Ed.* New York: Harper and Row.

Patterson, C.H. (1974). *Relationship counseling and psychotherapy.* New York: Harper and Row. Evanston, San Francisco, London.

Rogers, C. (1961). *On becoming a person.* Boston: Houghton Mifflin, 121.

Skinner. B.F. (1971). *Beyond freedom and dignity.* New York: Alfred A. Knopf.

CHAPTER 3

TRANCE-ITIONS: A PHILOSOPHY OF CHANGE

What I'm about to try to explain is difficult. It is the belief that the world in which we live and perceive is largely our own invention. This view is held by a group called constructionist philosophers and research supports it. It also comes from such thinkers as Hume and Vico, and it holds that the objective world can never be known and that our functioning in the world depends upon our own ordering of it. Before your objections get too strong, let's look at some evidence.

Sense Distortion Experiments

Most people believe that our senses give us an immediate and accurate representation of external reality. This is the position developed by Immanuel Kant about 200 years ago. To Kant this immediate knowledge by perception is linked with knowledge and truth intuitively. Like the grasping of a solution to a problem, understanding through perception is seen as an aha! experience (Gregory & Gombrich, 1974, p. 50).

But this view is challenged when we look at some perceptual illusions which are quite common. First of all are visual distortions. Take a common everyday occurrence as looking into a mirror. Every day you do it—to comb your hair, brush your teeth, and so on. How big is the image you see of your face? How large is the reflection? If you can, test this now. Most people believe the image they see is as large as their face which can be 11 inches or larger. They are surprised to find that, depending upon how far away you are from the mirror, the image you see in the mirror is one-third to one-half the actual size of your face. You will find it interesting if you do this with any object in your line of sight. Look at the roof of a house, close one eye, and measure some distance of the roof with a pencil (height or length, and you will be surprised to learn that the image you see is quite small).

Hold this book with your right hand and close your left eye and look at the star in Figure 3.1. Now hold the book about arm's length away from your eye and move it back and forth (towards you and away) until the round black dot disappears.

Figure 3.1. The blind spot in human vision.

This blindness is produced by the fact that at the back of the retina on which pictures are projected is a spot where all the fibers leading from the front of the eye converge and form the optic nerve. At this point of convergence, no vision is possible. But yet until we do this short demonstration, you are unaware that no vision is in this part of the eye. That is, a black spot does not appear in your vision but the missing pieces are filled in.

But an even more profound phenomenon occurs every time we look at something. We see things in three dimensions, yet the image projected onto our retina is a flat plane. The brain insists on seeing things in three dimensions. "The image of (three dimensional) space around what is projected onto the retina through the lens in our eye is also flat—that is two dimensional" (Locher, 1982). The brain insists on making two dimensional pictures spatial.

While vision can be distorted, hearing also can be. In these experiments, a single word is spoken into a tape recorder and then the tape is spliced into a loop so that it can be repeated over and over without any other noise. In high volume, the word is played back 50 to 150 times, then the word changes to an alternate. After 10 to 30 repetitions, a second alternate is played. All words are meaningful and clearly perceived. The following list contains some of the words reported to a playback of a single word "cogitate": agitate, annotate, arbitrate, back and forth, brevity, candidate, can't you see, can't you stay, Cape Cod you say, card estate, cardiotape, car district, catch a tape, cavitate, cha cha che, cogitate, computate, counter tape, count to ten, God to take, God you say, got a date, got your pay, got your tape, hard to take, majesty (von Foerster, 1984).

Many other experiments and demonstrations could be presented to show that what we perceive in the world is distorted and that our experience is subjective...our brains make the images we think we perceive (Bateson, 1979).

However, more important is the fact that humans also attach meaning to their perceptions and unlike other animals they look for relationships, patterns, and the meaning of existence as the next section shows.

Reality Construction

In research reported by von Foerster (1984) the experimenter reads to a subject a list of paired numbers (e.g., 31 and 80, 72 and 15). After each pair, the subject is supposed to say whether the two numbers "fit" or not. Subjects usually want to know in what sense are these numbers supposed to "fit?"; and the experimenter explains that the task is the discovery of these rules. Subjects in these experiments assume that the task is one of trial and error and that all he can do, therefore, is start out with random responses. At first, he/she is wrong every time, but gradually the performance begins to improve, and the "correct" responses increase. The subject thus arrives at a hypothesis that. although it is not entirely correct, turns out to be more and more reliable.

What the subject does not know is that no immediate connection exists between his/her guesses and the experimenters reactions. The experimenter gives "correct" responses on the basis of the lefthand side of the bell-shaped curve. That is, slowly at first and then with increasing frequency.

This creates in the subject an assumption of the order underlying the relation between the number pairs that can be so persistent that he/she is unwilling to relinquish it even after the experimenter has told the subject that the responses were not contingent upon anything. Some subjects are convinced of having discovered a regularity of which the experimenter was unaware.

What has happened here, in these "non-contingent reward" experiments, is that the subject has invented a reality. He/she has attached meaning and order where none, in fact, exists.

Cognitive Maps

While these experiments may be surprising to some, the results are not at all unusual. In fact, this searching to find lawful relationships and meaning in the world is a deeply embedded human trait. Humans are always so engaged. Making sense out of the world when even perhaps no sense exists is a human need—to live in a world without meaning, a world of chaos, would be intolerable.

This point can be underscored by the reactions of people put to death in Nazi death camps during World War II. Those put to death for resistance and fighting back died more peacefully than those put to death for a meaningless reason (e.g., having turned their heads away from an officer). Those who resisted felt their death had meaning. The others could not tolerate the capricious and seemingly meaningless death. Yet the end result remains the same.

The fact that an objective reality does not exist is unthinkable. Most feel that as long as we take the time and use our brains, ultimately we will get to know the rules and laws of nature.

But the world out there is not accessible through direct perception as we have shown earlier in the sense distortion descriptions. Nevertheless, as Hume pointed out, humans are fond of using the word "because" as explaining causality and relationships in the world. Hume said that the because, in fact, is not verifiable. Riedl (1984) gave one of Hume's examples saying we can never say that "the stone gets warm because the sun shines," but merely that "whenever the sun shines the stone gets warm" (p. 72).

Two hundred years ago, Hume argued that causalty in the world may be nothing more than a "need of the human mind." We must, in fact, realize that the sense we make out the world is a result of our thinking or opinion and is thus an image of the world.

Philosophy of "As If"

Vaihinger, in his philosophy of "As if" in 1935 began to give us the modern focus that ultimately would become part of existential philosophy and the foundation for Rogerian and Ericksonian models of counseling and psychotherapy. Vaihinger said, "It must be remembered that the object of the world of ideas as a whole is not a portrayal of reality—this would be utterly impossible—but rather an instrument for finding our way about more easily in this world" (p. 15).

For counseling purposes, this realization, that individuals live in a world of their own creation is adapted to its fullest by Watzlawick, Beavin, and Jackson (1967) and Bandler and Grinder (1975). In their excellent study of human communication, Watzlawick et al., stated that

> reality is not something objective, unalterable, "out there" with a benign or sinister meaning for our survival, but that for all intents and purpose our subjective experience of existence is reality—reality is our patterning of something that most probably is totally beyond objective human verification. (p. 267)

Bandler and Grinder (1975) used the idea of "maps" to illustrate this point of reality construction, "we as human beings do not operate behaviorly directly upon the world, but rather we operate through a map or model (a created representation) of what we believe the world to be" (p. 7).

Importance of Human Interaction

But, if reality is nothing more than my own invention, how can common ways of responding exist? How can I interact with another human if that person's model of the world is his/her own and different from mine? Doesn't this reflect the world of mental illness? A world where communication is impossible?

Certainly cases can be made for cognitions or maps of the world shared by most members of a society of culture. Whether these cognitions are good "fits" to "reality" is irrelevant. An illustration of this is the shared belief by most members of the culture that success if insured by hard work. This is a commonly shared view of reality, especially in the United States. But this view is not widely held in other cultures.

In our culture, we have cognitive maps for individuality. But contrast this with the Japanese whose workers carry with them very different cognitions which subordinate individuality for the good of the group (company).

But, beyond these cultural beliefs, how do we avoid the problem of countless individual realities which reflect that the world is simply in my own imagination, of which I am the center? As soon as we introduce other human beings with their own realities, then the "I am the center of the universe" falls apart.

According to von Foerster (1984), "Earthlings and Venusians may be consistent in claiming to be the center of the universe, but their claims fall to pieces if they should ever get together. The...claim falls to pieces when besides me I invent another autonomous organism" (p. 59).

To von Foerster, acceptance or rejection of "I am the center of the universe" is not the issue on constructing a reality but the acceptance of the third possibility which is the relation between I and you and the reality of a "community of people." The relationship between you and me becomes a third, perhaps more important reality, especially for therapy. As we shall show later, the quality of this relationship is what plays a major role in the counseling process. But this does not rule out variability in cognitions and individual perceptions of reality within accepted unstated cultural guidelines. These separate perceptions as agents of changes are what we need to try and understand. As Rogers said,

> I think that men and women, individually and collectively, are inwardly and organismically rejecting the view of one single, culture approved reality. I believe they are moving inevitably towards the acceptance of millions of separate challenging, exciting, informative, *individual* perceptions of reality. (Carl Rogers, 1980, p. 106)

These individual perceptions and maps of the world are what gives me my individual way of operating in the world and at times may cause me difficulty.

Trance as a Metaphor for Guiding and Changing Behavior

We can now turn to a fundamental view of this book, that a form of normal "trance" guides and influences are everyday behavior, and the beliefs, patterns, or maps of the world which we carry with us daily which influence our behavior play a major role in this trance. This metaphor of trance is useful for understanding ours and other people's behavior.

Milton Erickson, whose work contributes to the basis of this book stated that trance was "a special but normal type of behavior encountered when attention and the thinking processes are directed to the body of experiential learnings acquired from and achieved in the experience of learning" (Erickson, 1970, pp. 995-997).

Similarities can be seen between Erickson's definition of trance and Bandler and Grinder's map and models of the world or Watzlawick's patterns of beliefs and suggest that we use the idea of trance as a metaphor for how people function in the world.

This metaphor helps us to look at our own and other people's behavior. It gives us clues as to how we act as we do. And if change is desired or necessary, then we know where to start—we need to change the map.

Here is an example:

Suppose you are finding your way by car, with the aid of a map. Then you find you are lost. Some error has occurred—why has the error occurred? The car has not broken down, and you managed to control it without difficulty. The trouble could be: (a) you followed an incorrect route on the map; (b) the map was incorrect. Now there could be many reasons for missing your way on the map. But suppose the map is wrong. Suppose that the road system has changed since the map was printed. You are now dealing with the present according to a true record of the past, but the world has in the meantime changed. Now this kind of error is bound to occur when the world changes, if the present has to be dealt with in terms of scored information of the past. This is not a mechanical error, and it is inevitable whatever the mechanism employed to carry out the strategy be it map, computer or brain. (Gregory & Gombrich, 1974, p. 56)

And so it is with cognitive maps and strategies we use in our daily lives. When these are not productive, when they don't get us where we want to go, then the map needs to be changed.

This idea is not a new one, but it needs to be refocused. Epictetus, a 1st century A.D. philosopher, told us the things themselves do not trouble us, but our opinions which we have about things.

Araoz (1983) used the ancient Greek word *metanoia* to describe this process of change that had to do with early Christian conversion (see Chapter 8). In this view, change to be effective must come from the inner self. In Christianity, for the conversion to be genuine, the person has to accept the new belief and way of life from within—an inner transformation has to take place. And this is a dramatic change in one's *perception* of one's self and one's *world*. It is a change in one's world image.

My view is that a good deal of behavior and certainly important behavior is a result of trance especially when trance is viewed as beliefs and world images. Also my view is that people are open-ended systems that undergo change throughout their lives. As a humanistic psychologist, I adhere to the view that all humans have a drive toward growth and the utilization of their potential, as we discussed in Chapter 2. Allport's concept of "becoming" is appropriate here. This view is important for a therapist in two ways. First, all therapists must be growing therapists. Once I think I have reached all I can know about helping people, then the time has come to seek a new profession. Second, this philosophy also gives me a framework of hope for working with clients—a belief that people can change and utilize these potentials or else why bother to treat people?

People operate through a model of the world (trance) which is their own. Yet, this model changes as they experience new things. Subsequently behavior changes as they go through a transition from one stage of development to another. Hence, life is filled with *trance-itions.* As you will see, this metaphor for change *trance-itions* is something you will observe for yourself as you examine your own beliefs and develop your own personal counseling style.

TRANCE-ITIONS—ACTIVITIES

What follows are a quote from the artist Gianfranco Baruchello and a story from Gordon Allport. Both deal with the issue discussed in this chapter—that the world is our own invention. Read both, and then explore the questions. If you are not in a group, explore the question personally.

1. Baruchello, G., & Martin, H. (1985). *How to imagine,* p. 64. New Paltz, NY: McPherson & Co.

Duchamp never needed excuses for anything, and that's part of why his absurdities are never infantile. They are never contaminated with psychology or psychological explanations. They are about the mind and what the mind can learn about itself when it learns that one of the things it can do is be totally arbitrary.

2. Allport, G. (1964). Mental health: A generic attitude. *Journal of Religion and Health, 4,* 7-21.

In a provincial Austrian hospital, a man lay gravely ill—in fact, at death's door. The medical staff told him frankly that they could not diagnose his disease, but that if they knew the diagnosis, they could probably cure him. They told him further that a famous diagnostician was soon to visit the hospital and that perhaps he could spot the trouble.

Within a few days, the diagnostician arrived and proceeded to make the rounds. Coming to this man's bed, he merely glanced at the patient, murmured, "moribundus" and went on.

Some years later, the patient called on the diagnostician and said, "I've been wanting to thank you for the diagnosis. They told me if you could diagnose me I'd get well, and so the minute you said moribundus, I knew I'd recover."

Discussion Questions

1. What do these quotes mean to you personally?

2. Give an example of "mind as arbitrary."

3. What implications does quote number 2 have for psychotherapy?

4. What implications does quote number 1 have for psychotherapy?

Activities

On a sheet of paper, make a drawing—use large paper if you prefer. The title of the drawing is "The Mind is an Arbitrary Thing." Do not make recognizable figures. (40 minutes)

After completing your drawing, study it in light of viewpoints expressed so far in this book.

Next summarize your concepts of the mind.

REFERENCES

Allport, G. (1964). Mental health: A generic attitude. *Journal of Religion and Health, 4,* 7-21.

Aroaz, D. (1983, July). Transformation techniques of the new hypnosis. *Medical Hypnoanalysis, 4*(3), pp. 114-124.

Bandler, R., & Grinder, J. (1975). *The structure of magic: A book about language and therapy, I.* Palo Alto, CA: Science and Behavior Books.

Baruchello, G., & Martin, H. (1985). *How to imagine.* New Paltz, NY: McPherson & Co., p. 64.

Bateson, G. (1979). *Mind and nature: A necessary Unity.* New York: Dutton.

Erickson, M. (1970). Hypnosis. *Encyclopedia Britannica,* 14th Edition, Vol. 11, pp. 995-997.

Gregory, R.L., & Gombrich, E.H. (Eds.). (1974). *Illusion in nature and art.* New York: Charles Scribner's Sons.

Locher, J.L. (Ed.). (1982). *M.C. Escher.* New York: Harry N. Abrams.

Riedl, R. (1984). The consequences of causal thinking. In P. Watzlawick (Ed.), *The invented reality*. New York: W.W. Norton, 69-94.

Rogers, C. (1980). *Way of being*. Boston, MA: Houghton Mifflin.

Vaihinger, H. (1935). *The philosophy of "as if." A system of the theoretical, practical, and religious fictions of mankind*. New York: Barnes and Noble.

von Foerster, H. (1984). On constructing a reality. In P. Watzlawick (Ed.), *The invented reality*. New York: W.W. Norton, pp. 13-14.

Watzlawick, P., Beavin, J., & Jackson, D. (1967). *Pragmatics of human communication*. New York: W.W. Norton, pp. 261 and 266.

CHAPTER 4

A RADICAL VIEW
OF THE UNCONSCIOUS*

Until Freud, people thought important drives, wishes, and thoughts were in conscious awareness. But Freud "discovered" a reservoir of drives, wishes, and instincts, and he said these were largely unconscious and outside of our awareness. Freud used the analogy of the mind as an iceberg in which the smaller part (above the top of the water) represents the conscious part of the personality, while the much larger mass (below the water) represents the unconscious.

According to Freud, within this vast domain reside our instincts and drives which demand expression. Also included are repressed memories of past traumatic events in addition to repressed memories of significant interactions with others.

Freud felt that the unconscious had no direct access to awareness. Consequently, another part of the personality must develop which has conscious awareness and can interact with the world. This, of course, is the ego.

---

*A version of this chapter was presented at the International Congress of Hypnosis and Family Therapy: Ericksonian Methods, Rome, Italy, October 18, 1985.

Freud's view of the unconscious is negative. It continually puts pressure on the conscious part of the personality for expression and release of energy. One could liken Freud's unconscious to a hyperactive child who continually demands attention and does things that get him/her into trouble. While Freud's basic model of an unconscious (which lies outside of awareness and which affects behavior) has been widely accepted, the view of a negative unconscious which has no perceptual awareness is, however, changing. Present research supports a conception that goes against how we commonly think the mind works. Contemporary research supports the idea that much more important mental activity goes on in the unconscious and lies outside of our awareness.

Unconscious Functioning

Human beings are not robots; but the fact is that in many cases, we act as if we are robots. Milton Erickson continually emphasized how rigidly patterned we are in many of the things we do. Much of our behavior is unconscious and automatic, and this is as it should be for so many mundane things receive the needed attention in daily living that, if we had to be conscious of all of them, doing so would be too cumbersome (see Chapter 7). Take this task of writing. As I put the words on the page with the pen, all is going fast and smoothly. As I think the words, my hand writes them in order. It's only when I write *Hte* instead of *The* do I have any consciousness of what I am writing. In fact, consciousness can actually interfere with many behaviors that are necessary for everyday living.

Let's look at two general classes of functioning where behaviors are largely automatic and unconscious: biological functions and external behaviors.

Biological Functions. All of our biological workings which keep us alive and functioning lie outside of our awareness—and this is as it should be. Attending to all of those functions would be too much of a chore and would be too pre-occupying if we were required to monitor such things as our breathing, heartrate, and blood pressure. These are only a few of the functions which are monitored on an unconscious level. Only when these are not functioning properly (and this is not always the case) do we become consciously aware that something is not working properly and may need some adjustment. Recent innovations in biofeedback technology point toward all the automatic (involuntary) functioning that goes on outside of our awareness.

People, who for the first time receive a visual or auditory message showing them how tense their muscles are, often are surprised to find how unconsciously they were in a state of constant fear and readiness.

Unconscious Behaviors. Throughout the day, we engage in countless numbers of behaviors which allow us to function but which lie outside of our awareness. Until these are called to your attention, you are unaware of how you are sitting in the chair and of how your hands are placed. You probably have little recognition of how you picked up the book you are reading and which hand you used. Only when something goes wrong with these behaviors are we conscious of them—as I take the jar of just-used mustard and place it in the dishwasher next to the refrigerator and close the door, I realize my mistake. Do you remember putting the cap back on the toothpaste this morning? Which shoe did you put on first? Without looking, can you remember what color the shirt or blouse is that you are wearing?

These are only a few examples of the hundreds of behaviors in which we engage in daily that are largely automatic—outside of our awareness and unconsciousness.

Erickson's view of the unconscious included the biological and automatic behaviors for daily functioning, but his view included much more.

Erickson's View of the Unconscious

Outside of the automatic behaviors necessary for everyday living, Erickson's conception of the unconscious was radical, revolutionary, and controversial. He used the term unconscious with his patients as part of his therapy in addition to using it in his writing and teaching.

With his patients, he freely used the expression "unconscious mind" as something with which they already had familiarity and would accept as when he stated, "We know when you are sleeping your unconscious mind can dream" (Rossi, 1980a, Vol. I, p. 457). He also used it with colleagues in his teaching seminars, "What do I mean by the unconscious mind? I mean the back of the mind, the reservoir of learning. The unconscious constitutes a storehouse" (Rossi, 1980b, Vol. III, p. 27).

Beahrs (1981) said Erickson's unconscious was not the teeming caldron of untamed energy pressuring the ego for expression. But rather

Erickson saw the unconscious as the core or center of the person—a repository of all past experiences and learning that could be used beneficially. It was the source of growth lying mostly beneath the conscious level. An important characteristic of the unconscious (radical but typical of Erickson) was, "Let the unconscious do the work."

Freud and Erickson's views of the unconscious are different, but both agreed that it was necessary for therapy to get to the unconscious (but for different reasons). They also did not agree on how to gain access to it.

For Freud, the unconscious was to be made conscious so it could be analyzed. Therefore, for him dreams, slips of the tongue, and hypnosis were ways used to help the analyst find the material in the unconscious which was controlling behavior.

Erickson did not wish to make what was unconscious conscious. He felt that the unconscious with its positive drives needed only to be freed from the rigidity of the conscious mind so it could do its work. While Erickson reached the unconscious through hypnosis, he also attempted to talk to the unconscious through the use of puns, jokes, implications, and stories.

In Figure 4.1 are shown the different routes to the unconscious as considered by Freud and Erickson.

ROUTES TO THE UNCONSCIOUS

Freud	Erickson
Hypnosis	Hypnosis
Drugs	Puns
Dreams	Jokes
Free Association	Double Binds
Projective Techniques	Implications
	Interspersal Approach
	Stories

Figure 4.1. Routes to the unconscious.

Erickson (1979, p. 256) wrote regarding a client, "It is his conscious mind that is perplexed. I verify that by adding that his unconscious mind understands a lot more than he does....I say your unconscious knows." What Erickson meant by this simple, yet profound statement, may be understood further by the following quote: "Unconscious processes can operate in an intelligent, autonomous, and creative fashion—people have stored in their unconscious all the resources necessary to transform their experience" (Gunnison, 1985). What is of note here is the idea of the unconscious operating in an autonomous fashion. The quotation demonstrates that Erickson operated as if the unconscious, this storehouse of behaviors, had a perceptual awareness of its own which guides and influences behavior. In his review of Erickson's collected works, Hilgard (1984) pointed out, "Sometimes 'Erickson's' unconscious appears to have the characteristics of an autonomous personality...and that he treats it (unconscious) as if it had both coherence and wisdom" (p. 256). As we shall see later in the chapter, Rogers held similar views.

Ideas such as these perplex especially the more experimentally and research-oriented members of the psychological community when Erickson's work is described.

Hilgard further pointed out, that in both Freudian and Jungian views, the unconscious is known only by its derivatives; it has to be inferred, because it is really unconscious. This seems not to be the case for Erickson as he repeatedly "talks to the unconscious." Hilgard asked what does this "talking to the unconscious" mean? He further felt that what evidence there is needs to be examined more critically. Indeed, what evidence is there that the unconscious has its own perceptual awareness and can be talked to? These are important questions.

Unusual as the case may be, a number of studies independent of Erickson's work have been found with results which seem to support Erickson's notions. We examine these studies in detail in the next section because of their relationship to Erickson's work.

We See But We Are Not Aware

A note of caution is in order. These experiments may be difficult to follow because they are distilled for the purposes of this book. What is important is that the reader understand the support they show for

Erickson's notions of the unconscious. The reader is referred to the original studies for complete descriptions.

A patient, blind in the visual field due to a lesion, reported he was not aware of any stimulus. Yet, when forced to, he could reliably make certain shape discriminations and reach accurately for small light sources. The patient denied seeing anything and said he was guessing. However, researchers using a high speed camera found his movement quite precise. Tony Marcel (1983b), a researcher in reading development, called this "blindsight," and the work done by Marcel showed that normal sighted people also seem to have this capacity to know without an awareness that they know.

Unconscious Reading Experiments

Marcel's research, which demonstrates a perceptual awareness which lies outside of consciousness, began accidentally. He was studying how children and adults learn to read by flashing words or letters very fast (a few thousandths of a second), and subjects had to guess whether they saw anything or not. Marcel found, that while some responses had no graphic or auditory relationship to the stimulus word being presented, a striking relationship did exist as to the meaning of words presented. For example, the response "king" was made to the stimulus *queen* and "yellow" to the stimulus *green*. Because these results were so interesting, Marcel decided to study this phenomena more closely (Marcel, 1978, 1983a, 1983b). The following outlines a typical study:

> A. He presented a single word or a blank card followed by a
> *pattern mask*. A pattern mask is a meaningless jumble of
> lines made up of fragments of letters. This procedures is
> called *pattern masking*. In pattern masking, a visual pattern
> is briefly exposed (less than one second). The pattern can be
> some letters or a word.
>
> The subject is then asked to tell what they have seen.
> The stimuli are shown very briefly (a few thousandths of a
> second), and people say, "Well, I saw a U or Z. I know
> there were more things there, but I can't seem to tell you
> what they were." (Marcel, 1978)
>
> If a stimulus such as letters is followed with a second
> meaningless jumble of lines, then the shorter the time be-

tween the onset of the first stimulus and the onset of the second stimulus the less the observer can tell you of what has been shown in the first display. Again, the length of time between the mask and the stimulus itself is a few thousandths of a second. Since it seems to interfere with perceptions of the target stimulus because of the pattern on it, the second stimulus is called a *pattern mask*.

B. After each trial the subject had to make one of three decisions:

1. Was there anything before the mask or not?

2. Given two words, which of them was more similar visually to what had been presented? This is graphic similarity, e.g., *doctor-beater* is graphically similar. *Doctor-awe* is not.

3. Given two words, which of them was more similar in meaning to what had been presented? This is semantic similarity, e.g., *doctor-nurse* is similar. *Doctor-cause* is not.

The exposure time for the stimulus words was kept constant but was still very brief in the beginning—500 milliseconds. The time was gradually lowered to where the length of the flash was so fast that subjects reported they could not see anything when presented with the decision task—that is, a word or nothing.

Some subjects refused to continue when they could no longer see anything. Some thought it silly, but they continued answering questions. Marcel stated, "Obviously the experiment was bizarre in asking someone to judge something whose presence he or she is not aware." About two-thirds said although they could not see the point, they kept on guessing.

The results were as follows: When they reached chance on the presence or absence judgment (e.g., they were not able to tell whether a word was present or not), they were still guessing 90% correctly on the other two tasks (graphic similarity and semantic judgment). Eventually, they reached chance on all judgments with the judgment as to meaning being the last to reach chance. Marcel noted all subjects were guessing correctly while indicating that they could not see anything! This study indicates that subjects were making judgments while not consciously aware of how they were doing it. Marcel's work shows that the pattern mask interfered with the visual recognition of stimulus words, but yet the subjects did have some perceptual awareness of the stimulus words—otherwise, they could not have affected their scores on the test words.

Since subjects could not have a conscious awareness of these words (could not say whether a word was present or not), this awareness was unconscious.

Unconscious Effects on Behavior

As important as these discoveries are, they may be moot if the unconscious perceptions have no effect on behavior. Marcel's work has shown that indeed these unconscious perceptions can effect behavior. We turn to this issue now.

Lexical Decision Studies. In lexical decision studies a string of letters is presented to a subject, and he/she has to decide as quickly as possible whether the string of letters is a word or not. When it is not a word, it is pronouncible but has no meaning. For example, a subject would respond "yes" to *party* but "no" to *prain*.

The trials can be given in quick succession, and it has been shown in other studies (Meyer, Schvaneveldt, & Ruddy, 1972) that the decision of the second word comes faster if it is associated in meaning with the first word (e.g., *boy-man*). Examples of letter strings from Marcel are shown in Figure 4.2.

The method of this experiment was to compare the effects of the associated words on the amount of decision time. Before the experimental session, Marcel found the onset of time before the mask in which each subject was no longer able to detect the presence or absence of a word (above chance).

When the words are associated (e.g., *boy-man*), the reaction time is quicker. Therefore, one would expect the reaction time would be quickest to the words *child* and *infant* when *child* is left unmasked. Since masking has been shown to interfere with word identification, one would expect that the reaction time to *infant* after *child* has been masked would be slower than when it is not masked.

Pairs	String 1	String 2
non-word—non-word	Reet	Blager
word—non-word	Street	Blager
non-word—word	Reet	Mother
word—word (unassociated)	Avenue	Mother
word—word (associated)	Child	Mother

Figure 4.2. Example of word used in lexical decision making experiment. Letter string 1 is either unmasked or pattern masked. (Adapted from Marcel, 1978)

The results showed that the reaction time was significantly faster when compared to all other pairs when the words were associated by meaning (e.g., *child-infant*). However, the reaction time for the *associated* words, whether *masked* or *unmasked,* was not significantly different from each other.

Marcel took these results as an indication that the analysis of the masked words must have reached a stage at which words are associated with other words. The first word could not affect the second word unless some level of analysis had been reached. For analysis to take place, some perception of the stimulus had to have occurred. Marcel felt that the analysis has reached a stage at which the meaning is represented. Whatever the process, the first word could not affect the second word through meaning unless that level of analysis had been achieved. This level of analysis, of which the subject is unaware, takes place unconsciously.

However, one more experiment needs to be presented which more clearly meets the criteria of unconscious perception. In this experiment lexical decision was required to the first and third of three letter strings (in some cases the letter strings were words, in some cases they were not).

When all three were words, the second was a *polysemous word* (has 2 meanings) like *palm*. This could be followed by a word associated to one of its meanings (*wrist*) and preceded by a word related to the same meaning (*hand*), a different meaning (*tree*), or to neither meaning (*speed*). The second word (*palm*) was either masked (to prevent awareness) or left unmasked. When *palm* was masked to prevent consciousness, it helped the lexical classification of *wrist* whether it was preceded by *hand* or *tree*. But, when *palm* was not masked, and the subject was conscious of it, it had an inhibiting effect on the classification of *wrist* when preceded by *tree* (Marcel, 1983b). Thus both meanings (of palm) seem to be activated simultaneously unconsciously, but only one is activated consciously. This is consistent with the idea that only one interpretation of an event can be entertained by consciousness and prior context. The first word only selects the appropriate interpretation when choice becomes necessary, i.e., if the representation can become conscious (Marcel, 1978).

This experiment is of note because it also meets the criteria for unconscious perception as set forth by Dixon (1971). Dixon's criteria to justify unconscious perception is the occurrence of a contingent response without awareness of the stimulus that differs qualitatively from those elicited by the same stimulus when presented above the awareness threshold.

Results of this last experiment show that not only do pattern masked stimuli of which the subject is unaware produce facilitative effects (contingent responses) that is, *palm* helps *wrist* under a number of conditions, they produce more facilitative effects than nonmasked stimuli which are qualitatively different (*palm* helped *wrist* only when it was preceded by *hand* in the conscious condition).

Therapeutic Implications

Using the model of an independent unconscious awareness in therapy, Erickson's plan was to bypass the conscious part of the person and talk to the unconscious. Bypassing consciousness was important for Erickson because he thought consciousness was where resistance to change was most prevalent. As we shall see, this is an important idea in itself. We all have been surprised many times of changes in us of which we were unaware in addition to feeling frustrated when we consciously could not change a habit or behavior.

Erickson's idea in communication was to utilize a general context to fixate and distract consciousness while the individual associations of words, phrases, and sentences within that context are registered in the unconscious. (This is where they can work their effect.) This technique, though revolutionary and controversial, seems supported by the following conclusion which Marcel drew from his research.

Marcel pointed out that once we have learned to read, the meanings of individual words can be reached without the involvement of consciousness. This is a result of learning and development which pushes our consciousness to ever higher levels. Thus, we are aware of the significance of words instead of and before being aware of the cues. Describing what word was spoken is easier than describing what phoneme was spoken (Marcel, 1983b).

What makes Marcel's description interesting is that in 1976 Erickson and Rossi used a parallel description when referring to Ericksonian methods of hypnotherapy and psychotherapy:

> This situation can be made clear by analogy. The adult reader is usually searching for an author's meaning. Within certain limits it really doesn't matter what particular sentences or words are used. Many different sentences and combinations of words could be used to express the same meaning. It is the meaning or the general context of the sentences that register in consciousness while the particular sentences and words fall into the unconscious where they are "forgotten." (Erickson & Rossi, 1976, p. 167)

With this model, Erickson would use sentences, paragraphs, and stories distracting the conscious mind while key words (designed to effect growth and development) would be used individually within the sentence or paragraph *(interspersal approach)*. Erickson's notion is that these words would fall into the unconscious where they would be recognized and utilized by the unconscious.

Again, what has been difficult to accept is whether the unconscious could recognize anything independent of consciousness and whether this would have an effect on behavior. Marcel's research shows that an unconscious recognition does occur.

These experiments not only support Erickson's notions of the unconscious, but they also demonstrate what he seemed to understand intuitively and to utilize in his work—that is, distracting the conscious part of the person seems relatively easy since, as has been shown in the lexical decision with polysemous words study, consciousness has focusing limitations. Using confusing words, puns, and analogy (something Erickson was fond of) was obviously a way of bypassing consciousness and of "talking to the patient's unconscious."

For example, when Erickson used words with phonological similarities but with different meanings (e.g., *light* as in light in weight, or *light* as in a lamp, and *weight* or *wait*), he was intuitively using what has been shown in the polysemous experiment—that only one meaning would be identified consciously, but that the other representations would be recognized unconsciously.

These experiments show that no longer does a question exist of the accuracy of Erickson's model of the unconscious and conscious division of the mind. What is needed now is research using this division in carefully controlled clinical studies.

These findings have, of course, wide-reaching implications for anyone interested in human behavior and counseling. As we shall see in the next sections, learning to trust the unconscious is something not only clients need to do but therapists as well.

Unconscious and Its
Implications for Therapists

As we have said, Erickson did not have much faith in the conscious part of the personality, especially when it came to change. He felt consciousness was rigidly patterned and externally oriented.

While without doubt he placed value upon the unconscious, this still remains a fuzzy concept. As we have shown, much mental activity *does* go on outside of our awareness. Important activities and skills are carried out and learned unconsciously. This is probably what Erickson meant when he said, "...your unconscious mind knows more than your conscious mind does."

Rogers' View

Carl Rogers held similar views of an unconscious knowledge—a subception that seems to know more than we can express.

In something that sounds very similar to Erickson, Rogers (1980) said, "I have stated that we are wiser than our intellects, that our organisms as a whole have a wisdom and purposiveness which goes well beyond our conscious thought" (Rogers, 1980, p. 106).

The following 1985 quote from Rogers (see Chapter 6) gives his most recent ideas on the subject and is quite revealing:

> This was the kind of intuitive response which I have learned to trust. The expression just formed itself within me and wanted to be said. I advanced it very tentatively and from her initial blank puzzled look, I thought that perhaps it was completely irrelevant and unhelpful, but her next responses show that it touched something deep in her.
>
> I have come to value these intuitive responses. They occur infrequently (This is the first I have captured in a recording), but they are almost always helpful in advancing therapy. In those moments I am perhaps in a slightly altered state of consciousness in dwelling in the client's world completely in tune with that world. My nonconscious intellect takes over. I know much more than my conscious mind is aware of. I do not form any responses consciously, they simply arise in me from my nonconscious sense of the world of the other. (Rogers, 1985, p. 565)

The last observations are quite extraordinary. It's like the gifted baseball hitter who can actually see the ball hit the bat—a feat no hitter can do. Somehow Rogers' conscious is able to observe and give credit to an awareness that is both his and not his at the same time. It's his—because it's his unconscious, but not his—because it lies outside his awareness.

What Rogers had learned to do is to *trust* his unconscious. He allows it to make observations and also allows these observations to develop into responses. Learning this trust is something Erickson advocated in his clients and also himself. The following chapters, especially on techniques, are put together with this goal in mind: to help therapists trust their own unconscious so they can help clients do the same.

REFERENCES

Beahrs, J. (1981, October). The hypnotic psychotherapy of Milton H. Erickson. *American Journal of Clinical Hypnosis, 14*(2), 73-90.

Dixon, N. (1971). *Subliminal perception: The nature of a controversy*. London, England: McGraw Hill.

Erickson, M.H., & Rossi, E. (1976). Two level communication and the microdynamics of trance and suggestion. *American Journal of Clinical Hypnosis, 18*(3), 153-171.

Erickson, M.H., & Rossi, E. (1979). *Hypotherapy: An exploratory casebook.* New York: Irvington.

Erickson, M.H. (1980a). The nature of suggestion. In E.L. Rossi (Ed.), *The collected papers of Milton Erickson on hypnosis by Milton Erickson: Volume I,* 457. New York: Irvington.

Erickson, M.H. (1980b). Hypnotic investigation of the psychodynamic process. In E.L. Rossi (Ed.), *The collected papers of Milton Erickson on hypnosis by Milton Erickson: Volume III,* 1. New York: Irvington.

Gunnison, H. (1985, May). The uniqueness of similarities: Parallels of Milton Erickson and Carl Rogers. *Journal of Counseling and Development, 63,* 561-564.

Hilgard, E. (1984). Book review of the collected papers of Milton Erickson on hypnosis by Milton Erickson: Volumes I, II, III, and IV. E. Rossi (Ed.). New York: Irvington, 1980. *The International Journal of Clinical and Experimental Hypnosis, XXXII*(2), 256.

Marcel, A. (1978, Autumn). Unconscious reading. *Visible Language, XII*(4), 391-404.

Marcel, A. (1983a). Conscious and unconscious perception: Experiments on visual masking and word recognition. *Cognition Psychology, 15,* 197-237.

Marcel, A. (1983b). Conscious and unconscious perception: An approach to the relations between phenomenal experience and perceptual processes. *Cognitive Psychology, 15,* 238-300.

Meyer, D.E., Schvaneveldt, R.W., & Ruddy, M.G. (1972, November). *Activation of lexical memory.* Paper presented at meeting of Psychonomic Society, St. Louis, MO.

Rogers, C. (1980). *A way of being.* Boston, MA: Houghton Mifflin.

Rogers, C. (1985). Reaction to Gunnison's article on the similarities between Erickson and Rogers. *Journal of Counseling and Development,* 565-566.

SECTION II

READINGS IN ERICKSONIAN AND ROGERIAN THERAPY

INTRODUCTION TO SECTION II

This section contains, in my mind, some of the most important readings for anyone interested in the Ericksonian and Rogerian Psychotherapeutic Process. They can be read in any order, and they supplement rather well all else in this book.

INTRODUCTION TO CHAPTERS 5 AND 6

This section of readings begins with two chapters which show the conceptual similarities of Rogers and Erickson. The first article by Hugh Gunnison points to the common elements in theory, direction, and climate of the relationship that the two men held. Some of these concepts have already been introduced, but they are important and bear repeating here. Moreover, the second article is by Rogers himself, and there is no better way of hearing about someone's ideas than by hearing it in his words.

Carl Rogers, in his article, made some personal revelations about his own transcendent experiences as a therapist. Without question this article is an extremely important one for therapists. Yet, his experiences are human, and they point toward a higher functioning and awareness that can be reached by all of us.

In a way, when Rogers is at his best as he says, he is closest to his inner intuitive self, "when I am somehow in touch with the unknown in me" he is acting as an artist. He is being spontaneous, and his message is full of trust. Trusting his client sure, but trusting *himself.* And in this trust is an acceptance of feelings, thoughts, and impulses that come from parts of him that are unknown to him.

The importance of trusting oneself and becoming open to unknown experiences for both artist and therapist is quite clear in this presentation.

While Rogers had changed some of his ideas over the years in action, he is still the quintessential Rogerian. I saw one of his therapy demonstrations at the 1985 Evolution of Psychotherapy Conference, and he developed his usual empathy, positive regard, and warmth while respecting the clients' right to make their own decision.

Carl Rogers

(Drawing by the author)

62   *Psychotherapy: The Listening Voice*

CHAPTER 5

THE UNIQUENESS OF SIMILARITIES: PARALLELS OF MILTON H. ERICKSON AND CARL ROGERS

Hugh Gunnison*

The philosophy and values of Carl Rogers hold a central position in the counseling profession. Today the writings and work of Milton H. Erickson are beginning to have a similar influence. Erickson's strategies and techniques have been explored from many theoretical frames of reference, but little attention has been paid to his values regarding the human condition. It is these value assumptions of Rogers and Erickson that will be examined in this article.

Hugh Gunnison is Coordinator, Graduate Program, Counseling and Human Development, St. Lawrence University, Canton, New York.

*Gunnison, H. (May, 1985). The uniqueness of similarities: Parallels of Milton H. Erickson and Carl Rogers. *Journal of Counseling and Development, 63,* 561-564.

Although Milton H. Erickson did not identify with any particular theory in psychiatry or psychology, I will argue here that these values regarding human beings are aligned with humanistic psychology (Maslow, 1971) and more specifically the person-centered approach of Carl Rogers (1980).

It is hardly necessary to introduce the works of Carl Rogers; however, the seminal mind of the late Milton Erickson may be less familiar to the reader. Erickson is generally considered to be the world's leading authority on hypnotherapy and brief strategic psychotherapy (Haley, 1967). His work is so original and complex that he has been called "Mr. Hypnosis" (Weitzenhoffer, 1976). He was the founding leader and first president of the American Society for Clinical Hypnosis and the founder and editor of its journal. Zeig (1980) wrote that "it is not hyperbole to state that history will demonstrate that what Freud contributed to the theory of psychotherapy, Erickson will be known as contributing to the practice of psychotherapy" (p. xix).

One can analyze Erickson's techniques (Erickson & Rossi, 1979) through many theoretical templates and arrive at varying understandings. Zeig (1980) recounted how Haley (1973) approached Erickson's work through an interactional view, Grinder and Bandler (1981) through a linguistic view, and Rossi (Erickson & Rossi, 1979) through a Jungian-intrapsychic orientation, each providing another rich perspective. This article examines the works of Erickson and Rogers from a person-centered approach (Evans, 1975; Rogers, 1980).

In a recent survey of practicing counseling and clinical psychologists designed to ascertain the names of those who have had the most influence, Smith (1982) reported that Rogers' name led the list. Probably the influence of Rogers still remains because of his relentless belief in the importance of the therapeutic relationship, the value-belief system regarding the person, and intra-interpersonal communication—the now so increasingly familiar hallmarks of Erickson's hypnotic patterns and psychotherapy. Rogers (1980) put it this way: "I discern more sharply the theme of my life as having been built around the desire for clarity of communication, with all its ramifying results" (p. 66).

Throughout the writings of Erickson (Rossi, 1980a, b) one is struck by his brilliant communication abilities, the connecting with his patients at direct and indirect levels. Weitzenhoffer (1976) described Erickson as a master of verbal and nonverbal communication, the heart of his theory of intervention.

ON THE PERSON-CENTERED APPROACH

In summarizing the two central hypotheses of a person-centered approach, Rogers (1980) demonstrated a very positive and optimistic view of the human. He held that "individuals have within themselves vast resources for self-understanding and for altering their self-concepts, basic attitudes and self-directed behavior; these resources can be tapped if a definable climate of facilitative psychological attitudes can be provided" (p. 115). This quote has rich value implications. It suggests a belief that in this "definable climate," each person's potential can be achieved.

ON DIRECTION

The term "non-directive," originally used to describe Rogers's (1942) early therapeutic approach, became so thoroughly misunderstood that he tried to avoid it. By non-directive, Rogers meant not directing, advising, interpreting, or guiding the person, but rather allowing the person's actualizing tendency to emerge. Rogers (1977) began to realize that his very presence in a relationship had many powerful and "directive" aspects. He was keenly aware of the power of a therapeutic climate that allowed or assisted his client to change in growing directions.

Rogers's (1978) "direction" comes out of his strong belief that within each individual there are powerful instinct-like potentials. In 1942, he created great furor when he argued that counseling

relies much more heavily on the individual drive toward growth, health and adjustment. Therapy is not a matter of doing something *to* the individual, or of inducing him to do something about himself. It is instead a matter of freeing him for normal growth and development, of removing obstacles so that he can again move forward. (Rogers, 1942, p. 29)

"Person-centered" became a more accurate label of his approach. Erickson (Erickson & Rossi, 1979) may have been discussing a similar process. The utilization "approach is *patient-centered* and highly dependent on the momentary needs of the individual" (p. 14). The utilization approach focused on the person, utilizing and activating unconscious resources and learnings that were already within rather than imposing from without (Erickson, Rossi, & Rossi, 1976).

Rossi, in a dialogue with Erickson (Erickson et al., 1976), commented that: "Patients keep pulling at the therapist for the cure, the magic, the change, rather than looking at themselves as the change agent.

You are continually putting the responsibility for change back on the patient." Erickson replied: "On to them always!" (p. 27).

ON THE FORMATIVE TENDENCY
AND THE UNCONSCIOUS

Both Rogers and Erickson in their words and deeds emphasized the internal motivation of people—Rogers (1980) in his "growth or formative tendency" and Erickson in his view of the "unconscious."

Beahrs (1982) described Erickson's "unconscious" as being very different from Freud's, not the teeming caldron of untamed energy screaming to be suppressed and repressed for society's sake. Erickson saw the unconscious as the core or center of the person, a repository of all past experiences and learning, the source for growth lying mostly beneath the conscious level. Unlike so many of his time, he emphasized the positive aspects of the unconscious (Haley, 1967). To Secter (1982), one of the most important statements from Erickson was, "Let the unconscious do the work" (p. 450). This statement was so simple yet so profound in its implications. Gilligan (1982) quoted Erickson's notion: "Unconscious processes can operate in an intelligent, autonomous and creative fashion...people have stored in their unconscious all the resources necessary to transform their experience" (p. 89). In the same article, Gilligan described Erickson's view of the therapeutic task—arranging conditions that facilitate and elicit this unconscious processing.

As with Erickson, Rogers (1951, 1959, 1961) emphasized the importance of trusting the individual's potential toward growth. He (Rogers, 1961) stated that:

> There is one central source of energy in the human organism. This source is a trustworthy function of the whole system rather than of some portion of it; it is most simply conceptualized as a tendency toward fulfillment, toward actualization, involving not only the maintenance but also the enhancement of the organism. (p. 123)

As early as the 1940s, Rogers warned against diagnosing, advising, and interpreting (Evans, 1975). A person-centered approach holds that individuals have within themselves the basic wherewithal for growth. Rogers (1978) called it the formative tendency. Albert Szent-Gyoergyi (1974), a Nobel Prize winning biologist, called this tendency "syntropy," or the other side of the process of "entropy." Entropy has been traditionally described as the natural process in the universe whereby organized forms gradually disintegrate, not unlike a vast machine running down. Erickson assigned syntropy, or the growth process, to the unconscious and talked about "the wisdom of the unconscious" (Rosen, 1982b). Rogers (1961, 1978) used the phrase "wisdom of the organism" in much the same way.

ON THE THEORY

Rogers (1959) developed a theory for a person-centered approach, but he warned that theories can become dogma and highly rigid (Evans, 1975). I can recall, in a personal discussion with Rogers at St. Lawrence University in 1978, his emphasis on the person and on the concept "that the person becomes your theory." He also related to me that what he had "ultimately learned about people, was from people." Erickson, where queried as to where he obtained his psychiatric knowledge, responded, "From patients" (Secter, 1982, p. 451).

Rogers emphasized the importance of setting theory aside and letting the person emerge. Erickson similarly believed that theory was restrictive and could trap both patient and therapist (Zeig, 1980). He espoused the ideas of flexibility, indirection, permissiveness, and unique differences. How apt all of these terms are to Rogers' description of the attitudes of the effective counselor-therapist.

According to Rogers (1961), the process of effective counseling involves "a change in the manner of the client's experiencing...a *loosening* of the *cognitive maps* of experience" (p. 64). These are almost Erickson's very words: "Patients have problems because their conscious programming has too severely limited their capacities. The solution is to help them break through the limitations of their conscious attitudes to free their unconscious potential for problem solving" (Erickson et al., 1976, p. 18).

ON THE CLIMATE

For many years Rogers studied the specific characteristics of the therapeutic climate. He chose not to study the process of change through a theoretical framework; instead, he "approach[ed] the phenomena with as few preconceptions as possible, to take a naturalist's observational, descriptive approach....I used myself as a tool" (Rogers, 1961, p. 128).

In his study of hypnosis, Erickson also used himself as his own best instrument, spending countless hours as a youth reflecting on experiences in altered states and learning to relieve his own pain by focusing on relaxation, fatigue, heaviness, and so forth (Rossi, 1980a). He, too, was discovering through his own incredible facilities of observation and introspection. Both he and Rogers were able to look at different ways of "seeing" themselves, others, and the relativity of different world views.

Rogers emphasized the importance of empathy in the climate of the relationship. Empathy, along with realness or genuineness in the relationship and deep caring and trust in the potential of the person, was the basis for the "definable" climate so critical in Rogers's works (Rogers, 1957).

Empathy or deep understanding of the client is essentially an attitude of "desiring" to understand. For Rogers (1980), empathy is a process: "It means entering private perceptual world of the other and becoming thoroughly at home in it...you lay aside your own views and values in order to enter another's world without prejudice" (pp. 142-143).

As did Rogers, Erickson continually stressed the importance of empathy. In the preparation phase of his approach, the initial and most important factor is building "sound rapport—-that is, a positive feeling of understanding and mutual regard between therapist and patient" (Erickson & Rossi, 1979, p. 1). Erickson believed that "an attitude of empathy and respect on the part of the therapist is *crucial* to ensure successful change" (Erickson & Zeig, 1980, p. 336). He (Erickson & Rossi, 1979) amplified the concept of rapport that develops out of a sincere acceptance of another. Through the use of the client's own vocabulary and frames of reference, pacing, and matching (Grinder & Bandler, 1981) a powerful kind of empathy develops that forms the interpersonal connection. Erickson and Rossi (1979) commented on the similarity between this approach and Rogers's: "At this level our approach might appear similar to the *non-directive client centered approach of Rogers (1951)*" [italics added] (p. 51).

The second and probably the most critical ingredient within the climate has to be realness or genuineness, because if empathy and positive regard and respect are not genuinely felt or expressed, then the climate becomes toxic and phony. For the counselor-therapist, realness means being fully there with the client, matching the experiencing of the moment with clear and transparent communication.

> Sometimes a feeling "rises up in me" which seems to have no particular relationship to what is going on. Yet I have learned to accept and trust this feeling by my awareness and to try to communicate it to my client. (Rogers, 1980, p. 14)

I suggest that Rogers has moved into what Erickson might describe as an altered state, particularly when he accepts and trusts those sensations and images that "seem to have no particular relationship to what is going on." Rogers continually emphasizes that the counselor-therapist must trust and accept him or herself in the ongoing process. Erickson did this elegantly and naturally. He was so "in touch" with his own inner experiences and so trusted the "wisdom of *his* unconscious" that he was capable of incredible understandings of his patients' worlds (Zeig, 1982).

Erickson advised against limiting our approaches because of loyalty to a method, a school, or a mentor. He suggested that we learn and observe as widely as possible, but practice only those techniques and skills that allow us to express ourselves genuinely. "Remember that whatever way you choose to work must be your own way, because you cannot really imitate someone else" (Haley, 1967, p. 535).

Rogers argued that a third condition, positive regard or caring, was necessary in the creation of the therapeutic climate. When the therapist is experiencing positive, warm, and accepting feelings toward what is going on in the client, "it means that he [she] prizes the client, in a non-possessive way" (Rogers, 1961, p. 62).

Haley (1967) mentioned a similar deep caring in Erickson's work. Erickson told of working with a patient about whom he felt had little chance for successful change. Despite the poor prognosis, Erickson kept the doubt "to himself and he let [the patient] know by manner, tone of voice, by everything said that he [Erickson] was genuinely interested in him, was genuinely desirous of helping him" (Haley, 1967, p. 516).

Erickson's belief and respect in people were evident in his deep and abiding faith in the competence of people to work out things in their own lives, comfortably and confidently. Erickson believed that his patients each had the natural desire "to acquire mastery, to obtain understanding, to have fun, to have certainty and to have immediate results" (Lustig, 1982, p. 459).

ON YOUTH AND STORIES

The work of the counselor-therapist is inextricably intertwined with the early experiences that shape his or her philosophy of life and beliefs about the world, the self, and others.

In a line from his poem, *My Heart Leaps Up,* William Wordsworth wrote that "the child is the father of the man," and the childhoods and youth of Erickson and Rogers deserve mention.

Both grew up on farms. Both were struck by the growth processes that they witnessed and the experiences that permeated their values—the optimistic and positive joy in life and the simple everchanging world around them. Both emphasized and sensed the uniqueness of each living thing and prized above all these differences.

Erickson used stories, anecdotes, and metaphors as a significant part of his utilization approach. Conversely, anecdotes and metaphors were not a distinct part of Rogers's approach. But he would use them to make a point and, like Erickson, would often draw them from his youth and childhood. Both used "growing" metaphors in powerful ways.

Rogers (1961), in trying to describe the formative growth tendency, drew upon an experience from his youth.

> I remember that in my boyhood, the bin in which we stored our winter's supply of potatoes was in the basement, several feet below a small window. The conditions were unfavorable, but the potatoes would begin to sprout...But these sad, spindly sprouts would grow 2 or 3 feet in length as they reached toward the distant light of the window. The sprouts were, in their bizarre, futile growth, a sort of desperate expression of the directional tendency....But under the most adverse circumstances, they were striving to become. Life would not give up, even if it could not flourish. (p. 118)

Erickson regarded stories and metaphors as a central part of his approach, but he rarely ever explained them to patients. Instead, patients drew their *own* conclusions and created their *own* meanings by using their *own* experiences and resources. Erickson emphasized concepts such as

> growth and delight and joy....Life isn't something you can give an answer to today. You should enjoy the process of waiting, the process of becoming what you are. There is nothing more delightful than planting flower seeds and not knowing what kinds of flowers are going to come up. (Rosen, 1979, p. xii)

Probably Erickson is conveying the suggestion of becoming and growing as well as the excitement and patience in waiting.

Erickson's use of anecdotes, puns, metaphors, stories, and jokes has become legendary (Rosen, 1982a). A person probably grasps their general contextual meaning at the conscious level; however, each word and phrase has unique associations that go beyond the general context (Erickson et al., 1976). In this, his interspersal technique, Erickson (1966) inserted words and phrases that indirectly stimulated deeper focusing on the patient's experiences and interests. Through the interspersing of indirect suggestions, the unconscious is put to work. For example, when Erickson used as a metaphor a tomato seed in the process of becoming a tomato (Haley, 1967), the patient, a florist, had this general context within his conscious perceptual field. Erickson interspersed suggestions as he related the story, letting the "unconscious do the work." Gordon and Meyers-Anderson (1981) described a delightful and powerful metaphor that Erickson had recalled from his youth. It seems that a riderless horse appeared one day. There was no way of knowing to whom the horse belonged. Erickson volunteered to find the owners by mounting the horse and leading it to the road. As he approached the road, he let go of the reins and waited to see in which direction the horse would go. Erickson intervened only when the horse would wander off the road. After about 4 miles, the horse turned into a farmyard. The surprised owner asked young Erickson how he know where the horse belonged. "I didn't know. The *horse* knew. All I did was keep him on the road" (p. 6). What an elegant description of therapy; what an elegant description of the utilization and person-centered approaches!

ON CONCLUDING

Although this article has focused on the value assumptions of Erickson from a person-centered approach, the model could easily be reversed. Gunnison and Renick (in press) discuss the hidden hypnotic Ericksonian patterns in counseling about which the counselor is often unaware. Lankton and Lankton (1983) analyzed, from an Ericksonian model, the hypnotic patterns of Rogers's work in the film, *Gloria*. What appear to be highly divergent approaches assume the most interesting connections and similarities.

Rogers and Erickson had similar goals for their clients and patients: the utilizing of their directional tendencies, the evoking of the wisdom of the organism (the unconscious), and the providing of the greatest freedom. Each did it so genuinely and so differently. Rosen (1979) described this as "a typical Ericksonian paradox. The master manipulator [facilitator] allows and stimulates the greatest freedom" (p. xiii). And each did it so humanely and so uniquely.

REFERENCES

Beahrs, J.O. (1982). Understanding Erickson's approach. In J.K. Zeig (Ed.), *Ericksonian approaches to hypnosis and psychotherapy* (pp. 58-83). New York: Brunner/Mazel.

Erickson, M.H. (1966). The interspersal hypnotic technique for symptom correction and pain control. *American Journal of Clinical Hypnosis, 8,* 198-209.

Erickson, M.H, & Rossi, E.L. (1979). *Hypnotherapy: An exploratory casebook.* New York: John Wiley.

Erickson, M.H., & Rossi, E.L., & Rossi, S.I . (1976). *Hypnotic realities: The induction of clinical hypnosis and forms of indirect suggestion.* New York: John Wiley.

Erickson, M.H., & Zeig, J.K. (1980). Symptom prescription for expanding the psychotic's world view. In E.L. Rossi (Ed.), *The collected papers of Milton H. Erickson on hypnosis* (Vol. 4, pp. 335-337). New York: Irvington.

Evans, R.I. (Ed.). (1975). *Carl Rogers: The man and his ideas.* New York: E.P. Dutton.

Gilligan, S.G. (1982). Ericksonian approaches to clinical hypnosis. In J.K. Zeig (Ed.), *Ericksonian approaches to hypnosis and psychotherapy* (pp. 87-103). New York: Brunner/Mazel.

Gordon, D., & Meyers-Anderson, M. (1981). *Phoenix: Therapeutic patterns of Milton H. Erickson.* Cupertino, CA: Meta Publications.

Grinder, J., & Bandler, R. (1981). *Trance-formations: Neurolinguistic programming and the structure of hypnosis.* Moab, UT: Real People Press.

Gunnison, H., & Renick, T.F. (in press). Hidden hypnotic patterns in counseling and supervision. *Counselor Education and Supervision.*

Haley, J. (Ed.). (1967). *Advanced techniques of hypnosis and therapy: Selected papers of Milton H. Erickson, M.D.* New York: Grune & Stratton.

Haley, J. (1973). *Uncommon therapy: The psychiatric techniques of Milton H. Erickson, M.D.* New York: W.W. Norton.

Lankton, S.R., & Lankton, C.H. (1983). *The answer within: A clinical framework of Ericksonian hypnotherapy.* New York: Brunner/Mazel.

Lustig, H.S. (1982). Understanding Erickson and Ericksonian techniques. In J.K. Zeig (Ed.), *Ericksonian approaches to hypnosis and psychotherapy* (p. 455-561). New York: Brunner/Mazel.

Maslow, A.H. (1971). *The farther reaches of human nature.* New York: Viking Press.

Rogers, C.R. (1942). *Counseling and psychotherapy.* Boston: Houghton Mifflin.

Rogers, C.R. (1951). *Client-centered therapy.* Boston: Houghton Mifflin.

Rogers, C.R. (1957). The necessary and sufficient conditions of therapeutic personality change. *Journal of Consulting Psychology, 21,* 95-103.

Rogers, C.R. (1959). A theory of therapy, personality and interpersonal relationships, as developed in the client-centered framework. In S. Koch (Ed.), *Psychology: A study of a science. Formulations of the person and the social context* (Vol. 3, pp. 184-256). New York: McGraw-Hill.

Rogers, C.R. (1961). *On becoming a person.* Boston: Houghton Mifflin.

Rogers, C.R. (1977). *Carl Rogers on personal power.* New York: Dell.

Rogers, C.R. (1978). The formative tendency. *Journal of Humanistic Psychology, 18,* 1-24.

Rogers, C.R. (1980). *A way of being.* Boston: Houghton Mifflin.

Rosen, S. (1979). Foreward. In M.H. Erickson & E.L. Rossi, *Hypnotherapy: An exploratory casebook* (pp. ix-xiii). New York: John Wiley.

Rosen, S. (Ed.). (1982a). *My voice will go with you: The teaching tales of Milton H. Erickson, M.D.* New York: W.W. Norton.

Rosen, S. (1982b). The values and philosophy of Milton H. Erickson. In J.K. Zeig (Ed.), *Ericksonian approaches to hypnosis and psychotherapy* (pp. 462-476). New York: Brunner/Mazel.

Rossi, E.L. (Ed.). (1980a). *The collected papers of Milton H. Erickson on hypnosis* (Vol. 1). New York: Irvington.

Rossi, E.L. (Ed.). (1980b). *The collected papers of Milton H. Erickson on hypnosis* (Vol. 4). New York: Irvington.

Secter, I. (1982). Seminars with Erickson: The early years. In J.K. Zeig (Ed.), *Ericksonian approaches to hypnosis and psychotherapy* (pp. 447-454). New York: Brunner/Mazel).

Smith, D. (1982). Trends in counseling and psychotherapy. *American Psychologist, 37,* 802-809.

Szent-Gyoergyi, A. (1974, Spring). Drive in living matter to perfect itself. *Synthesis,* pp. 12-24.

Weitzenhoffer, A.M. (1976). Foreward. In M.H. Erickson, E.L. Rossi, and S.I. Rossi (Eds.), *Hypnotic realities: The induction of clinical hypnosis and forms of indirect suggestion* (pp. xiii-xix). New York: John Wiley.

Zeig, J.K. (Ed.). (1980). *Teaching seminar with Milton H. Erickson, M.D.* New York: Brunner/Mazel.

Zeig, J.K. (Ed.). (1982). *Ericksonian approaches to hypnosis and psychotherapy.* New York: Brunner/Mazel.

INTRODUCTION TO CARL ROGERS' ARTICLE (CHAPTER 6)*

Rogers and Erickson had no direct contact with each other's work. Whatever similarities exist developed independently. Rogers stresses his reliance on an intuitive relationship to the client's inner core and discusses the basis for this intuition. He also relies on a fundamental directional tendency which exists in every person. He trusts the client to choose his or her own goals. In these respects he sees some similarities between himself and Erickson, confirming Gunnison's points and going beyond them.

*As stated in the *Journal of Counseling and Development, 63,* 565.

CHAPTER 6

REACTION TO GUNNISON'S ARTICLE ON THE SIMILARITIES BETWEEN ERICKSON AND ROGERS

Carl R. Rogers*

I am profoundly impressed by the similarities that Gunnison found between my work and that of Milton Erickson. I never had direct personal contact with Erickson, except a very slight acquaintance when we were both undergraduate students at the University of Wisconsin. Nor have I read any appreciable proportion of his writings. This may seem strange, but many years ago I concluded that though I respected him for

Carl R. Rogers is a resident fellow at the Center for Studies of the Person.

*Rogers, C. (May 1985). Reaction to Gunnison's article on the similarities between Erickson and Rogers. *Journal of Counseling and Development, 63,* 565-566. "Copyright American Association for Counseling and Development. Reprinted with permission. No further reproduction authorized without written permission of AACD."

what I heard about his work, hypnosis was not my path into therapy. I was not really aware of the fact that his work went so far beyond hypnosis itself. Neither has Erickson ever had personal contact with my work. I do not know how well-acquainted he was with my writings.

I mention these things to indicate that whatever similarities exist developed quite independently—certainly not out of close contact or thorough knowledge of each other's writings. The similarities are therefore real and not simply derivative.

I believe that a lengthy quotation from my most recent writing will confirm many of Gunnison's points. I have just completed a chapter for Kutash and Wolf's (in press) *Psychotherapist's Casebook* in which I first describe the person-centered approach to therapy and then illustrate it by analyzing a single recorded interview. In my description I review the three conditions reported by Gunnison. Then I add "one more characteristic."

> I described above those characteristics of a growth-promoting relationship which have been investigated and supported by research. But recently my view has broadened into a new area which cannot as yet be studied empirically.
>
> When I am at my best as a group facilitator or a therapist, I discover another characteristic. I find that when I am closest to my inner, intuitive self, when I am somehow in touch with the unknown in me, when perhaps I am in a slightly altered state of consciousness in the relationship, then whatever I do seems to be full of healing. Then simply my *presence* is releasing and helpful. There is nothing I can do to force this experience, but when I can relax and be close to the transcendental core of me, then I may behave in strange and impulsive ways in the relationship, ways which I cannot justify rationally, which have nothing to do with my thought processes. But these strange behaviors turn out to be *right,* in some odd way. At those moments it seems that my inner spirit has reached out and touched the inner spirit of the other. Our relationship transcends itself, and has become a part of something larger. Profound growth and healing and energy are present.
>
> This kind of transcendent phenomenon is certainly experienced at times in groups in which I have worked, changing the lives of some of those involved. One participant in a workshop puts it eloquently. "I found it to be a profound spiritual experience. I felt the oneness of spirit in the community. We breathed together, felt together, even spoke for one another. I felt the power of the 'life force' that infuses each of us—whatever that is. I felt its presence without the usual barricades of 'me-ness' or 'you-ness'—it was like a meditative experience when I feel myself as a center of consciousness. And yet with that extraordinary sense of oneness, the separateness of each person present has never been more clearly preserved."

I realize that this account partakes of the mystical. Our experiences, it is clear, involve the transcendent, the indescribable, the spiritual. I am compelled to believe that I, like many others, have underestimated the importance of this mystical, spiritual dimension.

In this I am not unlike some of the more advanced thinkers in physics and chemistry. As they push their theories further, picturing a "reality" which has no solidity, which is no more than oscillations of energy, they too begin to talk in terms of the transcendent, the indescribable, the unexpected—the sort of phenomena which we have observed and experienced in the person-centered approach.

The person-centered approach, then, is primarily a way of being which finds its expression in attitudes and behaviors that create a growth-promoting climate. It is a basic philosophy rather than simply a technique or a method. When this philosophy is lived, it helps the person to expand the development of his or her own capacities. When it is lived, it also stimulates constructive change in others. It empowers the individuals, and when this personal power is sensed, experience shows that it tends to be used for personal and social transformation.

When this person-centered way of being is lived in psychotherapy, it leads to a process of self-exploration and self-discovery on the part of the client, and eventually to constructive changes in personality and behavior. As the therapist lives these conditions in the relationship, he or she becomes a companion to the client in this journey toward the core of self. (Rogers, in press)

In this same chapter I give a recorded instance of an intuitive response that has no rational connection with what is being said. I discuss it in these terms.

This was the kind of intuitive response which I have learned to trust. The expression just formed itself within me, and wanted to be said. I advanced it very tentatively, and from her initial blank and puzzled look, I thought that perhaps it was completely irrelevant and unhelpful, but her next response shows that it touched something deep in her.

I have come to value highly these intuitive responses. They occur infrequently (this is the first one I have captured in a recording) but they are almost always helpful in advancing therapy. In these moments I am perhaps in a slightly altered state of consciousness, indwelling in the client's world, completely in tune with that world. My nonconscious intellect takes over. I know much more than my conscious mind is aware of. I do not form my responses consciously, they simply arise in me, from my nonconscious sensing of the world of the other. (Rogers, in press)

When I use the term "nonconscious" mind or intellect, I am referring to the fact that "mind" covers much more territory than "brain," a view by Barbara Brown (1980), among others. What I mean is perhaps best illustrated from the field of biofeedback. If you ask me to raise the temperature of the middle finger of my right hand, my conscious mind is completely baffled. It cannot possibly do it. Yet if you show me a needle that indicates the temperature of that finger and ask me if I can make it move upward, I find that I can do it. How do I make all the analyses and discriminations necessary to accomplish this end? It is completely inexplicable if we limit ourselves to the conscious mind. But the nonconscious, organic mind is quite capable of the task.

Used in this sense, the nonconscious mind is very different from the Freudian "unconscious." It also seems to be different from Erickson's "unconscious," which appears to be more similar to my term "the actualizing tendency." I suspect, however, that Erickson would have found the concept of the nonconscious mind congenial. For me, at any rate, this concept helps to explain how I can know and relate to the inner core of my client without any conscious knowledge of that core. It seems that Erickson had a very great fit for this kind of mysterious communication.

To take up another point, I share Erickson's liking for the power of the metaphor, although we differ in the particulars. I am always encouraged when a client in therapy begins to use metaphors, because I believe that the client can express him or herself much more readily and deeply through a metaphor than through exact words. So when a client begins to speak of "this heavy bag that I am carrying around on my back" or speaks of the fear of "walking into darkness—out of the light and into the darkness," I feel sure that progress will be made, and I am eager to respond on the metaphorical level. For myself, I believe that metaphors generated by the client will be more powerful than metaphors that I generate. I do use my own metaphors in some intuitive responses, however, and this seems close to Erickson's approach.

One other quotation from this same recent chapter will confirm another of Gunnison's comparisons. It has to do with the nature of trust in psychotherapy.

Practice, theory and research make it clear that the person-centered approach is built upon a basic trust in the person. This is perhaps its sharpest point of difference from most of the institutions in our culture. Almost all of education, government, business, much of religion, much of family life, much of psychotherapy, is based upon a distrust of the person. Goals must be set, because the person is seen as incapable of choosing suitable aims. He or she must be guided toward these goals, since otherwise the individual might stray from the selected path. Teachers, parents, supervisors must develop procedures to make sure that the individual is progressing toward the goal—examinations, inspections, interrogations are some of the methods used. The individual is seen as innately sinful, destructive, lazy, or all three. This person must be constantly watched over.

But the person-centered approach depends upon the actualizing tendency which is present in every living organism—the tendency to grow, to develop, to realize its full potential. This way of being trusts the constructive directional flow of the human being toward a more complex and complete development. It is this directional flow that we aim to release. (Rogers, in press)

Although I am sure that there are many differences in Erickson's approach and my own, and perhaps a paper should be written on those, they may not be as important as the similarities. If in our work we both rely on the fundamental directional tendency of the client-patient, if we are intent on permitting the client to choose the directions for his or her life, if we rely on the wisdom of the organism in making such choices, and if we see our role as releasing the client from constraining self-perceptions to become a more complete potential self, then perhaps the differences are not so important as they might seem.

REFERENCES

Brown, B.B. (1980). *Supermind*. New York: Harper & Row.

Rogers, C.R. (in press). A client-centered, person-centered approach to therapy. In I.L. Kutash & A. Wolf (Eds.), *Psychotherapist's casebook: Theory and technique in practice.* San Francisco: Jossey-Bass.

INTRODUCTION TO CHAPTER 7

THE IMPORTANCE OF CONTEXT IN COUNSELING

Some years ago a news story appeared which told that riots had broken out in an underdeveloped country because human flesh was being sold in a store. The rumor was traced to food cans with a grinning boy on the label (Gombrich, 1982).

Normally, we do associate what is in a can with the picture on the outside of it. Vegetable or fruit pictures on the label of a can or jar usually refer to the can's contents. But in this case, the smiling baby referred to baby food. Here the switch of *context* was what caused the confusion.

In western societies, we immediately rule out the possibility that the can would contain human flesh. The fact that this ruling out is automatic and unconscious is shown by the fact that most, if not all reading this story, can reflect on their own experience of seeing smiling babies on cans and jars, and the possibility of the contents being human flesh never entered conscious awareness.

We correctly interpret the message of the can's contents through the *context* in which it occurs. All messages have this property—that the context in which the message occurs helps us to understand it.

Another way of looking at context is to see it as the fabric within which communication occurs. This fabric with its own patterning highlights the message communicated.

Context and Communication

Context is important for counseling, because it is a vital part of the communication process. For human beings, context is a product of communication between people. Failure to recognize the relationship between an event and the fabric in which it takes place can cause confusion. The observer who sees the event take place but is unaware of the meaning of the context in which it takes place then may attribute fake properties to the object in the context. Context may be part of the society's custom. In the baby food example the error was made because the context was related to tradition.

Another way of understanding how context is involved in communication is through what Gregory Bateson (1978) called "context markers." For Bateson, a context marker is something artificial. It is an abstraction which is imposed upon the situation by the observer.

Placebo as a Context Marker

One of the most striking examples of a context marker and its effect on communication and behavior is the placebo effect.

Many varieties of placebo(s) exist, but most are familiar with the sugar pill which, when administered by a physician and is seen as "real" medicine by the patient, actually has the effect of reducing pain or anxiety depending upon the symptoms.

A placebo actually has not curative or pain-reducing properties. It is a non-specific treatment with no known effects on the body.

Yet, placebos do work albeit the effects are short lived. One way of explaining placebo effect is that it sets up an expectation of relief, and this is partly due to the context of the situation and the context marker.

Involved in the context are the physician, his/her behavior, the office, and the actual placebo or pill. All provide a *context* in which the patient's definition, the abstraction imposed upon the situation by the patient, includes the expectation of relief.

An interesting context marker is supplied by young children who see bandaids as symbols for relief. While the bandaid itself actually gives no relief but only protection, the child expects that putting the bandage on the bruise actually has pain-reducing qualities. They attribute to this context, of putting on a bandage, pain reduction.

Another context marker are sirens for "fire" and "all clear." The importance of these as context markers occurs when we look at the village where the fire siren for volunteers sounds every noon as a test. Residents of this community hear this siren and go about their business since the context marker (siren) in the context of noon has a different meaning. Wilk points out that if a war broke out the enemy would be well served by timing its bombing attack with the noon siren test which would catch people completely unaware.

Physical Properties of
the Counseling Context

Part of the context in which communication takes place is situational and external to the communication, but the context affects the communication taking place in that it may restrict or help the communication process along. In a church setting, the verbal communication between church-goers is restricted, although the communication for the pastor with his flock is enhanced by the setting. The office, the building, the degrees on the wall all make up the properties of the physical context of counseling. If the counselor is working in the context of a public school where his/her office is situated, that context may affect how he/she is seen in that school. A counselor's office situated right next to the principal's office (another context marker) could have a negative affect and reduce the number of students the counselor sees.

Of course, the counselor wants to set up a context which will be conducive to the counseling process. In this sense, how the office is set up also provides information to the client. In any case within this knowledge context, the counselor must operate in a context of his/her own choosing and comfort.

The following article by Wilk focuses extensively on the importance of context mainly for the systemic or interactional point of view. The Wilk's article also shows how Erickson changed contexts to affect therapy.

Of all the articles in this section, this one may be seen to lie the furthest away from a Rogerian approach with its focus upon external prescriptions. Yet, all of the interventions discussed here need to be done within the fabric of warmth, respect, and positive regard for the client. In fact, as I mention in another section of this book, Bill O'Hanlon, who collaborated with Wilk on a book about contextual interventions, said in a workshop he was leading that, "all the Rogerian stuff" had to precede any intervention.

Finally, this article is important because of the context being related directly to how we perceive and construct the world—an important area we discussed in Chapter 3.

REFERENCES

Bateson, G. (1978). *Steps to an ecology of mind.* San Francisco: Chandler Publishing.

Gombrich, E.H. (1982). *The image and the eye.* Oxford: Phaidon Press.

.

CHAPTER 7

CONTEXT AND KNOW-HOW: A MODEL FOR ERICKSONIAN PSYCHOTHERAPY*

James Wilk, M.A. (Oxon.), M.Sc.**

Reprinted with permission from the author and the *Journal of Strategic and Systemic Therapies,* Vol. I, #4, pp. 1-20, 1982.

*The writer wishes to thank Bill O'Hanlon, M.S. of the Therapeutic Learning Center, Omaha, Nebraska, and Philip Booth, M.A.(Oxon.) of the Park Hospital for Children, Oxford, England, for their help in clarifying these ideas through many hours of discussion; and also the participants in the workshops where these ideas have been presented, whose thoughtful questions have forced me to clarify them still further. Thanks also to Martin E. Corbin for his help with the logistics.

**Consultant, Scientific Staff, The Grubb Institute of Behavioural Studies, London, England. Address for correspondence: James Wilk Associates, 12 Victor Road, TEDDINGTON, Middx., TW11 8SR, England.

ABSTRACT: A model of Ericksonian/strategic psychotherapy is presented as a framework for integrating Dr. Erickson's diverse therapeutic strategies and for aiding the clinician in devising interventions. The model is based on the concept of manipulating contexts to extricate the individual from the system.

"Brooke's Law:

Whenever a system becomes completely defined, some damn fool discovers something which either abolishes the system or expands it beyond recognition."

—Quoted in Arthur Block (1977)[1]

What follows is a working paper, no more and no less. It is to be taken as a report on work-in-progress, the fleshed-out version of which will be presented in the future[2] replete with more extensive clinical examples and fuller argument; the present work, in the meantime, is offered for whatever pragmatic value clinicians may find in it—or not. The model presented was originally derived by the writer, over years of studying and attempting to emulate the psychotherapeutic work of Milton H. Erickson, M.D., as a way of conceptualizing and integrating Dr. Erickson's unique and diverse therapeutic strategies as portrayed in his and others' extensive writings on the subject. The purpose of the model is to assist the practitioner of Ericksonian or strategic psychotherapy to devise therapeutic interventions. It is intended as a kind of map indicating and specifying the range of different routes to the same therapeutic destination and guiding the clinician in selecting the route of choice. The model employs the central concepts of (a) *recontextualization/decontextualization* (through the introduction or obliteration of context-markers) and (b) *know-how* ('learning' in the Ericksonian sense), in a theory of systemic change which does justice to the importance of meaning and of free will in human life.

I. PATTERNED INTERACTION AND BEHAVIORAL OPTIONS

A. The Necessity and Desirability of Rigidly Patterned Behavior

"Human beings are not robots, and they often behave *as if* they were robots."[3] That is, they often behave as if in situation S at time T they had only one choice—tantamount to no choice at all. Throughout his work, Erickson emphasized how rigidly patterned we all are without our knowing it. So much of our functioning goes on automatically, unconsciously, autonomously, and follows rigidly recurring patterns. Bateson and Erickson alike insisted that, indeed, it could not be any other way. Bateson writes:

> In the cliché system of Anglo-Saxons, it is commonly assumed that it would be somehow better if what is unconscious were made conscious. . . . This view is the product of an almost totally distorted epistemology and a totally distorted view of what sort of thing a man, or any other organism, is.

Unconsciousness, except in the special and anomalous sense implied in the Freudian theory of repression, is, according to Bateson, *necessary.* He considers "the impossibility of constructing a television set which would report upon its screen *all* the workings of its component parts, including especially those parts concerned in this reporting." He writes:

> Consciousness, for obvious mechanical reasons, must always be limited to a rather small fraction of mental process. If useful at all, it must therefore be husbanded. The unconsciousness associated with habit is an economy both of thought and of consciousness; and the same is true of the inaccessibility of the processes of perception. The conscious organism does not require to know *how* it perceives—only to know *what* it perceives.

Bateson goes on to draw attention to the fact of *skill* "as indicating the presence of large unconscious components in the performance."[4]

What is efficiently mastered in consciousness is promptly 'sunk' into unconsciousness. To use a crude analogy, what is programmed on keyboard and video screen is transferred as soon as possible to tape or disk. Motor-cortical patterns, once worked out in sufficient detail as it were, are accorded the highest accolade of being deposited in the archives of the cerebellum, which specializes in supplying stereotyped motor patterns for ready reference on the open shelves.* Lewis Thomas[5] reacts with horror to the thought of biofeedback technology ever succeeding in giving him conscious stewardship of his liver function—the way any of us non-pilots would feel, aboard a jumbo jet, if the pilot offered to hand over to us the controls of the aircraft. The liver operates with millions of years of accumulated evolutionary wisdom embodied in rigid patterns of unconscious, autonomous functioning. Bateson reminds us that unaided purposive rationality is pathogenic due to the "circumstance that life depends upon interlocking *circuits* of contingency, while consciousness can see only such short arcs of circuits as human purpose may direct."[6]

---

*The metaphor is mine; it describes what I think are broad trends of consensus amidst the continuing disagreement over the details of cerebelar function (1982).

Erickson talks about learning to ride a bike: first learning to turn the pedals until that becomes automatic, then adding on the learning of how to steer until that in turn becomes automatic too, and then taking off the training-wheels to learn how to keep one's balance until that too becomes automatic, unconscious, and rigidly patterned. This is how we learn skills and develop them—including the skills involved in interacting with our fellow humans.

Such rigid, automatic patterning is equally important in the interaction between people who are in an ongoing relationship. The musicians in an orchestra, indeed even two lead guitarists in a rock band, cannot be continually working out a *modus operandi* for their mutual interaction—else they would never play a single note. Albert Scheflen's work, particularly *Body Language and Social Order*[7] demonstrates the necessity for predictable, rigid, automatic patterns (different on the whole for each culture, and, to an extent, for groups within that culture) for interaction—even a simple conversation—to be possible at all. Individuals' behavior becomes, as it were, "locked-in" in complementary ("fitting-together") fashion with that of others with whom they are in an ongoing relationship, as in a family. To take but one example here, each family will have a set of fairly rigid (= regular = predictable = stable = redundant = . . . &c.) patterns 'governing' behavior at the dinner table. Otherwise all would be unmitigated chaos.

B. The Interactional System and Individual Functioning

If I may state (what is, among family therapists) the almost universally ignored obvious, rigid patterning only becomes problematic in itself *when problems arise.* Intervention to change a rigid pattern of individual behavior, or the larger interactional pattern (or "system": the pattern considered metaphorically in terms of its "machine-*like*" sequenced automaticity) of which the individual's pattern (typically) forms a part, is called for *when and only when (a) problems arise and (b) the pattern does not include behavioral options necessary to eliminate the problem. In such instances the individual finds his present pattern of behavior to be unsatisfactory and yet acts AS IF his behavioral options were limited.* (This illusion of limitations appears in perhaps its most compelling form where the individual's behavior *has the appearance* of being 'locked in' with the behavior of others in an interactional system, or where the symptomatic pattern in question is, according to prevailing cultural assumptions, reified and regarded as involuntary and mechanistically determined.)

In the most general terms, the *aim* of intervention in the pattern/system would be to extricate the individual from the rigid pattern or interactional system and enable him to exercise alternative behavioral options, in order that a new, equally rigid, automatic, unconscious, autonomously functioning pattern or interactional system can be inaugurated; but a pattern which is non-problematic, i.e. produces the desired results and does not contain the 'symptom' or any other undesired 'symptom.'

In the fuzzier versions of purported systems thinking, individual behavior is described as if it were somehow the deterministic product of the functioning of the interactional system: a glaring example of Whitehead's "fallacy of misplaced concreteness." * Self-styled systems thinkers sometimes write or talk as if they thought an individual's behavior were "caused" by the behavior of others with whom he interacts, and as if they thought that, given the behavior of others in the interactional system and the way in which their behavior all appears to "interlock," the individual can do no other than he does. This of course is nonsense. Such sophistical thinking is also *anything but* systems thinking—it is old lineal wine in new circular (Klein) bottles, old-fashioned lineal chain-reaction causality tied 'round in a circle, the snake biting its tail. And it ignores the fact that individuals can act purposively, consciously, and exercise free choice. (Not to exercise such choice would itself be a choice.)

In Bateson's famous example of the man felling a tree with an axe, in which "each stroke of the axe is modified or corrected, according to the shape of the cut face of the tree left by the previous stroke," it is true that we might consider the self-corrective system to be, as Bateson suggests, "(differences in tree)—(differences in retina)—(differences in brain)—(differences in muscles)—(differences in movement of axe)—(differences in tree), &c."[8] This is the case at least where the man is a skilled woodcutter relying on unconscious, automatic patterns. When performing most efficiently, he allows himself to function as a machine, to let his muscles and retina and brain and axe function within the circuit described above, without having to think about it.

---

*Cf. O'Hanlon. Occam's Razor states that "Entities are not to be multiplied without necessity." Wilk's Machete states that "Non-entities are not to be multiplied without necessity either."

But at any point—say when the lunch whistle blows or when he decides he's had enough—the woodcutter can act quite independently of that self-corrective system, and do something else—like put down the axe, for instance. The circuit can at any time be over-rided, and without so much as a by-your-leave. The machine analogy draws attention to the fact of circuitry, but every analogy breaks down at some point—and the point at which this analogy breaks down is precisely that the man, unlike the tree, can say "that's enough," and 'extricate' self from the pattern. Interpersonal interactions too displays rigidly recurring patterns— sequenced automatcity—but this in no way constrains the individuals concerned from acting outside those patterns and just doing their own thing. A rigid interactional pattern many not *contain* certain behavioral options—but neither does it *constrain* the individual from exercising those options.

C. Extricating the Individual from the Interactional Context

There are two general classes of ways of extricating the individual from his interactional context.

First, he can be provided with the requisite know-how or aided in using his existing know-how, to exercise new behavioral options in the problem-context. The result will be the abolition of the existing pattern (system) or its expansion beyond recognition.

Alternatively, the pattern (system) can be abolished or expanded beyond recognition, thus throwing the individual back on his own devices (resources, know-how) and initiating a search for new options.

Either way, if all goes well, new rigid, automatic patterns will emerge which do not contain the problem or symptom and which are otherwise satisfactory.

These two classes of intervention are outlined in what follows.

II. DECONTEXTUALIZATION AND RECONTEXTUALIZATION

A. Contexts and Context-Markers

For human beings, reality is necessarily contextual. We live in a world of meaning, in which "what a thing is" involves/includes what it means for us—its significance. On a biological level of explanation we might refer to its "signal value." Human beings do not simply live in a billiard-ball world of forces and impacts, but a world in which the context of a "thing" is part of what that thing is. For the same "thing" in different contexts will *mean* something different and therefore *be* something different. An utterance, or action, or communication, or piece of interaction, &c. would have a completely different significance (and therefore would *be* something completely different) in a different context. (Indeed, it is difficult to even *talk* about all this precisely *because* the context is *part of* what something is; and here "we are so befuddled by language that we cannot think straight," as Bateson points out.[9])

A fist at the end of an outstretched arm with the thumb pointing heavenward, may be a request for a car to stop to offer transportation to the thumb's owner. At least in some part of Asia Minor, I believe, the same (physical) gesture may "be" (or will be taken to be) an obscene gesture employed as an aggressive insult. (Hence the mayhem committed upon the persons of unsuspecting Western hitch-hikers.) The same thumb may equally well "be" (at least in England) any of the following, depending on the context: a show of approval or support (the non-verbal equivalent of "I agree" or "Right on!"); a "Good luck" wish; a parting salutation—"Goodbye, all the best!"; a reminder or affirmation of who is "number one" (usually, depending on the context, the thumb's owner or some group to which he belongs, where the recipient of the non-verbal communication is typically also a member of that group—i.e. "Up the Lions!"); a display of affiliation (as in a political poster urging one to "vote for Bloggs," illustrated by the ubiquitous thumb); an "O.K." indicating the thumb's owner's acceptance of what he has been requested to do; or a simple "thanks for your help." The earliest recorded upstanding thumb was a plea of "let the Christian live" and an applauding of his bravery, a signal from crowd to gladiator to get off his case. (The alternative was thumbs down and socially sanctioned murder.)* And, needless to say, the thumb becomes a horse of a different color as soon as its context is altered by dint of the bending of the arm and the juxtaposition of the thumb's owner's nose.

The work of Ray Birdwhistell,[10] Albert Scheflen,[11, 12] and Gregory Bateson[13] painstakingly demonstrated the vital importance of context in human (and animal) communication. And they demonstrated, at the same time, the vital importance of human communication in the creation and maintenance of contexts. For human beings, context is a product of

---

*This, of course, is how the story is commonly told. In actuality, 'thumbs down' indicated a reprieve and 'thumbs up' a go-ahead for the kill.

communication between people, present and past, ongoing (as in kinesics) or enduring (as in written traces such as stop signs). The communication may include verbal and non-verbal communication, rules, laws, customs, traditions, institutions, and even *Weltanschauungen.* We may, for heuristic purposes, abstract from the stream of communication those aspects which serve to signal, to classify, to differentiate contexts; following Bateson,[14] we will call these (abstracted parts of communication) "context-markers." As these context-markers are artificial abstractions, something imposed on the data by the observer, there is no question of ever being able to count context-markers or to decide how many can dance on the head of a pin. But we can consider the sources of information heralding the news that this is one sort of context rather than another. Bateson[15] gives these examples from among "the diverse set of events [falling] within the category of context markers":

(a) The Pope's throne from which he makes announcements *ex cathedra,* which announcements are thereby endowed with a special order of validity.

(b) The placebo, by which the doctor sets the stage for a change in the patient's subjective experience.

(c) The shining object used by some hypnotists in 'inducing trance.'

(d) The air raid siren and the 'all clear.'

(e) The handshake of boxers before the fight.

(f) The observances of etiquette.

Context is more like a hot-air balloon than a zeppelin, the former sort of airship requiring the constant input of heated air to maintain its distinctive shape. Context needs to be *maintained,* either by a continuing stream of context-markers or by context-markers with some durability through time (such as police uniforms or stop signs or chessboards or houses of parliament). If not continually maintained, contexts tend to fade, wither, decay, evaporate, or generally evanesce in the special way contexts have of evanescing: they become ambiguous. Once ambiguous, the very context is at the mercy of the first unambiguous context-marker to happen along and exploit the situation by claiming the context for its own. Unmaintained contexts quickly come to be up-for-grabs, and like unmaintained roads can contribute to causing accidents.

The psychological counterpart of "context" is "frame"—though Bateson would argue perhaps that "frame" isn't quite yet "psychological" either. "Frame" is at least the *intraorganismic* counterpart of context, the part of the context that the *organism* contributes: what Mohammed brings to the mountain. This is, if you will, "the internal state of the organism *into* which the information must be received"; for, "message material, or information, comes out of a context into a context...."[16] (For further elucidation of the concept of frame, and hence of reframing, the reader is referred to Bateson's paper on "A Theory of Play and Fantasy"[17] and to the work of Watzlawick and others.[18, 19, 20]

In any event, it should now be self-evident from the above discussion that the introduction of new context-markers into a context, or the obscuring or obliteration of existing context-markers, can dramatically transform *what something is* by dramatically altering the context.

B. The Obliteration or Obscuring of Existing Context-Markers: Decontextualization

During some road construction on the one-way traffic system in Oxford a few years ago, just before rush hour, a practical joker obscured a carefully selected detour-sign, resulting in the establishment of a loop that the diverted traffic could get onto but not off of. A bumper-to-bumper jam of cars soon formed a slowly-moving complete circle such that no further traffic could even get *onto* the loop, thus snarling up traffic throughout the city, virtually within minutes. Clearly, obscuring one judiciously selected context-marker can produce major ramifications reverberating throughout an entire system.

The obliteration or obscuring of context-markers is the blotting-out of *information* of a certain kind—information about the differentiation and the classification of contexts. In radio communications and the like, one would speak of "jamming"—"introducing noise"—preventing the reception of certain signals by sending out other signals of approximately the same frequency. In counter-espionage one might speak of "disinformation"; Watzlawick in *How Real Is Real?* devotes considerable discussion to examples from deception in wartime counter-intelligence work.[21] Since information is "a difference that makes a difference" (McCulloch), information can be obliterated either by obliterating the difference or by obliterating the-difference-it-makes.

To obliterate the difference is to prevent reception of the signal in the first place, by somehow introducing other signs indistinguishable from the signs used in the signalling—so that the signal cannot be differentiated *as a signal.* This is the case of the boy who cried wolf. The context-marker of the fire-alarm, signalling a context of evacuation, can be obscured/obliterated/rendered-meaningless, by repeated "false alarms." The sign used in signalling/marking the evacuation-context (a bell of a particular kind) is now indistinguishable from the sign (the same bell) used to signal a malfunction in the fire-detector system. Therefore when there *is* a real fire, that sign will fail to signal the news of an evacuation-context. In the classic situation-comedy scene of a large office after hours, a phone is ringing and the poor moonlighter has to answer every phone before he finds the right one. *This* phone's ring is not detectably different from any other's, so *this* sign (a particular ring) is insufficiently differentiated to signal the news that *this* phone is ringing. (In the daytime the ring would be distinguished by its nearness, and so the person at that particular desk would answer it.)

To obliterate the-difference-it-makes is, whilst allowing the signal to be received *as* a familiar and identifiable signal, ensuring that it makes no difference in terms of the response to that signal—i.e., the response in its presence is no different from the response in its absence, as it were. With a well-functioning fire-alarm system, it might be announced that a test will be carried out on such-and-such a day at such-and-such a time. (When I was a child there was a test of the town's air-raid siren every Saturday at 12:00 noon, and I can remember thinking frequently, "What a wonderful time for the enemy to attack!") When American cities introduced the right-turn-on-red, the red light could still be detected but it no longer *necessarily* specified a context of stopping (more than momentarily)—it was a difference (distinct from green) that no longer made a difference (distinct from the difference green made), at least once the driver had paused briefly and looked for oncoming traffic.

The distinction we have introduced (between obscuring the difference and obscuring the-difference-that-that-difference-makes) is a purely heuristic distinction. There will be considerable overlap; and often the same situation can be looked at equally validly from either point of view. (Though of course it doesn't cease to be true that black is distinct from white just because there are all shades of gray in between.) Equally there will be overlap of this kind between the category of obscuring existing context-markers (decontextualization) and the next category of intervention—introducing new context-markers (recontextualization).

We can "introduce noise" or do some "jamming" to prevent a context-marker from being perceived, either by introducing new behavior, &c. which is indistinguishable from the behavior currently serving as a context-marker, or *merely by attribution*—attributing in advance an alternative sense to that behavior (whenever it would occur 'naturally"), in this way: If A is the person who performs behavior x,y,z, which serves as a context-marker for B of a context $\emptyset$, we can merely *request* of A *in the presence of B* that A additionally perform that x,y,z behavior to signal the news of some other context ψ (where $\emptyset$ and ψ are incompatible and, preferably, require opposite courses of action from B). Whether A complies with this request or not, noise will have been introduced, just as broadcasting the news that large numbers of counterfeit $5 bills are about to be put into circulation will have the same effect on behavior whether or not those bills are subsequently circulated. (News of an impending fuel shortage will have the same effect on increasing fuel sales and decreasing net available supplies, irrespective of whether the gross amount of supplies subsequently *is* diminished.) Note that A's behavior x,y,z may now disappear altogether, either because it is no longer of value to A (its raison d'être having been to serve as a context-maker for B of context $\emptyset$), or because B, now 'robbed' of information, behaves differently, and so the context-into-which-the-information-comes is now changed (perhaps breaking a communicational loop in which more of the same x,y,z elicited more of the same x',y',z' from B,...eliciting more of the same x,y,z from A and so on).

A child whose fits (in a 1980 case of Gilles de la Tourette's Syndrome) were responded to by protectiveness and concern from mother ("he can't help it") and impatience and threats from father ("he's just showing off"), was told (in his parents' presence) that his parents obviously aren't very good at distinguishing real fits from "put-on" fits, and that at least once each day he must have a "faked" fit to help his parents learn the difference. Even had the child ignored (or not even heard!) the prescription, the noise—and ambiguity and doubt—introduced into the situation would have reduced the polarity between the parents when the fits occurred, reduced the double-messages, &c. In this case, the child's fits disappeared before the next session a fortnight later.

In an elegant case of Haley's[22] a husband who had been referred for *ejaculatio praecox* had been crusading for years to give his wife an orgasm. (If we follow Masters and Johnson, no doubt it was the husband's over-attentiveness to his wife's sensations and consequent inattentiveness to his own which maintained the problem.) The wife was told in the husband's presence that one day she might experience some sexual pleasure but she was to say she did not enjoy it. If asked whether she really did not enjoy it or was just saying that, she was to insist she did not enjoy it. Robbed of his source of information as to his wife's enjoyment, the husband could no longer focus his attention on his wife's sensations, and so the husband's potency was soon restored and with it his wife's pleasure in sex.

Into this category too fall most of the "pretending" interventions (cf. Madanes 1980)[23], particularly those instances in which an individual who regularly x's is told to pretend to x.

If we wish to introduce noise at another 'level', obscuring the-difference-it-makes (*rather than* introducing ambiguity at the level of the sign itself) we can simply—whether in the presence of or absence of A, but usually preferably in A's absence—tell B that A's x,y,z do sometimes classify the context as $\emptyset$, *and also may sometimes classify the context as* ψ (Where, again, $\emptyset$ and ψ are mutually exclusive).

To take just one example here, in a case of John Weakland's,[24] a family came in for therapy because the children were all in open rebellion about not doing their chores. The eldest daughter had just returned home from a stay in a mental hospital following a breakdown and was lounging around the house refusing to lift a finger. Father was extremely protective of her and treated her as very fragile. Mother felt she was just malingering and getting off easy. The younger kids were refusing to do their part until the eldest daughter did hers, and mother subtly supported their campaign. The main intervention was given to Mother and Father alone at the end of the session. They were told to err on the side of caution because there was no way of telling how much the daughter still needed time to recuperate; of course people *can* sometimes *use* their illness to get out of doing things they can very well do, but (this was directed straight at father:) "you mustn't let that doubt enter your mind." In the meantime, they must err on the side of caution and go easy on her.

There are many levels to this intervention as I understand it, but for our purposes here note (1) the way in which the girl's malingering behavior (which it was) is now a context-marker not for a battle but for Mother to go easy on her and tell the other kids, "never mind your sister—the doctor said she must take it easy; the rest of you get on with it" (see below on introducing new context-markers), and more to the point, (2) for father, that behavior can no longer be an unambiguous context-marker for going easy on her, because the therapist has ineradicably planted the seeds of doubt and ambiguity.

In summary, existing context-markers can be obscured/obliterated: (1) by getting A to introduce new behavior—the 'same' behavior x,y,z at additional times to mark additional contexts (ψ *as well as* $\emptyset$); (2) by requesting of A, in B's presence, that A introduce such behavior; or (3) by attributing, in B's presence (even in A's absence), a further significance to A's behavior x,y,z to wit, that it marks the context as ψ or $\emptyset$.

The above considerations all apply equally where there are *more than* two individuals involved, and, *also, in the limiting case where A and B are the same person.* For it is in the self-reflexive nature of human beings that we can both behave and be the observers/interpreters of our own behavior. We are at once producer, director, author, actor, audience, critic, and board of censors.* Our own behavior can serve as context-markers for further behavior on our part, particularly where we regard some of this behavior as involuntary. This brings us back to the subject that we do not realize just how rigidly patterned we all are.

C. Introducing New Context-Markers: Recontextualization

Sometimes we may decontextualize *and* recontextualize a situation by introducing an entirely new context-marker or markers, u,v,w in the form of *new behavior.* This is one case in which we will speak of introducing new context-markers. Here is a brief example: Parents came in for help because of the violent quarrels their teenage sons were getting into at home; the boys refused to have anything to do with any "shrink." I told the parents to tell the boys that since they couldn't come in so I could hear their arguments in person, I needed the parents to bring me some good 'data.' The parents followed the boys around with a tape-recorder to get the kind of data I insisted on, each time the boys showed signs of getting near to starting an argument with each other. They cockily assured their parents, "you'll never catch *us* arguing—you're gonna go back to that shrink empty-handed!" They were right.

The other situation in which we will speak of introducing *new* context-markers is that in which we aim to do *more than* simply in-

---

*Not to mention casting director, prompter, make-up artist, ticket-collector, usher, bouncer, and so on.

troduce noise or ambiguity. Rather than simply turning an unambiguous context $\emptyset$ into one which may be *either-* $\emptyset$ *-or-* $\mathcal{Y}$ so that the context is now "up for grabs," we may wish to create, through manipulation of the context-markers, some very specific new context. We *may* use previously existing markers (behavior) and assign new meanings to them through attribution, but the intervention is designed to create an unambiguous context selected in advance by us. *

In the above example of the arguing boys, when the parents eventually dropped their tape-recording intervention the arguments eventually resumed (though no longer so violently), and the parents made "secret" tape-recordings and brought them to me. After listening to the tapes I made a tape for the boys which I gave to the parents. I told the boys it was clear why they argued so much—they didn't know the first thing about arguing *properly,* and so, just squabbling like a couple of old ladies or a couple of little girls, nothing was ever resolved. The art of arguing properly, I explained, involved remaining one-up whilst putting your opponent one-down by trying to "push his buttons," all the while staying in control of yourself by not letting your own buttons be pushed. They were to give each other plenty of practice, trying to provoke the other deliberately—push his buttons—so he could practice staying one-up and in control of himself. They would, I assured them, find it difficult at first to stay cool and one-up, but with practice—and they needed to give each other plenty—it would become difficult to push their buttons. (I reassured the parents privately that if the practice sessions got out-of-hand, they knew that all they needed to do was turn on the tape-recorder!) The arguments stopped and the boys took a new pride in outdoing each other in being "the coolest of them all."

Once again, all of these considerations apply equally to the limiting case of one individual and to the case of two or more individuals in an interactional system.

An alcoholic came to Dr. Erickson for help with his drinking problem. He would go into a bar and set up two boiler-makers, drinking one whisky and washing it down with a beer and then drinking the other whisky and washing it down with a beer, and then he would be off on his drinking binge. He had been a flying ace in the First World War, and, though now a lush full of self-pity, he was still proud of his

---

*This use of introducing new context-markers using existing behavior, comprising a whole class of therapeutic interventions, we may call "colonization"—see below.

achievements. He brought in his scrapbook for Erickson to see—full of newspaper clippings, photographs of himself, the full record of his times of glory. Erickson perused the album and threw it in the trash, saying, "This has nothing to do with you." Then he told the man what he was to do. He was to go to the bar and set up two boiler-makers as usual. As he finished off the first one he was to say to himself, "Here's to that bastard Milton Erickson, may he choke on his own spit." And as he finished off the second one he was to say, "Here's to that bastard Milton Erickson, may he rot in hell." Then Erickson dismissed him. That was the end of his drinking problem.[25]

In discussion with Bateson, Stewart Brand characterized this man's fate and Bateson heartily agreed: "He's been colonized."[26]

This time, and forevermore, it was Erickson who set up those boiler-makers: he set them up as context-markers of another context altogether. This context we may, with some interpolation, characterize as one in which the man's indignant, self-righteous anger confronted Erickson's glib dismissal, an anger full of his inner insistence that these achievements—the man he was, full of self-confidence, self-discipline, and stoical courage—did *so* have *everything* to do with him. And this—in place of the old context of self-pity, self-indulgence, and compulsion—was now the context those boiler-makers unambiguously marked.

In a rigid, automatic, recurrent pattern of symptomatic (i.e., undesired) behavior, each step in the familiar sequence marks the context, *inter alia,* as one of compulsion and immutability, of behavior following its predictable and pre-determined course. To introduce one small piece of new behavior—so small that the individual can easily incorporate it in the pattern—is to introduce a new context-marker marking the context as therapeutic, and as one of change, of choice, of mutability, and of subsuming an 'automatic' pattern under voluntary control. (It also, incidentally, marks the context as one of hope rather than hopelessness.)

At the same time, if the sequence is L-M-N-O-P, L may be a context-marker marking the context as one in which M is the next step, and M may play the same role for N and so on, or it may be that it is the sequence L-M which is the context-marker "summoning up" N (rather than it being the occurrence of M alone), and so on; and therefore to introduce a new behavior W (however small) between L and M or anywhere else (L-W-M-N-O-P) is to eliminate L as an unalterable context-marker for M, or L-M for N, and to set up W as the new context-marker signalling that it's time to M, or, as the case may be, that it's time for T. Because, as the next intervention, T can come after W and before M, and why not? W's only been "calling forth" M since yesterday! Thus: L-W-T-M-N-O-P. Likewise, one can insert L again just before the end: L-M-N-O-L-P...L-M-N-O-L-P...L-M-N-O-L-P...L-M-N-O-L-P... and evntually one can just go L-P...L-P...L-P...: "In my beginning is my end."[27] [Cf. "shortcircuiting" in O'Hanlon's "Strategic Pattern Intervention" (1982a)[28] and see this paper also for further examples which may be additionally understood from the standpoint of introducing new behavior into the pattern to manipulate context-markers.]

New behavior can also be introduced in such a way that the symptom itself is transformed into a context-marker for self-improvement, by linking occurrence of the symptom with accomplishment of some beneficial activity such as getting much-needed exercise or improving one's handwriting. There are numerous examples in Erickson's work of this particular variation.

This variation of the technique is not to be confused with an equally Ericksonian approach in which the new behavior introduced is a "benevolent ordeal" (in Haley's terminology[29]) so that the symptom becomes a context-marker for some arduous and unpleasant activity of the sort that human beings, given human nature, are naturally good at finding ways—conscious or unconscious—of postponing or avoiding altogether. And even if it means failing to produce the symptom which is now a context-marker for the start of the ordeal.

Just as there was an overlap between obscuring a difference and obscuring the-difference-it-makes, and between obscuring existing context-markers and introducing new ones, there is an overlap between all of the above categories on the one hand, and the second broad class of interventions to be considered: know-how. So far we have considered extricating the individual from the interactional context by transforming that context so that the individual is thrown back on his own resources. If all of the traffic lights in the city were disconnected, drivers would be thrown back on their own resources; and if the situation became a permanent one, various hand-signals, &c. and customs would develop over time and become standard, so that a new rigid system would be established. Sometimes it may be necessary, in addition to abolishing the old pattern through decontextualization or recontextualization, to supply the individual with at least one viable behavioral alternative; sometimes, however, it may be sufficient to break the previous pattern of behavior around the problem (sometimes *but not always* by interdicting/reversing the attempted solution) which had been maintaining the problem. Below we will consider interventions based on intervening in, as it were, the *opposite* direction: "supplying" the individual with the know-how he needs to behave satisfactorily in the problem-situation, which will itself break up the old pattern or system and lead to the establishment of a new one.

III. KNOW-HOW

A. "The Same Damn Thing"

It is, I believe, to Dick Fisch that we owe the currency among strategic therapists of the homily that "life is just one damn thing after another" and when it's not it's "the same damn thing over and over again." Now when it's the same damn thing over and over again some problem-solving may be in order, and a therapist *may* have a job to do. And if it's the same damn thing over and over again in numerous settings—work, home, college, &c. and at different times in the individual's life, we had best be careful in selecting our level of intervention. Just to alter, however dramatically, the family system, may be insufficient to have any real impact on the problem except as it appears in the family setting. And that small change may or may not generalize. Likewise, we may successfully help someone who has trouble asking for a date because he is looking for the perfect opening line, and have him reappear in our office a year later unable to finish his dissertation because he can't write a chapter until he finds the perfect chapter title.

There is no question of any "symptom substitution" having occurred at all. Nor is there any hypothesized Freudian "compulsion to repeat." Rather it's just another isomorphic or homologous instance of the same damn thing over and over again. The client may not even be aware of "the pattern that connects," nor need we help him to become aware. As therapists *we* must be aware in selecting our definition of the pattern in which we are seeking to intervene. In the above example, it may be something like "not getting started on anything until he's devised a 'perfect' beginning." Our client may keep *doing* the "same damn thing over and over again" because he keeps *seeing* each situation the same damn way over and over again: he keeps bringing the same damn frame. And psychoanalysts have on the whole been better than family therapists (at least strategic family therapists) at recognizing that individuals may bring the same frame/behavior to repeated interactional contexts of a certain kind, elicit complementary behavior in response, and thereby recreate the same interactional system repeatedly.

In the present model, wherever it is a case of the same damn thing over and over again across different times and places and problem-settings, and so on, it is the individual and his limiting frame which is the focus of our intervention, once we have carefully selected the relevant "more-of-the-same"[30]—the pattern that connects.

B. Not Carrying Coals to Newcastle

The majority of the time, clients already have all the resources, all of the 'learnings' they need to solve their problems. They know how to solve them and they don't know that they know. Dr. Erickson would sometimes quote Josh Billings's, "The trouble ain't that people are ignorant, it's that they know so much that ain't so," and then he'd add *"And the even bigger trouble is that they know so much they don't know they know."* Perhaps the word Erickson used more than any other in both his teaching and his therapeutic work was "learning." And he was talking about *learning* pure and simple—not the technical concept of "learning *to*"* of behaviorist conditioning theory, but everyday "learning *how,"* the acquisition of skills—from learning how to ride a bike to learning how to be comfortable in uncomfortable situations: He was talking about know-how.

No matter for how long or with what severe consequences it's been the same damn thing over and over again, only a small change is usually called for. An intermediate class of interventions between abolishing the old pattern or interactional system and supplying the individual(s) with the requisite know-how (that they may have and not know they have) to solve their problem, is simply to reverse, through behavioral prescription, the direction of the attempted solution. Weakland, Fisch, Segal, Watzlawick, and others at the Brief Therapy Center of the Mental Research Institute have already written so much on this approach[31,32,33,34] that we will say no more about it here. (In the present writer's view, many of the interventions of the BTC do not fall strictly into this category and are covered elsewhere in the present model.) Sometimes it is *only* the attempt to solve the problem, or the direction of that attempt, which is maintaining the problem, and to get the client(s) to reverse the main thrust of their attempted solution is sufficient to break the pattern

---

*In colloquial English, "learning how to X" is sometimes abbreviated to "learning to X" as in "learning to swim."

and/or give them access to the know-how they need to solve it. Here we will be concerned with interventions based on "merely" altering the individual's frame without even needing to prescribe the now "obvious" behavior.

Whatever know-how the individual may need to solve his problem and break free of the limiting pattern or interactional system, the therapist can *usually* find some area of the client's life now or at some time in the past where the client has demonstrated/applied such know-how in another context. The therapist's job here is then to reframe the problem-context so that the individual can see it—frame it—as sufficiently similar in the relevant respects to the context in which he already has applied the know-how, so that he can apply that know-how in the problem-context. Watzlawick et al.[35] define "reframing" as changing "the conceptual and/or emotional setting or viewpoint in relation to which a situation is experienced and to place it in another frame which fits the 'facts' of the same concrete situation equally well or even better, and thereby changes its entire meaning." In the present use of reframing, the new frame is typically one broad enough to include both the problem-context and the "native" context of the applied know-how as two sub-classes or examples from the same class of contexts.

This reframing, *helping the client to frame the problem-context and a non-problematic context as two versions of the same thing,* may be accomplished in a great variety of ways including simple redefinition, metaphor, anecdotes, describing the problem-context in terms borrowed from the "native context" of the applied know-how, and so on. O'Hanlon's model of Erickson's use of metaphor is relevant here.[36] There is *some* overlap between this class of intervention and that described above (p. 95) as "colonizing" to create a new unambiguous context selected by us in advance. The main distinction is that the reframing described here requires that the client consciously *accept* the new frame before he can apply his know-how; whereas in "colonizing" interventions the context is radically altered *whether or not* the client consciously "buys" the connection we are making.

C. First Providing a Context for the Acquisition of Know-How

Sometimes the client does not have the know-how required to solve his problem, or at least the therapist cannot readily find any area of his life in which the required know-how is, or ever has been applied. Where this is the case the therapist must, additionally, first arrange a context where this know-how can readily be acquired—a context related *at most tangentially* to the problem-context. It should be, above all, a context in which the acquisition of this know-how is the *natural* response that this individual would have to being in this context—given what we know about his patterns of responsiveness. Frequently we need rely only on the fact that our client is a human being and on our knowledge of human nature.

1. *Providing a context in the therapy room.* Whether or not trance is employed, the client can often be guided by the therapist in developing the necessary know-how and in practicing it in the office. This is particularly so where the client needs to learn how to alter his affective or behavioral response to some situational stimulus, or to alter how he behaves whenever he feels a certain way.

A nine-year-old boy who was readily provoked into fights whenever the other kids baited him by calling him names, and who "couldn't help it"—he just "got so mad"—was able to acquire the know-how he needed through the simple expedient of my calling him all the names in the (other kids') book. He *had to* 'control himself' in my office and soon he was beside himself with giggles. In Dr. Lustig's film of Erickson, *The Artistry of Milton H. Erickson, M.D., Part 1,*[37] Monde, in the trance state, was helped, *inter alia,* to develop and practice a different response to situations where she would previously have felt anxious and insecure, and she was taught a "cue" to help her trigger this response in daily life. Typically, Erickson would elicit the response—the know-how—in his office; have the client practice it; monitor it; and send the client out to practice it in the problem setting.

2. *Providing a context out in the world.* Erickson knew more than anyone else about using life as a teacher, and he would frequently arrange a context out in the world where the relevant know-how would be acquired naturally. Once again, this context would be one in which *this* individual's (or *any* individual's) natural response to being in this context would be to develop the required know-how.

Once the individual has acquired the know-how in another context —in the therapy room or outside in the world—reframing can be employed as described above to complete the transfer of this know-how to the problem-context. The seedlings can thus be transplanted from greenhouse to garden.

D. Unhooking

Where the only obstacle to the individual's applying the necessary know-how is some limiting belief on which he has got himself hooked, the intervention of choice—because it is the simplest—is to unhook the client from that limiting belief.

Where parents are hamstrung because they are hooked on the belief that they must *agree* about everything regarding rules for their children and the sanctions for breaking those rules, all that may be necessary may be to tell them there's no law that says they've got to agree. And that their kids need to learn to deal with different people and different standards and to adapt their behavior to the person they're with.

The unhooking can often—perhaps most often—be accomplished by providing counterexamples from the client's own experience. If he is hooked on a belief that when he *feels* like doing X he must then *do* X (i.e., that feeling a certain way *causes* him to behave in accordance with that feeling) he can be asked, for example, whether he has ever wanted desperately not to attend some social function and then has gone anyway because it was important for his career. Or he can be told that 99% of all people feel "desperately" like going back to sleep when the alarm rings in the morning and, still feeling that way, they then get themselves out of bed: if everyone did just whatever they felt, the world would end because there would be no one left to run it—they would all be under the covers. A depressed person who is failing to take the necessary action because he takes the depth and darkness of his feelings of gloom as proof of the hopelessness of the situation, may never have had the experience of coming out a deep depression, yet will undoubtedly have known times when "after the rain comes the sunshine." The experience of sunshine after the rain is one of the universal life experiences or learnings on which Erickson would draw (examples as irrefutable as they are simple) in unhooking clients from limiting beliefs. There is an overlap between (a) unhooking, and (b) reframing-to-allow-the-transfer-of-know-how, in so far as, for example, we can view the "getting out of bed" counterexample as enabling the transfer of the know-how of feeling-one-way-and-acting-another from the morning context to the problem context; and the sunshine after the rain is a reframing enabling the client to see the problem-context and a non-problematic context as two versions of the same thing, so that he can re-apply his know-how of maintaining his hope and planning for a breakthrough at times when all seems gloomiest.

IV. SUMMARY

In this model, the aim of therapeutic intervention is to extricate the individual from a problematic rigid pattern or interactional system so that he can exercise new behavioral options and inaugurate a new, equally rigid but non-problematic pattern or interactional system. This can be accomplished in one or both of two ways:

I. Abolishing the system so that the individual is thrown back on his own devices, so that he must initiate a search for new options.

A. By decontextualization, obliterating or obscuring an existing context-marker (a difference that makes a difference as to the context) so that the context becomes ambiguous: *either*

    (1) By obliterating a difference. EITHER

        (a) getting A to produce the context-marking behavior at additional times to mark additional contexts mutually exclusive of the contexts originally marked, OR

        (b) merely requesting this of A in B's presence; *or*

    (2) By obliterating the-difference-it-makes: in B's presence attributing to that context-marking behavior an alternative and mutually exclusive sense.

B. By recontextualization, introducing new context-markers: *either*

    (1) By introducing new behavior interfering with the functioning of existing context-markers and serving as new ones; *or*

(2) By "colonization": attributing new meanings to previously occurring context-markers, to create a new, specific, unambiguous context selected in advance.

II. Providing the individual with new behavioral options, so that the system is abolished.

A. By prescribing a reversal in the direction of the attempted solution.

B. By reframing the problem context so that the individual can apply know-how which he has previously applied only in some other context: helping the client to see both contexts as two versions of the same thing.

C. By reframing as above (B), after first providing/arranging this latter context so that the know-how can be acquired through the occurrence of the client's own natural responses in that context: *either*

(1) In the therapy room, *or*

(2) Outside in the world.

D. By unhooking the individual from limiting beliefs which keep him from applying the necessary know-how.

E. By straightforward advice (in therapy, *rarely* necessary or sufficient: sufficient only where *un*necessary).

V. DISCUSSION

A. Implementation Strategies: Reframings, Requisitions, Spoiling Interventions, and Incantations

The above outline attempts to describe in broad terms the range of strategies for intervention in this model of Ericksonian psychotherapy. It is useful to distinguish four categories of strategies for *implementing* these types of intervention, a distinction introduced by the present writer in an earlier work[38] :

(1) *Reframing:* As defined by Watzlawick, et al. (see above, p. 27): may be achieved through redefinition, presuposition, implication, metaphor, anecdotes, and many other forms of verbal therapeutic communication, often with multiple levels. To achieve its effect, the client must come to accept the reframing at a conscious level (though he need not be conscious of having done so).

(2) *Requisition:* A behavioral prescription which, to achieve its therapeutic effect, must be carried out by the client.

(3) *Spoiling Intervention (Errand):* A behavioral prescription which need not be actually carried out to achieve its effect, but which the client must somehow be induced to keep in mind at some level.

(4) *Incantation:* 'A spell which need only be uttered and taken in,' but need *not* be accepted to achieve its effect; may have the form of a behavioral prescription or of a statement making a direct or implied re-attribution of meaning.

These implementation strategies may be employed in carrying out the strategies outlined in Figure 7.1.

B. Reframing: A Multitude of 'Sinns'

One area clarified by this model, is that of where "reframing" comes in—in strategic therapy generally. Reframing may be used:

(1) As an implementation strategy (IIB, IIC, IID)

(2) To 'sell' tasks which are requisitions—hooking them either to the client's current beliefs, or to current behavior in a way that makes sense to the client, or

(3) Providing a rationale (where necessary or desirable—this is usually a matter of taste, personal style, and confidence in giving interventions unbacked by rationales) for spoiling interventions and incantations.

Intervention Strategy \ Implementation Strategy	Reframing	Requisition	Spoiling Intervention (Errand)	Incantation
Decontextualizing (IA)	—	IA(1)(a)	IA(2)	IA(1)(b)
Recontextualizing (IB)	—	IB(1)	IB(2)	IB(2)
Using Existing Know-How (IIA,B,D,E)	IIB, IID	IIE	IIA	—
Using New Know-How (IIA,C,E)	IIC	IIA, IIC, IIE	—	—

Figure 7.1. Intervention Strategies and Implementation Strategies. (The numbers refer to the Summary outline.)

All of these uses of reframing are typically lumped together in the therapy literature, as well as overgeneralizing the concept to include many other types of intervention as well. This tends to render the concept all but useless. Many, many useful distinctions can be made here—the subject of another paper.

C. Who Mentioned Paradox?

Another feature of this model is that it seems to render the concept of therapeutic paradox entirely unnecessary. Symptom prescription and the prescription of other already occurring behavior can readily be understood as ways of decontextualizing or recontextualizing the symptom, and therefore, by changing the context, *eo ipso* changing the symptom itself. Although symptom prescription is rarely employed *tout simple* without prescribing an alteration in some aspect (time, place, attentional set, &c.), even prescribing it unchanged alters the context considerably though *not always* significantly. Since Haley's (1963) *Strategies*[39] and Watzlawick et al.'s *Pragmatics* (1967)[40] strategic therapists have referred glibly to 'the world of difference between doing something spontaneously and doing it when you have been told to do it,' without specifying the nature of that difference. *The difference is context.* A child who screams to annoy his mother for the sake of getting what he wants, will have the contextual rug pulled out from under him if mother cooly insists that he scream louder: the scream is no longer what it was, no longer a member of the class of "things that bother mother," and so of no further value to him.

D. Even People are People Too

Another implication of all this is that it puts systems theory in its (rightful) place. If one really takes systems theory seriously, one can no longer get away with passing off as "systemic" any model which uses old-fashioned, chain-reaction, lineal cause-effect, whether the chain is drawn out straight or tied in a circle under the name of "circular causality." *The pattern is the thing* (Bateson). And that pattern is not to be reified. People are not cogs in any machine and their behavior is not in any sense the deterministic product of the functioning of the interactional system. They of course can and do behave in rigid, automatic patterns. And at any point they can act purposively, consciously, and quite independently of the system of which their *automatic* functioning is a part. Purposive rationality has its own problems, as Bateson knew, but we cannot eliminate those problems by pretending that humans do not behave purposively.

E. "It's What We Know That Ain't So That Gives Us Trouble"

Here is a laundry list of presuppositions *NOT* held by the present writer, presuppositions which are rendered unnecessary by this model: that the problem or symptom serves a function in the family or for the individual; that clients/families are resistant to change or simply do not want to change; that "symptoms" are symptoms *of* something—such as an underlying dysfunction or conflict; that family systems exhibit homeostatic mechanisms or processes which tend to respond to a therapeutic change by attempting to undo it; that family systems can be pathological or pathogenic; that rigid patterns are bad news; that clients with problems are damaged people; that problems in the child indicate overt or covert conflict between the parents or between parent and child or parent and grandparent(s); that it is always *necessary* to change the whole family system to bring about change in an individual; that it is always *sufficient* to do so; that conscious functioning is *always* better than unconscious functioning; that it is *never* better; that it is not sufficient to deal therapeutically with the presenting problem or symptom alone; that strategic therapy needs to involve trickiness or disingenuousness; that therapy involves a contest between client and therapist; that psychotherapy is a difficult and highly technical business; that difficult human problems require complex solutions.

This bundle of presuppositions, a bundle containing many other presuppositions as well, is still waiting for us at the laundry.

But we have lost the ticket.

WORKS CITED

1. Bloch, Arthur (1977) *Murphy's Law and other reasons why things go wrong*, p. 51.

2. Wilk, J. (1983) "Ericksonian Therapeutic Patterns: A Pattern Which Connects." [In J. Zeig (Ed.), *Ericksonian Psychotherapy Vol. II: Clinical Applications*, New York: Brunner Mazel, 1985.]

3. O'Hanlon, Bill (1982) Personal communication.

4. Bateson, G. (1967), "Style, Grace and Information in Primitive Art," in *Steps to an Ecology of Mind* (1978), pp. 108-110. London: Paladin.

5. Thomas, L. (1974), *The Lives of a Cell.* London: Allen Lane.

6. Bateson, G., ibid., p. 119

7. Scheflen, A. (1973). *Body Language and Social Order: Communication as Behavioral Control.* Englewood Cliffs, NJ: Prentice-Hall.

8. Bateson, G. (1971) "The Cybernetics of 'Self': A Theory of Alcoholism," In *Steps* (1978), p. 288.

9. Bateson, G. (1969) "Double Bind, 1969," in *Steps* (1978), p. 246.

10. Birdwhistell, R. (1970) *Kinesics and Context.* London: Allen Lane.

11. Scheflen, A. (1973) *Body Language and Social Order: Communication As Behavioral Control.* Englewood Cliffs, NJ: Prentice-Hall.

12. Scheflen, A. (1973) *How Behavior Means.* New York: Gordon and Breach.

13. Bateson, G. (1978) *Steps to an Ecology of Mind* (Paladin edition).

14. Bateson, G. (1964/1971) "The Logical Categories of Learning and Communication," in *Steps* (1978), p. 260.

15. Ibid., p. 261.

16. Bateson, G. (1978) *Steps,* p. 370.

17. Bateson, G. (1978). "A Theory of Play and Fantasy," in *Steps,* 150-66.

18. Watzlawick, P., Beavin, J., and Jackson, D. (1967) *Pragmatics of Human Communication.* New York: Norton.

19. Watzlawick, P., Weakland, J., and Fisch, R. (1974) *Change.* New York: Norton.

20. Watzlawick, P. (1976). *How Real is Real?* New York: Random House.

21. Ibid.

22. Haley, J. (1963) *Strategies of Psychotherapy.* New York: Norton.

23. Madanes, C. (1981). *Strategic Family Therapy.* San Francisco: Jossey-Bass.

24. Weakland, John (1982) Personal communication.

25. O'Hanlon, Bill (1982) Personal communication; and G. Bateson in *CoEvolution Quarterly,* Fall 1975, p. 33.

26. *Co-Evolution Quarterly,* Fall 1975, p. 33.

27. Eliot, T.S. (1944). *The Four Quartets.* London: Faber.

28. O'Hanlon, Bill (1982) "Strategic Pattern Intervention," *Journal of Strategic and Systemic Therapies* I, 4.

29. Haley, J. (1973) *Uncommon Therapy*. New York: Norton.

30. Watzlawick, P. et al. (1974) *Change*. New York: Norton.

31. Ibid.

32. Fisch, R., Weakland, J., and Segal, L. (1982) *Tactics of Change*. New York: Jossey Bass.

33. Fisch, R., Weakland, J., Watzlawick, P., Segal, L., Hoebel, F.C., and Deardoff, C.M. (1975) *Learning Brief Therapy: An Introductory Manual* (Privately circulated)

34. Weakland, J., Fisch, R., Watzlawick, P., and Bodin, A. (1974) "Brief Therapy: Focused Problem Resolution," In *Family Process*.

35. Watzlawick, P. et al. (1974) *Change*.

36. O'Hanlon, B. (1983) "Class of Problems/Class of Solutions: A Model for Parallel Communication in Therapy," (in preparation)*

37. Lustig, H.S. (1975) "The Artistry of Milton H. Erickson, M.D." (Film and videotape.)

38. Wilk, J. (1980) *Techniques and Theories of Change in Strategic Psychotherapy*, Unpublished M.Sc. Dissertation, University of Oxford.

39. Haley, J. (1963). *Strategies of Psychotherapy*. New York: Norton.

40. Watzlawick, P. et al. (1967) *Pragmatics of Human Communication*. New York: Norton.

*See also the more recent model of therapeutic metaphor found in J. Wilk & B. O'Hanlon (1987) *Shifting Contexts: The Generation of Effective Psychotherapy*. New York: Guilford Press.

INTRODUCTION TO CHAPTER 8

An earlier chapter introduced the philosophy that our minds actually create the world in which we live. If this is so, then why not create a world we enjoy and in which we function productively. This next article by Daniel Aroaz begins with a continuation of this concept of the importance of ideas. He began the article with his concept of *Metanoia,* a Greek term coined to reflect that in order for people to change, they must change their *perceptions* of themselves and their perceptions or beliefs of the world.

He then offered a number of techniques which can be utilized to effect those changed perceptions. Although the format of the article is written for counselors and can be used by counselors, each of the techniques is easily understandable and simple enough to be used by anyone interested in self-growth.

The article also is a good introduction to hypnosis, a technique discussed in more detail in Section III.

CHAPTER 8

TRANSFORMATION TECHNIQUES OF THE NEW HYPNOSIS

Daniel L. Araoz, Ed.D.*

INTRODUCTION

The ultimate goal of any hypnotic intervention in therapy is change. But since change, to be effective, must come from one's inner self, I prefer the ancient Greek expression, *Metanoia,* associated with early Christian conversion. For a conversion to be genuine, the person had to

---

*Dr. Araoz is the author of a new book, *Hypnosis and Sex Therapy,* New York: Brunner/Mazel, 1982.

Aroaz, D.L. (July, 1983). Transformation techniques of the new hypnosis. *Medical Hypnoanalysis,* *4*(3), 114-124.

accept the new belief and way of life "from within." He had to undergo an *inner* transformation. Anything less did not count. *Metanoia* means, then, a drastic change in one's perception of oneself and one's *world image,* the constant element at the root of all human emotional problems. The world image, as explained by Existentialists, is the mental image I have formed of my world. This often does not correspond exactly to what my real world is. This discrepancy leads me frequently to want to conform the world to my world image. As long as this is impossible, I suffer emotional stress and pain. The solution to this conflict is the change in my world image, which slowly has to become more in harmony with the external world.

To effect this *metanoia* or special transformation there are several major techniques used by the New Hypnosis. This article will describe them and give practical applications for each. These techniques fall under several categories as the chart shows. For brevity's sake and to avoid repetition, twelve techniques will be discussed, though many more could be listed. However, upon close consideration, all other techniques fall under one of the twelve.

NEW HYPNOSIS TECHNIQUE

Somatic

Relaxation
Somatic Bridge
Subjective Biofeedback

Mental

Dissociative	Temporal	Paralogical
Dissociation	Transfer	Paradox
Personality	Reliving	Parable
Activation	Rehearsal	
Materialization	Emotional Bridge	

SOMATIC TECHNIQUES

These are techniques which focus on the bodily experience. In *Relaxation,* for instance, frequently the simple and constant act of breathing becomes a focus of attention, leading to an expanded awareness of one self. In *Somatic Bridge,* a slight pain or discomfort in any part of one's body is the beginning of greater awareness and integration. In *Subjective Biofeedback* one uses one's body to monitor emotional reactions.

Relaxation

Most professionals interested in hypnosis know the value of relaxation. The point I want to make is that relaxation is the means to give the parasympathetic a chance. By learning to relax, one allows the parasympathetic to take over. Tension or lack of relaxation occurs when the sympathetic nervous system is active longer than it is necessary to face a threat or danger. What this technique of relaxation attempts to achieve is to activate the parasympathetic nervous system, that mechanism which brings all our bodily systems to optimal functioning. In practice I find that as long as the person does not have any breathing difficulties, it is helpful to start with one's normal breathing (later on I will discuss how to achieve relaxation with someone who has any form of breathing difficulty such as asthma, emphysema, hyperventilation or similar conditions). The approach may be simple. For instance one may say something like this: "You are breathing now. Please, pay attention to the way your body likes to breathe. Don't force anything. Just breathe and find out what is your body's rhythm of breathing—its breathing tempo. Let it happen. Plenty of time. No rush. Just breathe. While you breathe, think of relaxation. As if you were watching your whole body—your whole body—relax—really r-e-l-a-x. Enjoy the relaxation. Let it happen. Right now.''

By learning to relax one allows
the parasympathetic to take over

The relaxation chatter continues as long as the person needs it to enter the relaxed state. It is always useful to encourage clients to close their eyes when they blink naturally. I find myself saying something like this: "You just blinked. Next time it happens notice how restful it is to blink. Perhaps you may even want to put your blinking in slow motion, while your whole body enjoys this experience of relaxation. All systems slow down while you enjoy the experience," and so on.

For those who have some breathing difficulty and consequently may have associated breathing with discomfort, the technique of relaxation must start elsewhere. In this case, one may use any of the traditional hypnotic techniques (eye fixation, arm levitation, different kinds of visualization, etc.) or one may ask the client to remember a situation in which he felt very relaxed. Once the situation is decided upon, more and more details are introduced in order to "reproduce" the same somatic experience of relaxation the person experienced in the situation he is currently remembering. Let's assume the person identifies as a relaxing scene one night in a ski trip, when he could not sleep and sat by a dying fire while the snow was falling outside and everybody else in his party was deeply asleep. One can then build on this scene until the person re-experiences the peace and relaxation he experienced in the original situation. (The 25 "images" suggested by Kroger and Fezler (1976) are very helpful to build on the relaxing scene offered by the client).

As a back-up technique, in these cases where a person is too tense or distracted to follow our instructions to relax, the paradoxical approach of muscle tensing and relaxing in fairly rapid succession is beneficial. It demonstrates dramatically to the client the sensation of relaxation: after tensing up one's muscles, it is easy to experience and enjoy the general feeling of relaxation. Once this is accomplished, one may proceed to the other methods described earlier.

Relaxation is a general technique since practically every person we deal with can benefit from it. But, as implied before, the main point is not so much muscle relaxation but inner peace. This is important to remember because a person worried, guilty or anxious with negative thoughts cannot obtain the type of relaxation I am dealing with. In practice this means that the hypnotherapist must address himself to the client's inner reality. It can be done in conjunction with the instructions suggested in the previous paragraphs. For instance: "While letting your breathing blow away your tensions—like tiny particles of dust leaving your tense muscles—let your breathing fill your mind with good thoughts. Let your breathing fill you with peace and inner serenity. Breathing in comfort. Breathing in good feelings—peace, quiet, tranquil thoughts. Distractions will come and go. Let them fly just through you. Your inner peace is the important thing right now,'' and so forth.

The main point is not so much
muscle relaxation but
inner peace

Somatic Bridge

The general concept of this technique is taken from Wright's (1971) affect bridge. Rather than using it to activate older ego states by focusing on a feeling common to something current and something past, the somatic bridge is similar to the Oriental "taitoku" or body-thinking. This is a way of utilizing one's awareness of the body to facilitate awareness of repressed feelings, since authentic self transformation—*metanoia*—must include the whole being rather than be merely intellectual. Because of this, the somatic bridge is effective with people who are too left-hemispheric, or who have never developed intuitive, symbolic and emotional capacities—the functions of the right cerebral hemisphere.

The technique is introduced when clients feel "they have nothing to talk about," or they are feeling "flat," with no emotion. The hypnotherapist invites the person to simply sit there and pay attention to her body. "The goal here is not to talk about it but to experience. What parts of your body are you aware of now?" the clinician may ask, "Just become aware of one part. Stay with the awareness. Don't talk. Don't do anything. Let distractions come and go. Just enter the awareness of your body more fully."

Only after the person has become involved in her body awareness, she may describe what she is experiencing. Then the hypnotherapist may continue: "Now, let the awareness of your body lead you to something which is hidden in the recesses of your mind. I wonder what will come up: memories, images, joys, pains. Whatever comes is O.K. Your inner mind will speak to you in a new way through your body. Take your time. Let it happen and you'll learn important things about yourself. You'll be surprised, pleased," etc.

Many mental health workers believe that clients must get in touch with their feelings. The somatic bridge is a surprisingly quick and effective technique to facilitate this. Frequently a host of meaningful memories and psychological connections rush to awareness, giving the client significant therapeutic material to work.

This technique is rich in therapeutic potential. Often when the client concentrates on one part of his body, mental images occur. These, then, should be followed, as in the case of the man who started to be aware of his left foot, "More like a slight itch on my big toe." I invited him to concentrate on that itch, "to get more into it." At that point the man frowned and said, "Like a line going up to my groin." I invited him to visualize the line: its color, thickness, the material it was made of. He saw it as of a silvery color, perhaps even made of silver and added, "But I don't know what it means." Typical of most people in our culture is the importance *to know,* the discomfort with mere experiencing and being. I replied: "You will soon enough. Now, just stay with that silvery line: *feel* it going from your right toe to your groin. Does it end there? What happens there? Take your time and stay with the silvery line." This sensitive respect for any material coming from the subconscious mind is not anti-intellectualism but rather a holistic approach to being alive. The silvery line did not end there. It soon became a powerful light that enveloped his whole body. I encouraged him to enjoy the new energy he was experiencing. He connected it with "the energy that keeps me alive, the force of life in me, life itself." After this experience he talked about his mental attitude in the last few days which had been rather negative and pessimistic. He had been ready "to fold his tent," as he put it. This experience made him think more positively about his future, about enjoying life more, about giving himself more time to play, have fun and relax.

Often when the client
concentrates on one part of his
body, mental images occur

This example is typical. Much meaning is discovered through this approach, but the meaning seems to emerge without the laborious left hemispheric activity of analyzing, evaluating, "thinking." And, what makes this therapy always interesting and full of surprises is that the hypnotherapist does not have to wonder where to go next, what to do next. The therapist simply follows carefully and respectfully what the client's inner mind offers naturally, spontaneously and, at times, even playfully; as if the inner mind is waiting to "communicate" with the person's conscious mind.

The somatic bridge may be used any time a client expresses any somatic awareness. If it is tiredness, a slight pain, a headache or anything similar, it becomes surprisingly therapeutic to stay with it, to allow it to become the focus of attention and then to let it develop any way it goes, paying attention to mental images, memories and psychological connections.

Subjective Biofeedback

Here one starts with a mental image, an event or memory. Then attention is paid to the way the body reacts to that mental activity. Finally, meaning emerges out of this connection. Let's test it first with ourselves. Imagine a very sad experience; visualize it in detail. Then attend to your body's reaction to it. Just notice it and become aware of the fact that there is harmony between mind and body. The Cartesian separation between the two is more didactic than real, as Oriental philosophy and medicine teach us. Do the same again but this time think of something very exciting and joyful. Stay with it and relive as many details as possible. Next notice how your body—some part of your body—is reacting to the joyful and exciting experience. At the end, check if any sense emerges from this spontaneous connection. If not, repeat the exercise until your conscious mind becomes aware of this link and understands—in a uniquely subjective manner what this connection means to you.

It is important to experience this first in ourselves before we try it as a technique with clients because, generally speaking, most Westerners are very unfamiliar with these experiences. We tend to concentrate too much on thinking (left hemisphere) at the expense of inner experience and feeling (right hemisphere). A remarkable exception to the rule is the mystics who have frequently been labeled as anti-intellectual. One of them stated it succinctly: "What satisfies the soul is not to know much but to taste and savor things internally." He was Ignatius Loyola, the founder of one of the most intellectual and highly educated groups in the Catholic church.

> What satisfies the soul is not
> to know much but to taste
> and savor things internally.

After having tasted and savored this experience internally, we may think of applying it in our clinical work to help clients "get in touch with their feelings." The Ikemi's (1983) refer to the inability to express feelings as *alexithymia* and have coined the term *alexisomia* for the condition that makes it difficult for a person to express how his body feels. This technique helps overcome these conditions. The same subjective biofeedback may be used with important statements (e.g., "I really love this woman") or gestures (a spontaneous fist or both hands going to one's chest or any other spontaneous and non-planned movement.) The client is asked to close his eyes and to repeat the statement (to himself or out loud) or the gesture several times checking what happens in his body; "how is your body reacting to this (statement/gesture)." Whatever emerges from the inner mind becomes then the next focus of attention in which the therapeutic work continues.

MENTAL TECHNIQUES

Although all of the twelve techniques we are discussing are essentially "mental," i.e., involving one's mental capacities, the next group does not focus primarily on the bodily experience as the first category of techniques did. These are more specifically "mind tricks" used to alter our perception of our problems and to facilitate the *metanoia*—the difficult transformation which starts at our world image and translates itself at the behavioral and relational levels.

DISSOCIATIVE TECHNIQUES

Dissociation

Let's start with an example. A woman is very angry, sad and frustrated because her three grown children have "abandoned" her after her three year separation from her husband of 36 years. She has tried to talk to them, to explain, to confront them but all to no avail. They promise they'll call and keep in touch but long weeks go on without any sign from them. When she finally calls, they respond with surprise at her complaint or clearly tell her there is nothing to talk about and that's the reason they have not contacted her. She had been in therapy discussing this for six months. No progress was noticed either in her children's behavior or in her depressed mood, though she had become more involved in outside activities with different groups of mature adults. Many years could be spent analyzing her reaction to the children's "abandonment." Another (emergency) procedure is to use dissociation. She was asked to have a pleasant or funny daydream. The daydream is in order to leave the emotional pain behind, "so that you don't have to be with the pain all day long." This is a method she can learn in order to stop the emotional pain, at least for awhile. In the office she is kept in her pleasant daydream for several minutes at a time. She is made aware of how different (even good) she feels while she is "daydreaming." She is asked to practice this exercise every day. Later this technique is coupled with mental rehearsal, which will be explained later.

In many cases where the therapist feels frustrated and helpless, dissociation is a first step to lead a client to further growth. In the case of the woman just mentioned, her "little journey of the mind," as she started to call it, gave her relief several times a day. Later she started rehearsing mentally new things she would do, other people she could start to count on and in less than two months *she* had decided that her children were toxic to her, emotionally, and that she would not contact them unless they did. This was a sad decision, indeed, but by that time, she had prepared herself for her "new life" at the ripe age of 66.

Activation of Personality Parts

This technique is taken also from Watkins (1978) but modified in the sense that the emphasis is less psychoanalytical. I often call it *healthy personality split*. It consists in making a habit *not* to consider any feeling, thought, mood, or action as emanating from me but as "coming from a part of me." Every time the client says, "I feel this way," or "I keep thinking..." the hypnotherapist reminds her to check what an opposite part in her is thinking, feeling or saying. The client is asked to keep doing this in private. "Check the parts in you," becomes the constant injunction. If the person is depressed, for instance, one may ask to check what the depressed part is saying inside. Then, "Is there another little part, perhaps, that is not agreeing with the depressed part? Let's hear what that part is saying." This is a way of enlarging one's awareness by realizing in practice that one's whole being is seldom involved in any inner experience. It is a way of looking at the whole picture of one's existence to realize that "at least a tiny part of me is not in total agreement with the depressed (angry, frustrated, etc.) part." Gestalt as well as T.A. therapists have used this technique in many similar ways. What the hypnotherapist does is to allow the client to really identify with the new part, to become the new part completely and to be aware of how the new part of himself feels. Rather than just talk as the new part, it is imperative to help the person experientially become that part of himself. Then and only after this experience it may be useful to discuss what the part may mean, why it triggered the memories it did, etc. Rather than ask the client to describe the part to me, I suggest that he take his time to deeply experience that new part which is also he. Later we talk.

The general idea is to check
whether the problem appears
symbolically.

This technique has also many possibilities, limited only by the hypnotherapist's and the client's imagination and willingness to "sound silly."

Materialization

This is another form of dissociation in that it separates the client from his problem. However, the difference is essential. Here the problem is not left behind but visualized and experienced differently. Let's suppose a person starts the session by stating she is confused. (Notice that traditional therapy would probably encourage the person to talk more about it, to explain the confusion). The New Hypnosis would encourage something experiential (right hemispheric) but suggesting that the client imagine his confusion as some material from or object familiar to him. Can the confusion become a fog or a deep darkness or a kakophonic sound or like the experience of falling from a great height? Is there any mental image for the confusion? The client is asked to close his eyes, to relax according to the way relaxation was explained earlier in this paper and then to concentrate on some mental image that the thought of his confusion might trigger. Usually and if the hypnotherapist gives the client options for visual, kinetic, auditory and even olfactory and gustatory mental images or representations, the client gets in touch with some symbol of his psychological state. If not, memories or other associations are readily made.

This might be the place to note that techniques are always means to an end. If one does not work, another one can be used for the same purpose the hypnotherapist has in mind in helping the client. The main point is to remember Mahrer's (1983) model for experiential therapy, namely, the purpose for which any intervention, any technique, any operation, as he calls it, is engaged in.

The general idea is to check whether the problem appears symbolically. Then, as in all other techniques explained here, the therapist follows the mental image or symbol, asking the client to stay with it, concentrate on the feelings and inner experiences in order to make them his own completely. At this point, an expansion of consciousness or awareness takes place. Even though we are discussing techniques individually and separately, the expert hypnotherapist will be quick to mix and combine different techniques in order to attain the desired effect which, to repeat, can be said to be, in general terms, a change in one's perception or world image so as to be able to react differently to the situation or issue which produces the problem or symptoms.

TEMPORAL TECHNIQUES

These are interventions which use time distortion in one way or another. Three of them refer to the past and one to the future. Even though the New Hypnosis, because of its experiential nature, deals mostly with the present, it is simply naive to attempt to avoid references to past or future. As humans, we are trapped by time and we are free because of time. These temporal techniques utilize our temporal reality experientially; not to analyze the lessons of the past or the dreams for the future; not to make sense of them and understand them, but to experience fully the inner reality of things past or projected into the future in order to own completely that aspect of our being.

Transfer of Inner Resources

When clients feel helpless or discouraged by current situations, many interventions can be used if the therapeutic purpose is to alter that affect so that the person feels more positive about himself. The transfer technique may take several variations but essentially it consists of focusing on past situations in which the person acted extraordinarily well and felt unusually good about himself. This situation is used hypnotically, reliving it in great detail, eliciting as much of the positive affect as possible and recreating the experience several times if needed. Then, the person is asked to check—again, experientially—whether any of the inner resources he used in that positive situation might have some value in the current situation making the person feel helpless, discouraged or, in general, negative. As in all these techniques, allowance must be made for slowness of movement; "There is no rush, take your time, try to stay with that question. Check whether any of the personality traits you used then could be helpful now," etc.

Another way of applying this transfer technique is to start with the negative situation and the affect it elicits, then go to a positive situation of the past with all the good feelings it engenders and finally return to the negative scene with some of the resources which, used in the past, made the person feel good and positive.

Most hypnotherapists combine
techniques so that in practice
there is a generous overlap
of them.

An example may help. A 39 year old woman divorced for the last five years had just broken up with a man with whom she had been very involved for the last four months. She wanted to make the relationship more serious and he didn't. She decided to stop seeing him but later became very unhappy, lonely and anxious to meet "the ideal man." At the therapy session after the break I employed a transfer technique.

Cl. *As I told you over the phone, I still feel miserable. Though I know I had to break with him. And I also feel proud that I did.*

Th. *Check now if you experience the sadness someplace in your body. Take your time to become aware of your body, breathing, sitting there. Your eyes closed, trying to feel some peace.*

Cl. (After about 90 seconds) *I'm becoming my sadness. It's painful* (starting to cry silently).

Th. *Stay with the sadness and pain just for a few more moments. You are the sadness, the pain.*

Cl. (Quiet, but with the beginning of a frown; concentrating but breathing in a relaxed manner).

Th. *Now, when you are satisfied that you have experienced your pain and sadness, change the mental picture to something completely different. Think now of another situation in your past that was very good for you, that made you feel terrific, happy, in control, competent, proud of yourself. Let that memory fill your mental screen. Take your time and let it happen. Your inner mind will choose a very positive scene for your to relive now.*

Cl. (Silence for about two minutes of relaxed breathing and general body relaxation. Then a bit of a smile, slowly becoming a full smile).

Th. *Whenever you're ready, you may want to tell me what scene is coming up. Don't rush. Stay with it and absorb completely. You are there, you feel terrific.*

Cl. (After about four minutes) *My new apartment. No husband. He's gone forever. My own place, finally. I made it!*

(This woman had been in a very violent marriage. Her husband had beaten her and threatened the life of Nicole, their two year old girl. She had left him in the middle of the night, moved in with her parents who protected her until she found her own apartment. Her husband, in the meantime, had been taken to jail for stealing from a large corporation where he was an officer).

Th. *Stay with all these good feelings. You are safe, you're free. You are proud of yourself. You saved yourself and your child. Now this is your place; all yours to share with Nicole whom you* *have saved.* (After about five minutes of encouraging her to fully relieve all the good feelings she had experienced then, I continued). *Now go back to the sad scene, to your present pain and sadness. But take with you some of the good feelings you had when you were first in your apartment. Use some of those good things in your current sadness and pain.*

Cl. (After a few moments) *Yes, it feels good. I'm doing it. This sadness is O.K. It will pass. I'll be O.K."*

The session continued along the same lines. It should be remembered that seldom is one technique used in a pure way. In this case, for instance, I added a form of mental rehearsal (to be explained later in this article) so she could experience herself beyond the current sadness. Most hypnotherapists combine techniques so that in practice there is a generous overlap of them.

Emotional Bridge

Although this intervention is also taken from Watkins (1971) who calls it the *affect bridge,* to avoid calling it "the modified affect bridge" or some other such name, I have labeled it *emotional bridge.* The reason is that this technique is less psychoanalytical than Watkins'. When the person is experiencing a particular emotion and the therapist has indications that it may be related to past experiences or events, the emotional bridge is very helpful intervention. Let's assume the client is feeling a general confusion, whose origin cannot be understood in terms of current events in the person's life. At this point, I may suggest that he stay with the confusion, that he concentrate on physically (bodily) experiencing his confusion to the utmost; that he let any memories and mental images connected generally in any way with confusion emerge slowly or quickly. "Your whole being is now confusion." This often is enough to establish a psychological link between the present confusion and significant past events where confusion was also experienced.

If there is no immediate reaction I become more explicit and say something like this: "You have been confused before. Perhaps not exactly like now. Allow now your inner mind to connect this confusion with some other confusion of the past. Take your time, relax and just let confusion—here and in the past—absorb all your being."

The current emotion, in this way, acts as a bridge to other past instances of the same feeling, allowing the person to broaden his awareness and thus to learn something new about himself. This learning about one self—frequently mentioned by Erickson while working with his clients—is the main purpose of the emotional bridge.

Regression

Somehow regression has obtained a negative connotation for many therapists and clients. However, regression in the service of the ego is by no means a new technique in psychotherapy. I prefer to refer to it as *reliving* of previous experiences. Others have described this intervention in detail (see Weitzenhoffer, 1957; Wolberg, 1964). I want to stress that this technique is essential when a person seems to be fixated on some traumatic event of the past. By reliving it, under the guidance of the hypnotherapist, the client usually obtains a new control over the event. This approach, combined with *activation of personality parts,* works well with many people who have experienced emotional deprivation in childhood. With a woman whose mother kept her in a small closet at the age of 4-6 while she went about the house chores, this technique became an important part of her therapy. She relived the event but at that point she saw herself as she was now, a grown up woman who knew how to deal with little children, consoling the young self, providing the young self all the support, understanding, and protection she needed. This woman learned to do this every time she felt depressed since she had realized that her depression was tied up to those cruel scenes of her past.

Mental Rehearsal

In our Western world, we have been taught to think logically, to test reality, to be objective—all functions of the left hemisphere. Mental rehearsal bypasses logic and moves ahead in time. It operates in the future, as opposed to the other Temporal Techniques which move back into the past. Mental rehearsal is the imaginative effort to experience oneself in the future, the way one believes one can be. "Now, jump ahead and experience in your imagination the self you are without the problem you have. The problem is gone, resolved, finished. *Like* yourself, *enjoy* being without the problem. You are O.K., now. How does it feel? Check the way your body reacts to this new reality of being," etc.

Athletes are being taught to mentally rehearse as much as they practice *in vivo.* Businessmen and women are encouraged to fantasize successful situations and to experience in their minds the feelings they elicit.

Actors are taught to become the character they portray by using their imagination to do it. Many methods of therapy employ psychovisualization, "in the mind's eye" technique and "movies of the mind." In other words, mental rehearsal has become a valued method of facilitating change in many diverse situations.

It should be remembered that often when people "worry" about a forthcoming event, what they are doing is simply to mentally rehearse *against themselves*. They use the same mental mechanism, but negatively. And in most cases, it works! It keeps up the negative feelings and "prepares" the person to fail or suffer in the upcoming situation. What mental rehearsal does is to utilize the same process for one's benefit and fulfillment. Every time a person in therapy talks about accomplishing something, about changing in some way or other I suggest that he "see" himself changed. The centuries old Virgilian statement—They change their being because *they see themselves* changing—was a brief definition of mental rehearsal.

PARALOGICAL TECHNIQUES

These are interventions which attempt to communicate directly with the right hemisphere of the brain. Watzlawick (1978) has discussed masterfully the language of the subconscious mind and the reader is encouraged to become acquainted with his work. Paradox and parables have been used by many of the great masters both in Oriental and Western civilizations.

Paradox

The point of the paradox is to obtain results by an indirect method when using a direct one would encounter resistance. The work by Weeks and L'Abet (1982) should be read carefully in order to understand clearly the value and uses of paradoxical interventions. Within the New Hypnosis approach paradox is made experiential. The woman whose daughter was looking for reasons to commit her to a mental hospital, said one day that "she was falling to pieces, she was in a real hole." I suggested that she see herself, in her mind's eye, becoming crazy, falling apart at the seams. We spent some time with this exercise and at the end she said very firmly: "I won't give her (the daughter) the satisfaction of seeing me crazy. I'm not crazy. I'm very upset but I can manage it."

Another client, considering leaving his wife because he was so much in love with another woman who was pressuring him to move in with her, was told to see himself with the other woman; to go over in detail the circumstances of living with her, keeping house, buying groceries, cooking meals, etc. After this exercise, he realized that he was not ready to make the decision to leave his wife, that he did not want to take the next step (moving in with the other woman) at this point.

The paradox—to mentally live something which is considered incredible but possible—helps the person confront the whole truth about the dilemma and, by so doing, to make a decision rather than remain between the two horns of the issue.

Parable

Some authors call it metaphor (e.g., Gordon, 1978) but the word which indicates the technique of presenting a short story conveying a message (moral) unique to the person addressed, though not explicit, is more accurate. This is why the parable is a very delicate tool. The hypnotherapist must be very sensitive to the person's need before using this technique since the parable is always a subtle form of interpretation of what the client is experiencing in order to present to him some material which will "connect" with that state of mind. The parable can be personal, as Erickson showed often (When I was a youngster, there was a horse...) or not (The woods, asleep through the winter, burst into life when spring called), but in any case, the point is to bypass consciousness—resistance, evaluation, analysis, intellectualization. Watzlawick (1978)has called this technique a "dream in reverse," citing as an example the woman who complained of "frigidity," whom Erickson told the story of defrosting her refrigerator. What could have been a story dreamt by that woman, the therapist presented as a means of reaching the subconscious level of mind activity.

The more cultured the hypnotherapist, the richer his repertoire of possible parables. Those stories that have survived the centuries hold eternal truths which can be used effectively in therapy, rather than the inane stories novice therapists create on the spur of the moment attempting to utter profound wisdom.

I also find that the parable can be used symbolically. For instance in case of impotence, arm levitation becomes a very meaningful analogy of how the inner mind can influence the conduct of one's body.

CONCLUSION

Techniques are always means to an end. Consequently, no technique is justified—ever!—unless the hypnotherapist knows what the current situation of the client is and what effects can be expected from that operation, intervention or technique. No technique has value in itself. Because of this, the experienced hypnotherapist usually mixes techniques in his clinical practice.

The novice should avoid the temptation to "collect" techniques the way a cook collects recipes. A therapeutic technique is always *a response* to a given situation; it is part of the interaction taking place between two human beings—in the unique situation of therapy—one of which is the hypnotherapist and the other the client. But, regardless of the situational role, the human interaction between these two persons must remain the most important aspect of this special relationship. The response given by the hypnotherapist to what the client needs or is experiencing at the time, takes the form of a technique. If any therapeutic technique is not this—a response—it is as best useless and at worst damaging to the relationship between a client and the hypnotherapist. Because of these reasons, the therapist will do well in being extremely respectful of the client. Rather than to say, "I now want you to do this or that," (Why should another human being do anything because *you* want it?) a more permissive approach is more effective. Such permissiveness is more affective. It could be expressed in terms of "inviting," "suggesting," or "proposing." For instance: "You may now want to try this or that," "I might suggest that you try this or that," "May I propose that you do this or that?"

Resistance is often a healthy reaction of the client to the intrusive approach of the therapist. If the therapist's approach is changed, often what appeared before as resistance, disappears all together.

It was mentioned in the beginning that the techniques described here are used by the New Hypnosis. The truth is that traditional hypnosis employs them as well. The main differences between the two approaches should be outlined once more (Araoz, 1982, 1983a, 1983b). First, the New Hypnosis assumes that hypnosis, being a natural mental function, is at the reach of every normal person with the motivation to learn this easy way of "thinking" or using one's mind, called hypnosis. The second difference, a corollary of the first, is that hypnosis is considered a skill, not a trial, which can be learned with proper guidance by anyone wanting to learn this skill. The therapist, then, is mainly a teacher or facilitator and the focus of control lies on the client, not the therapist. Consequently, the notion of hypnotizability is disregarded. Clients are not tested for the ability to be hypnotized, but the therapist is ready to try diverse approaches to help the person into the mental activity, primarily right-hemispheric in nature, designated as hypnosis. The concern is on the therapist's ability and flexibility to help the client use hypnosis; not on the client's ability which is always assumed.

Hypnosis is a skill, not a trait
which can be learned with
proper guidance by anyone
wanting to learn this skill.

The third difference is that the process of induction into hypnosis is not ritualized but "naturalistic," starting with the reality of the client's inner experience of the moment. The fourth difference is that the depth of hypnosis is of much less concern than in the traditional approach. Finally, the understanding of what hypnosis is all about is independent of the classic-psychoanalytic background prevalent in traditional hypnosis.

The techniques described fit within this context. There is no intention "to own" these techniques nor to imply that they were developed by the New Hypnosis advocates. They simply lend themselves to comfortable use by those who do not follow the traditional approach to hypnosis.

Mineola, New York 11501
1517 Franklin Avenue

REFERENCES

Araoz, D.L., *Hypnosis and sex therapy*. New York: Brunner/Mazel, 1982.

Araoz, D.L., Ericksonian hypnosis, the quientessence of client-centeredness. Paper presented at the 2nd. International Congress of Ericksonian Psychotherapy. Phoenix, December, 1983.

Araoz, D.L., The paradox of the New Hypnosis. Paper presented at the Annual Scientific Meeting of the American Society of Clinical Hypnosis, Dallas, November, 1983.

Gordon, D., *Therapeutic metaphors*. Cupertino, CA: Meta Publications, 1978.

Ikemi, Y. and Ikemi, A., Psychosomatic medicine: A meeting ground of Eastern and Western medicine. *Journal of the American Society of Psychosomatic Dentistry and Medicine*, 1983, *30*, 3-16.

Kroger, W.S. & Fezler, W.D., *Hypnosis and behavior modification: Imagery conditioning*. Philadelphia: Lippincott, 1976.

Mahrer, A.R., *Experiential psychotherapy: Basic practices*. New York: Brunner/Mazel, 1983.

Watkins, J., *The therapeutic self*. New York: Human Sciences Press, 1978.

Watzlawick, P., *The language of change*. New York: Basic Books, 1978.

Weeks, G.R. & L'Abate, L., *Paradoxical psychotherapy: Theory and practice with individuals, couples and families*. New York: Brunner/Mazel, 1982.

Weitzenhoffer, A.M., *General techniques of hypnotism*. New York: Grune & Stratton, 1957.

Wolberg, L.R., *Hypnoanalysis*. New York: Grune & Stratton, 1964.

INTRODUCTION TO CHAPTER 9

So much has been said about Milton Erickson and his use of language that this book would not be complete without a sample of his use of language in therapy and hypnosis. The following classic article demonstrates his uncommon use of language. In addition, his knowledge of what lies behind the words is shown in his and Dr. Rossi's comments.

He also outlined in this article his basic ideas of how therapy takes place and his use of the conscious/unconscious dichotomy.

CHAPTER 9

TWO LEVEL COMMUNICATION AND THE MICRODYNAMICS OF TRANCE AND SUGGESTION[1]

Milton H. Erickson, M.D. and Ernest L. Rossi, Ph.D.*

Phoenix, Arizona[2]   Los Angeles, California

[1]The commentaries of this paper were recorded on equipment provided by a grant from the American Society of Clinical Hypnosis. The actual induction was recorded at a hypnosis seminar of ASCH in 1958. Portions of this paper are adapted from the authors' work (Erickson, Rossi & Rossi, 1976).

*Erickson, M.H., and Rossi, E.L. (1976). Two level communication and the microdynamics of trance and suggestion. *The American Journal of Clinical Hypnosis, 18*(3), pp. 153-171. Reprinted with permission of Ernest L. Rossi and *The American Journal of Clinical Hypnosis.*

[2]1201 E. Hayward.

The authors provide the transcript and commentaries of an hypnotic induction and an effort to achieve automatic writing. An unusual blend of Erickson's approaches to two level communication, dissociation, voice dynamics and indirect suggestion are made explicitly in the commentaries. The junior author offers a "context theory of two level communication" that conceptualizes Erickson's clinical approaches in terms consonant with Jenkins' (1974) recent contextual approach to verbal associations and memory. A summary of the microdynamics of Erickson's approach to trance induction and suggestion is outlined together with a utilization theory of hypnotic suggestion.

A professional woman, Dr. Erickson, and a number of other psychiatrists and psychologists are discussing the nature of hypnosis, the double bind, suggestions on two levels, etc. She mentions that she has never personally succeeded in performing automatic writing. Erickson undertakes to help her with the dialogue and hypnotic induction listed on the left side of the following pages. On the right side of each page, Erickson and Rossi comment on the varieties of indirect suggestion and two level communication that are taking place.

INDUCTION   **COMMENTARY**

**Shifting Frames of Reference:
Displacing Doubt Resistance and Failure**

Subject: Now I have been trying for two years to automatically write something and I can't get it. How do I go about getting it?

E: She is telling me, "I have been trying for two years." Her emphasis is entirely on "trying."

Erickson: Do you want to get it?

E: I'm shifting her focus of attention with this question. I put the emphasis on "Do you want?" It is an unrecognizable shift from her concern with failure to the question of her motivation.

Rossi: You emphasize wanting rather than trying and failing. You are immediately shifting her out of her negative, failure frame of reference and reorienting her to her positive motivation.

S: Yes! I wouldn't have been trying this long if I didn't want to.

E: Yes and she does not even realize it.

R: Now in this sentence she immediately responds with your differentiation: she is speaking of "trying" and "want to" as different things.

Shock and Surprise to Break Old Frames of Reference

E: Ever try writing with your left hand?

S: I don't think I have.

E: She wants to do automatic writing and she has proved for two years that she cannot do it. By asking her if she has ever tried writing with her left hand and getting a "no" response from her I imply there is *another* way of writing.

R: You open up another possibility that has not been associated with failure. You are again dislodging her from her failure frame of reference.

E: The geographical shift to her left hand is so unrealistic that her unconscious is going to be alerted.

R: Many associations and search programs are activated by your unrealistic introduction of the left hand. It is a surprise or shock to jog her out of her failure set and thus activate a search on the unconscious level for something new (Rossi, 1972, 1973).

E: Ever try writing backwards with your left hand?

S: I don't think I could.

E: Here I'm opening up still another possibility. Whenever you do the unexpected you jog a person out of their setting.

E: You probably couldn't do that. (pause)

E: "You probably couldn't do that." That is where her failure is!

R: Oh, I see! You first dislodge her from her past failure in automatic writing with her right hand and then you shift her failure and place it on her probable inability to write backwards with her left hand. You reify her failure, you dislodge it from the task at hand and then shift it to something irrelevant. This is a neat paradigm of your general approach to discharging and displacing doubt, resistance or failure. You treat the resistance as a concrete thing that the patient must first express to get it out of his system. You then relocate the failure and resistance to a place where it will not interfere with constructive work on the problem at hand.

Distraction in the Dynamics of Two-Level Communication

Are you willing (pause)

to find that out? (Spoken softly with voice dropping.)

S: Yes.

E: Really?!

E: Again this involves a shift from trying to the question of conscious motivation: *are you willing* is to the conscious level; *find that out* is to the unconscious level because I've attracted conscious attention with the *are you willing?* By adding *find that out,* I'm also implying there is something to find out. (Communications to the conscious level are in italics while communication to the unconscious are in bold print.)

R: A pause and voice dynamics separate the two levels. In the critical sentence, *"Are you willing* **to find that out,"** your voice emphasis on *"willing"* catches the conscious mind. But the more softly spoken, **"to find that out..."**

E: ...Catches the unconscious.

R: Why? Because all her conscious attention went to the emphasis on *"willing?"*

E: Yes, she had two years of failure yet I'm questioning her willingness. The willingness to fail for two years and the willingness to write are two different things. I'm differentiating between them.

R: You recognize that for two years she has been stalemated between (a) her willingness to do automatic writing and (b) her willingness to fail at it (Erickson, 1965). By questioning her willingness to do automatic writing, you are actually challenging and thus fixating the attention of her conscious mind. Since her conscious is fixated on the first half of the sentence (*Are you willing*) it is distracted from the second half (**find that out**). This is the essential dynamic of communication on two levels: you activate, attract and fixate attention with one item and then add another item that will be received but not noticed. This is actually related to the classical notion of hypnosis as the fixation and distraction of attention.

S: *Writing backward with my left hand?*

E: *No,* **to find out.**
(pause)

To find out (very softly).

E: Her question is on the conscious level so the first part of my response *"No"* is on the conscious level but the last part **"to find out"** is actually contradictory and does not make much sense in that context. Therefore, it goes to the unconscious as a suggestion implying, **find out with your right hand.**

S: *I think I am willing.*

E: Do you think *you are willing* to find out? (softly)

R: Here again she responds on the conscious level with this statement about *willing,* but you return by repeating your question on two levels.

S: *How do I do this? How do I set it up?*

E: You don't set it up. You don't need to.

R: She again emphasizes her conscious orientation with her very rational questions about how she is to set up the automatic handwriting. Your response that she does not need to set it up is a direct effort to depotentiate that rational orientation.

Just find out

(pause)

E: I break up her conscious set. Her questions are on the conscious level but the answers require that she make a search on the unconscious level.

Trance Induction by Two Level Communication

Just find out.

R: You again emphasize the unconscious level with your softly spoken phrase **"Just find out."**

E: She does not realize I'm telling her to go into a trance. She thinks I said, **"Just find out."** But I said, **"Just find out"** to her unconscious mind and having spoken to her unconscious mind her unconscious mind has to come forth.

R: That coming forth of the unconscious defines the trance situation. You frequently induce trance by asking a question or assigning a task that cannot be dealt with by the patient's momentary conscious frame of reference. This momentarily depotentiates conscious sets and the patient retreats to an unconscious level in search for an adequate response.

Do you mind if J takes your cigarette?

Just find out.

(S's eyelids begin to blink slowly.)

R: This question about J taking her cigarette is the first direct indication that you are structuring a trance situation.

E: All the foregoing was a trance induction by the two levels of speaking.

R: She was speaking on the conscious level but her unconscious was picking up your suggestions on another level. To accommodate your suggestions on the unconscious level....

E: It (her unconscious) had to wipe out the conscious.

That's it, **close your eyes.**
(pause)

E: "That's it," tells her conscious mind that her unconscious is doing something.

And just close your eyes and sleep more and more deeply.
(pause)

R: You repeated your suggestion "**to find out**" to the unconscious so often that it finally depotentiated consciousness so she could easily enter trance.

E: I noticed the slowing of her eyelid blinking as I said that. I had to get rid of her cigarette because you can't go into trance smoking a cigarette since it is a conscious act. I removed the last vestige of her need for conscious thinking.

"Wonder" as a Two Level Suggestion

And now what I'd like to have you do is **wonder** about that writing.

R: You emphasize **wonder** to introduce an exploratory set?

E: When a person **wonders** it implies that they don't know.

R: "Wonder" depotentiates conscious sets on one level while stimulating exploratory efforts on the unconscious level. It is a two level suggestion all by itself. Many other words like "try, explore, imagine, feel, sense" tend to evoke two level communication. When confronted with such words people tend to get that far away look in their eyes that is characteristic of the common everyday trance (Erickson & Rossi, 1975). These words orient a person within themselves in a manner conducive to trance.

Dynamics of Dissociation and Need for Closure in Evoking Automatic Writing

I'd like to have you get the **feeling**

E: She has many times in the past had the feeling of writing with her right hand. I isolate that feeling and put it in the left hand where it does not belong. But everybody likes to put together things that belong together.

that you have **written** it.

But just the **feeling** that you have **written** it, just the **feeling.**

And get that **feeling** in your **left hand.**

(pause)

And get the **feeling** in your **left hand.**
(pause)

And now in a different way I'd like to have you get the *knowledge* of how *to write in your right hand.*

R: You set up a tension by evoking the feeling of having written in her left hand. There is going to be a natural tendency to get that feeling in her right hand where it belongs. The only way to get that feeling is to do the automatic writing. You set up an expectancy or need for closure in her right hand that can only be fulfilled by automatic writing.

E: Yes.

R: This suggestion of getting a *knowledge of how to write in her right hand* is a sort of truism that evokes many familiar associations and, as

The *knowledge* of how to write in your *right hand.*

such, tends to reinforce the suggestion of getting a **feeling of having written in the left hand:** That in turn strengthens the need for closure by doing the automatic writing so that feeling of having written can get back to the right hand where it belongs.

These dynamics come into play at an unconscious level, however, so consciousness is further depotentiated and automatism facilitated.

Cognitive Overloading to Depotentiate Conscious Sets to Facilitate Hypnotic Responsiveness

But the **feeling** that you **have written** it in your **left hand.**

And while you are enjoying those two separate sensations

you might be interested in a third realization.

R: There is also a cognitive overload and confusion introduced when you almost simultaneously evoke and carefully partition associations along those dimensions as follows:

Left Hand	Right Hand
Feeling	Knowledge
Past	Present

The reader can observe how you have associated **left hand, feeling** and **past tense** *in some of your sentences and* **right hand, knowledge,** and *present tense in others.* Her conscious mind cannot understand the significance of this dissociation and therefore, the controlling and directing function of her ego is depotentiated to the point where automatism tends to set in.

E: Yes. You are overloading the conscious mind, you are getting it off balance. It has to escape from that tension situation. I've been talking to the unconscious and it is feeling comfort-

	able because I'm putting all the discomfort into the conscious mind.
A third experiential learning.	**R:** You then overload further with this introduction of a "third experiential learning." (Erickson now gives a number of illustrations of how the conscious mind can be overloaded, startled, or mystified in order to fixate attention while the therapist unobtrusively adds other suggestions that automatically drop into the unconscious because consciousness cannot cope with them while so fixated.)
You say that you want to do a **certain** *amount of writing.* *Just what it is* **you don't know.**	**E:** She didn't say she wanted to do a **certain** amount I've overloaded her conscious mind with it. She has to search in her mind, "What makes you think it is a **certain** amount?"
But you say you want to *and you really do*	**R:** There are multiple meanings of the word **certain** that come in here: **certain** can mean positive affirmation as well as a limitation of amount. It can also mean a particular item of special interest. There could be a **certain** subject that she wants to deal with via automatic writing.
	E: We don't know which meanings her unconscious will act upon. But we do know that the word **certain** is a highly specific unspecific.

Voice Dynamics in Two Level Communication

At least I believe you. *I don't know if you believe* **you**	**E:** I'm telling her she can have her conscious *false* beliefs about not being able to do automatic writing but **I believe she can.** Again I'm speaking to her unconscious.

But I believe you
(softly)

R: Your initial phrase *"I don't know if you believe you"* acts as a challenge that catches her conscious attention. While she is attending to that you softly say **"but I believe you"** which acts as a suggestion that drops into her unconscious, since her consciousness was too occupied to heed it at that precise moment. You frequently use such compound statements wherein you fixate conscious attention with the first half so you can then unobtrusively drop a suggestion into the unconscious in the second half.

E: Yes, the phrase to the unconscious is spoken softly. I use one tone of voice to speak to the conscious mind and another to speak to the unconscious. When you use one tone of voice that pertains to conscious thinking and another tone of voice that expresses other ideas which you intend for the unconscious, you are establishing a duality.

The Double Bind

And the only question is

when will you do it?

R: You then immediately follow up with the phrase "the only question is when" which displaces her from the question of success or failure in writing to the mere question of *when*.

E: That is a double bind.

Will you do it expectedly

or unexpectedly? You are interested in experiments. You in your own mind can set up the experiment.

R: "Will you do it expectedly or unexpectedly?" is another double bind. It is not a question she can dispute and, therefore, it plants the actual suggestion of writing very strongly. Structuring such forms of mutually exclusive response (expectedly or unexpectedly) is actually another form of double bind: on one level her unconscious is free to choose its own form of response; you have, however, structured the alternatives so that on another level (the metalevel) the range of her response possibilities are determined by you.

Covering All Possibilities of Responses: Multiple Form of Double Bind

You can write as Mary does.

A word here,
a word there.

A syllable here,
a syllable there.

A letter here,
a letter there.

A word following a syllable, a letter.

You can misspell a word.

You can write the wrong word.

R: Here you outline a whole series of suggestions covering all possibilities of response so that unconscious processes can be facilitated. Whatever response she does manifest is acceptable as a correct step toward the ultimate goal of automatic handwriting. Covering all possibilities of response is actually a multiple form of the double bind. Rather than binding, however it gives free reign to the patient's creative process. You don't know what mechanisms the patient's unconscious can use so you give it carte blanche to use any available mechanism.

E: Yes, these are all just so many interlocking double binds.

The Double Dissociation Double Bind

You can write that material without ever knowing what it is.

R: In this first statement you suggest a dissociation between writing and knowing what she has written.

Then you can go back and discover you know what it is without knowing that you've written it.

In this second statement you offer the reverse dissociation: she can know what she has written but not know she has written it. Together these two statements effect a double dissociation in the form of a double bind that appears to cover all possibilities of response. It is an extremely powerful form of suggestion that so befuddles consciousness that it must rely on the unconscious to sort out the response possibilities.[3]

And as you continue

E: This is a very strong instruction to her unconscious that follows the double bind.

R: Conscious sets are momentarily depotentiated by the double bind so whatever follows tends to drop directly into the unconscious.

Utilizing Disequilibrium to Evoke Hypnotic Phenomena

That feeling of having written in your left hand

it can be most interesting.

R: You again return to your tripart division of **feeling, past tense,** and **left hand** versus *knowledge, present tense* and *right hand.*

And the *knowledge* that you *can write* with *your right* hand

E: It evokes a need to pull together the things that belong together: to get the feeling of writing in the right hand. There is only one way to get that feeling in the right hand: doing automatic writing.

---

[3]Another example of the double dissociation double bind that is analyzed in more detail by the authors (Erickson, Rossi, & Rossi, 1976) goes as follows. "You can as a person awaken but you need not awaken as a body, (pause), or you can waken when your body awakes but without a recognition of your body."

is also most interesting.

E: Here I'm getting the *present* tense ("is") into automatic writing. That is a bridging association from the past **(feeling of having written)** to *present.* To do the automatic writing she's got to have that **feeling now.**

R: You create a tension by suggesting a feeling in her left hand that really belongs in her right hand. You dissociate a feeling, and take it out of its natural context so that a tension is created until it can return to its rightful place by executing the hypnotic phenomenon of automatic writing. This is a general principle for evoking hypnotic phenomena: THE THERAPIST ARRANGES TO UTILIZE INTERNAL STATES OR TENSION, DISSOCIATION OR DISEQUILIBRIUM THAT CAN ONLY BE RESOLVED BY THE EXECUTION OF SOME DESIRED HYPNOTIC PHENOMENA.

E: If you observe children you learn they do this sort of thing all the time.

R: Yes, the Zeigarnik (Woodworth and Schlosberg, 1956) effect, for example, illustrates how children will return to an incompleted task after an interruption because of the tension or disequilibrium aroused by their set for closure.

Two Level Communication by Implication

And you want something at a two level suggestion.

Here and now

R: Here you talk about giving her a two level suggestion but I cannot find it.

and in the presence of all
the others

I'm going to say something
to you

in a two level suggestion.

And you can wonder what it is	**E:** I'm having her unconscious define what it is to be wondered about and what is worth waiting for.
And why. (pause) And you can wait And you can wonder	**R:** By waiting and wondering her unconscious is going through all its programs in search of something worthwhile?

(pause)	
And you can wait and you can wonder	**E:** Her problem was her difficulties with automatic handwriting. I'm really talking about that.
and you can wait and you can wonder.	**R:** On the conscious level you are talking about wondering and waiting but to the unconscious you are implying automatic writing. Is that the two level suggestion?
Because what will that suggestion be? And you wait and you can wonder.	**E:** Yes, I told her I would give her a two level suggestion. I'm illustrating two levels by two different kinds of behavior, waiting and wondering. A choice between two things is also two; I'm illustrating twoness.
(pause)	
	R: In a very concrete way.

Association and Two Level Communication:
Childhood Associations and Automatic Writing

And I taught my sister that two plus two is four.	**E:** The unconscious works without your knowledge and that is the way it

And four and four is eight.

And she didn't quite believe me when I told her that three and five is eight. Because she said that I had told her that four and four is eight.

(Long pause)

prefers. I'm evoking the patient's own childhood patterns here by simply talking about childhood.

R: Why?

E: Automatic handwriting usually does have a childlike character.

R: So you introduce childhood associations to facilitate a regressive or autonomous process of automatic handwriting.

E: Yes, and on two levels.

R: On one level it implies that the conscious mind does not always understand things (like the child's initial puzzlement about arithmetic) and on another level you are also facilitating regression by the simple process of association; talking about childhood reactivates memory traces of response tendencies appropriate to childhood. Since the conscious mind does not understand it tends to be depotentiated. With consciousness momentarily puzzled and depotentiated, your associations about childhood can now reach her unconscious where they may also reactivate memory traces and response tendencies appropriate to childhood and autonomous processes like automatic handwriting.

Dissociation to Facilitate Automatic Writing

And writing is one thing and reading is another.

E: Knowing what you are writing is an awareness while automatic writing is an unawareness. I'm dividing up the entire process of automatic writing and

And knowing what should be written is a third.

And concealment of the writing from the self is another thing.

(Long pause as S apparently does some automatic writing.)

And keep right on because you are interested.

giving her permission to do only one of those parts.

R: You are breaking up what seems to be one unitary act of writing, reading and awareness of what was written into its three component parts so the possibility of writing without awareness is introduced. Many hypnotic phenomena are simply dissociated forms of normal behavior.

E: Yes, this is actually an instruction of how to do automatic writing.

Non-Sequitur to Facilitate Two Level Communication

And the feeling in your left hand is so important

that you don't want to know that feeling.

(pause)

R: The second half of this sentence ("You don't want to know that feeling") seems to be a non-sequitur to the conscious mind but it makes sense to the unconscious?

E: It is an important feeling but you don't want to know it. The feeling is the essential thing. Knowing about it is not the essential thing.

R: What seems to be a non-sequitur to the conscious mind is actually a way of depotentiating consciousness. You are actually telling the unconscious that the feeling is important but consciousness is so unimportant that it need not know, recognize or register that feeling.

And concealing it from you

is interesting.

And enjoy that.

"Concealing it from you" effects a dissociation that depotentiates consciousness. It permits the unconsciousness to express itself in privacy and safety from consciousness.

Implied Directive and Two Level Communication

And as soon as you feel that you are through writing

you can rouse up.

(A tear begins to roll down her cheek.)

And are you going to hide that tear?

And are you going to hide that tear?

(Long pause)

S: (Awakens and sighs.)

R: This is an implied directive wherein you suggest an overt piece of behavior (awakening in this case) to signal when an indirectly formulated suggestion, the implied directive ("as soon as you feel you are through writing"), has taken place on the unconscious level. Many forms of ideomotor response (*e.g.,* finger, hand or head signaling) can be used as signals to let the therapist know when a question has been answered (Cheek & LeCron, 1968) or a suggestion implemented on an unconscious level. The signaling response is actually a form of biofeedback without the use of electronic instrumentation. We can hypothesize that the implied directive and biofeedback are similar in that both function on an unconscious level (The subject does not know how he does it.) and both use a signal to indicate when the desired response takes place. It would be fascinating to test whether ideomotor responses could be calibrated to give immediate knowledge of results and therefore reinforcement to any degree of the desired response just as electronic instrumentation does for biofeedback. The implied directive and biofeedback are both forms of two level communication whereby a signal expressed on the conscious level is an index of activity on an unconscious level.

A general conversation about other matters now takes place for about five minutes. Erickson then casually shows S the sheet on which she had been writing and continues as follows:

Protection of the Unconscious and Initial
Stages of Hypnotic Learning

E: Now you recognize, of course, that this is automatic writing, don't you? And you recognize it is not written for me or for anybody else to read.

(pause)

Would you recognize that hand writing?

You recognize it is not for anybody else to read and it is not for you to read at the present time.

So close your eyes

And when you want to read it

when you want to put it together in proper fashion

I'd like to have you do it before I leave Philadelphia.

And so

R: Apparently the writing was illegible as the first efforts of automatic writing frequently are. You emphasize that it is automatic writing to forestall criticism from the conscious attitude that it is not comprehensible and, therefore, worthless. This is an example of how the therapist must frequently protect the initial stages of learning a new hypnotic phenomena because the conscious mind, particularly in our rationalistic age, tends to down grade and thus destroy accomplishments of the unconscious.

E: (Erickson tells an interesting story of how useful automatic writing can be to help a person learn something they know without knowing they know it. A woman wrote something in automatic handwriting but then, on suggestion, she carefully folded it up without reading it and placed it absentmindedly in her pocket book. A few months later after making an important change in her marriage plans she "accidently" rediscovered the folded paper. She found her unconscious had worked on and had written about her change in plans automatically months earlier. It is thus a facilitative procedure to allow the unconscious to protect itself by taking cautionary measures that permit the automatic writing to remain hidden from the conscious until it is appropriate for the consciousness to know. Ideomotor signaling can be used to determine if the unconscious is ready to allow the conscious to learn what was written.)

Let's postpone the task
for a while.
(pause)
And now rouse up.

E: You can make the unconscious known without making it known. You make it known by automatic writing. You make it unknown by folding the paper and putting it away till consciousness is ready for it.

Hi!

S: Hi!

The group breaks up and goes to dinner with no further discussion. It is important during the initial stages of learning to experience trance that the therapist prevent the rationally oriented individual from building associative bridges between the nascent and autonomous aspects of trance phenomena and their usual every day awareness. Talking about trance immediately after experiencing it builds associative connections between trance and every day awareness that destroys the dissociation between them. Talking amalgamates the nascent and autonomous qualities of trance phenomena into the individual's usual, "normal" state of awareness to the point where many researchers (Barber, Spanos & Chaves, 1974) have come to believe that trance, as an altered state of consciousness, does not exist (Erickson & Rossi, 1974).

A CONTEXT THEORY OF
TWO LEVEL COMMUNICATION

In the commentary we analyzed the dynamics of two level communication in terms of the classical notion of hypnosis as the fixation and distraction of attention. In what follows we propose a more comprehensive analysis that encompasses a broader range of phenomena ranging from the conceptions of the recent contextual theory of verbal associations (Jenkins, 1974) and literalism to the use of shock, surprise, analogy and metaphor which are so common in Erickson's approach.

The question, *"Are you willing* (pause) **to find that out?"** has as a general context a query about motivation (Are you willing?) which fixates or structures the subject's conscious frame of reference or sense of meaning. The individual words and phrases used to articulate that general context, however, have their own individual and literal associations that do not belong to that general context. These individual and literal associations are, of course, usually suppressed and excluded from consciousness in its effort to grasp the general context. These suppressed associations do remain in the unconscious, however, and under the special circumstances of trance where dissociation and literalness are heightened, they can play a significant role in facilitating responsive behavior that is surprising to consciousness.

This situation can be made clear by analogy. The adult reader is usually searching for an author's meaning. Within certain limits it really doesn't matter what particular sentences or words are used. Many different sentences and combinations of words could be used to express the same meaning. It is the meaning of the general context of the sentences that registered in consciousness while the particular sentences and words used fall into the unconscious where they are "forgotten." In the same way one "reads" the meaning of a whole word rather than the individual letters used to make up the word. The general context of the letters register as the conscious meaning of a word rather than the individual associations of each letter. Jenkins (1974) has summarized the data of recent experimental work in the area of verbal association, event recognition, information integration and memory that places a similar emphasis on the significance of context to understand these phenomena. In any discourse or phenomena using words, it is usually the general context that establishes meaning rather than the structural units that create the discourse.

The obvious exceptions to this, of course, is in puns, allusions, and all sorts of verbal jokes where the punch line depends upon literal or individual verbal associations to words and phrases that originally escaped the attention of consciousness. Verbal jokes depend upon literal or individual associations that are usually suppressed.

In the same way, Erickson's two level communication utilizes a general context to fixate the attention of consciousness while the individual associations of words, phrases, or sentences within that context are registered in the unconscious where they can work their effects. From this point of view Erickson's Interspersal Technique (1966) is the clearest example of two level communication wherein subject matter of interest to a particular patient is utilized as a general context to fixate conscious attention while interspersed suggestions are received for their effects on an unconscious level.

Erickson has devised a number of other techniques to activate the individual, literal and unconscious associations to words, phrases or sentences buried within a more general context. Turns of phrase that are shocking, surprising, mystifying, non-sequitur, too difficult or incomprehensible for the general conscious context, for example, all tend to momentarily depotentiate the patient's conscious sets and activate a search on the unconscious level that will turn up the literal and individual associations that were previously suppressed. When Erickson overloads the general context with many words, phrases or sentences that have common individual associations, those associations (the interspersed suggestion) gain ascendency in the unconscious until they finally spill over into responsive behavior that the conscious mind now registers with a sense of surprise. The conscious mind is surprised because it is presented with a response within itself that it cannot account for. The response is then described as having occurred "all by itself" without the intervention of the subject's ego or conscious motivation; the response appears to be autonomous or "hypnotic."

Analogy and metaphor as well as jokes can be understood as exerting their powerful effects through the same mechanism of activating unconscious association patterns and response tendencies that suddenly summate to present consciousness with an apparently "new" datum or behavioral response.

THE MICRODYNAMICS OF SUGGESTION

Once Erickson has fixated and focused a patient's attention with a question or general context of interest (*e.g.*, ideally the possibility of dealing with the patient's problem) he then introduces a number of approaches designed to "depotentiate conscious sets." By depotentiating conscious sets we do not mean there is a loss of awareness in the sense of going to sleep; we are not confusing trance with the condition of sleep. Trance is a condition wherein there is a reduction of the patient's foci of attention to a few inner realities; consciousness has been fixated and focused to a relatively narrow frame of attention rather than being diffused over a broad area as in the more typical general reality orientation (Shor, 1959) of our usual everyday awareness. When fixated and focused in such a narrow frame, consciousness is in a state of unstable equilibrium; it can be "depotentiated" by being shifted, transformed or bypassed with relative ease.

Erickson believes that the purpose of clinical induction is to focus attention inward and alter some of the ego's habitual patterns of functioning. Because of the limitations of a patient's habitual frames of reference, his usual everyday consciousness cannot cope with certain inner and/or outer realities and the patient recognizes he has a "problem." Depotentiating a patient's usual everyday conscious sets is thus a way of depotentiating facets of his personal limitations; it is a way of deautomatizing (Deikman, 1972) an individual's habitual modes of functioning so that dissociation and many of its attendant classical hypnotic phenomena (*e.g.,* age regression, amnesia, sensory-perceptual distortions, catalepsies, etc.) are frequently manifest in an entirely spontaneous manner (Erickson & Rossi, 1975). Depotentiating the limitations of the individual's usual patterns of awareness thus opens up the possibility that new combinations of associations and mental skills may be evolved for creative problem solving within that individual.

Erickson's approaches to depotentiating consciousness are so subtle and pervasive in the manner with which they are interwoven with the actual process of induction and suggestion that they are usually unrecognized even when studying a written transcript of his words. In order to place them in perspective we outlined the microdynamics of induction and suggestion in Table 1 as (a) Fixation of attention, (b) Depotentiating Conscious sets, (c) Unconscious Search, (d) Unconscious Processes and (e) Hypnotic Response. We have also listed a number of Erickson's approaches to facilitating each state. Most of these approaches are illustrated in this paper and discussed in more detail elsewhere (Erickson & Rossi, 1974; Erickson & Rossi, 1975; Erickson, Rossi & Rossi, 1976; Haley, 1967; Rossi, 1973). Although we may outline these processes as stages of a sequence in Table 1 for the purpose of analysis, they usually function as one simultaneous process. When we succeed in fixating attention we automatically narrow the focus of attention to the point where one's usual frames of reference are vulnerable to being depotentiated. At such moments there is an automatic search on the unconscious level for new associations that can restructure a more stable frame of reference via the summation of unconscious processes. There is thus a certain arbitrariness to the order and the headings under which we assign some of the approaches Erickson used in this paper. He could equally well begin with an interesting story or pun as with a shock, surprise or a formal induction of trance. Once the conditions in the first three columns have been set in motion by the therapist, however, the patient's own individual unconscious dynamics automatically carries out the processes of the last two columns.

TABLE 1

THE MICRODYNAMICS OF TRANCE
INDUCTION AND SUGGESTION

(1) Fixation of Attention	(2) Depotentiating Consciousness
1. Stories that motivate Interest, Fascination etc.	1. Shock, Surprise, the Unrealistic and Unusual
2. Standard Eye Fixation	2. Shifting Frames of Reference: Displacing Doubt Resistance and Failure
3. Pantomine Approaches 4. Imagination and Visualization Approaches.	3. Distraction 4. Dissociation and Disequilibrium
5. Hand Levitation 6. Relaxation and All Forms of Inner Sensory Perceptual or Emotional Experience.	5. Cognitive Overloading 6. Confusion Non-Sequiturs
7. Etc.	7. Paradox
	8. Conditioning Via Voice Dynamics, etc. 9. Structured Amnesias 10. Etc.

TABLE 1. Continued.

(3) Unconscious Search	(4) Unconscious Processes	(5) Hypnotic Response
Indirect Forms of Suggestion		

1. Allusions, puns, jokes	1. Summation of:
	  a. Interspersal Suggestions
	  b. Literal Associations
	  c. Individual Associations
		''New''
		Datum or
		Behavioral
		Response Ex-
		perienced as
		Hypnotic or
		Happening
		All by itself

2. Metaphor, Analogy Folk Language	2. Autonomous, Sensory and Perceptual Processes	
3. Implication 4. Implied Directive	3. Freudian Primary Processes 4. Personality Mechanisms of Defense	
5. Double Binds 6. Words initiating Exploratory sets	5. Ziegarnik Effect 6. Etc.	
7. Questions and Tasks Requiring Unconscious Search		
8. Pause with Therapist Attitude of Expectancy 9. Open-ended Suggestions 10. Covering All Possibili- ties of Response 11. Compound Statements 12. Etc.		

A number of Erickson's most interesting approaches to facilitating hypnotic response are listed in Column 3 of Table 1. All these approaches are designed to evoke a search on the unconscious level. Allusions, puns, metaphors, implications, etc. are usually not grasped immediately by consciousness. There is a momentary delay before one "gets" a joke and, in part, that is what is funny about it. In that delay period there obviously is a search and processes on an unconscious level (column four) that finally summate to present a new datum to consciousness so it gets the joke. All the approaches listed in Column 3 are communication devices that initiate a search for new combinations of associations and mental processes that can present consciousness with useful results in everyday life as well as in hypnosis. The approaches listed in Column 3 are also the essence of Erickson's indirect approach to suggestion (Erickson, Rossi & Rossi, 1976). The study of these approaches may be regarded as a contribution to the newly defined science of pragmatics: the relation between signs and the users of signs (Watzlawick, Beavin & Jackson, 1967). Erickson relies upon the skill utilization of such forms of communication to evoke hypnotic behavior rather than hypersuggestibility *per se*.

It is important to recognize that while Erickson does think of trance as a special state (of reduced foci of attention) he does not believe hypersuggestibility is a necessary characteristic of trance (Erickson, 1932). That is, just because a patient is experiencing trance, it does not mean he is going to accept and act upon the therapist's direct suggestions. This is a major misconception that accounts for many of the failures of hypnotherapy; it has frustrated and discouraged many clinical workers in the past and has impeded the scientific exploration of hypnosis in the laboratory. Trance is a special state that intensifies the therapeutic relationship and focuses the patients attention on a few inner realities; *trance does not insure the acceptance of suggestions.* Erickson depends upon certain communication devices such as those listed in column three to evoke, mobilize and move a patient's associative processes and mental processes in ways that skills in certain directions to *sometimes* achieve certain therapeutic goals. He believes that hypnotic suggestion is actually this process of evoking and *utilizing* a patient's own mental processes in ways that are outside his usual range of ego control. This *utilization theory of hypnotic suggestion* can be validated, if it is found that other therapists and researchers can also effect more reliable results by carefully utilizing whatever associations and mental skills a particular patient already has that can be mobilized, extended, displaced, or transformed to achieve specific "hypnotic" phenomena and therapeutic goals.

In the formal trance situation, the successful utilization of unconscious processes leads to an autonomous response; the ego is surprised to find itself confronted with a new datum or behavior (Column 5). The same situation is in evidence in every day life, however, whenever attention is fixated with a question or an experience of the amazing, the unusual or anything that *holds* a person's interest. At such moments people experience the common everyday trance; they tend to gaze off (to the right or left depending upon which cerebral hemisphere is most dominant, Baken, 1969) and get that "far away" or "black" look. Their eyes may actually close, their body tends to become immobile (a form of catalepsy), certain reflexes (*e.g., swallowing, respiration, etc.)* may be suppressed and they seem momentarily oblivious to their surroundings until they have completed their inner search on the unconscious level for the new idea, response or frames of reference that will restabilize their general reality orientation. We hypothesize that in everyday life consciousness is in a continual state of flux between the general reality orientation and the momentary microdynamics of trance as outlined in Table 1. The well trained hypnotherapist is one who is acutely aware of these dynamics and their behavioral manifestations. Trance experience and hypnotherapy are simply the extension and utilization of these normal psychodynamic processes. Altered states of consciousness, wherein attention is fixated and the resulting narrow frame of reference shattered, shifted, and/or transformed with the help of drugs, sensory deprivation, meditation, biofeedback or whatever, follow essentially the same pattern but with varying emphasis on the different stages. We may thus understand Table 1 as a general paradigm for understanding the genesis and microdynamics of altered states and their effects upon behavior.

REFERENCES

Baken, P. Hypnotizability, laterality of eye-movements and functional brain asymmetry. *Perceptual and Motor Skills,* 1969, *28,* 927-932.

Barber, T.X., Spanos, N.P., & Chaves, J.F. *Hypnotism, imagination and human potentialities.* New York: Pergamon Press, 1974.

Cheek, D.B., LeCron, L.M. *Clinical hypnotherapy.* New York: Grune & Stratton, 1968.

Deikman, A.J. Deautomatization in the mystic experience. In C.T. Tart (Ed.), *Altered States of Consciousness.* New York: Doubleday, 1972.

Erickson, M.H. Possible detrimental effects of experimental hypnosis. *The Journal of Abnormal and Social Psychology,* 1932, *27,* 321-327.

Erickson, M.H. Hypnotherapy: The patient's right to both success and failure. *The American Journal of Clinical Hypnosis,* 1965, *7,* 254-257.

Erickson, M.H. The intersperal hypnotic technique for symptom correction and pain control. *The American Journal of Clinical Hypnosis,* 1966, *3,* 198-209.

Erickson, M.H., & Rossi, E.L. Varieties of hypnotic amnesia. *The American Journal of Clinical Hypnosis,* 1974, *16,* 225-239.

Erickson, M.H., & Rossi, E.L. Varieties of double bind. *The American Journal of Clinical Hypnosis,* 1975, *17,* 143-157.

Erickson, M.H., Rossi, E.L., & Rossi, S.I. *Hypnotic realities: The induction of clinical hypnosis and the indirect forms of suggestion.* New York: Irving Publishers, Halsted-Wiley Press, 1976.

Haley, J. (Ed.). *Advanced techniques of hypnosis and therapy: Selected papers of Milton H. Erickson.* New York: Grune & Stratton, 1967.

Jenkins, J.J. Remember that old theory of memory? Well, forget it! *American Psychology,* 1974, *29,* 785-795.

Rossi, E.L. *Dreams and the growth of personality: Expanding awareness in psychotherapy.* Elmsford, New York: Pergamon Press, 1972.

Rossi, E.L. Psychological shocks and creative moments in psychotherapy. *The American Journal of Clinical Hypnosis,* 1973, *16,* 9-22.

Shor, R.E. Hypnosis and the concept of the generalized reality-orientation. *American Journal of Psychotherapy,* 1959, *13,* 582-602.

Watzlawick, P., Beavin, J.H., & Jackson, D.D. *Pragmatics of human communication.* New York: Norton, 1967.

Woodworth, R.S., & Schlosberg, H. *Experimental psychology,* New York: Holt & Co. 1956.

INTRODUCTION TO CHAPTER 10

The following article by Ronald Havens underlines something both Rogers and Erickson stressed throughout their careers: That any therapist must find his/her own style and be creative and flexible in dealing with each client. Erickson often admonished his students, "Don't watch me; look at the client!" We will not find any secrets or formulas on how to deal with clients in Erickson's or Rogers's work. We can adopt them as partners in a sense, as I wrote in Chapter 1, but the key to our success lies within finding ourselves.

While in Section III we discuss and outline some basic techniques (Rogerian and Ericksonian) to be utilized in therapy, these are designed mainly as a way of creating the proper climate and atmosphere which will be conducive to therapy.

As Havens pointed out, those looking for formulas in Ericksonian therapy will be disappointed. Keep in mind the same is true of Rogers. Both men repeatedly pointed out that therapists must learn to be themselves and find what works for them in therapy.

CHAPTER 10

TRADITIONAL DELUSIONS VERSUS ERICKSONIAN REALITIES

by Ronald A. Havens*

Milton H. Erickson was a prodigiously fertile prototype who spawned an incredible array of innovative therapeutic approaches and techniques. In addition to the information provided in his numerous journal articles, lectures and teaching seminars, Erickson developed a large coterie of prolific and creative followers, each of whom has pro-

---

*Reprint requests and other communications should be sent to: Ronald A. Havens, Ph.D., Psychology Program, Office G-7, Samgamon State University, Springfield, Illinois 62708.

Havens, R.A. (1982). Traditional delusions versus Ericksonian realities. *Journal of Strategic and Systemic Therapies, 1*(4), 45-49. Reprinted with permission from Journal of Strategic and Systemic Therapies, 1982, Vol. 1, No. 4, pp. 45-59 and the author.

vided unique insights into his therapeutic style. Jay Haley, for example, developed the fundamental propositions of strategic therapy during his hours of study with Erickson and the brief therapy models developed at the Mental Research Institute in Palo Alto, California also were heavily influenced by Erickson's work. Numerous other followers have focused less upon the derivation of such general rules for the process of therapy and more upon the use of specific Ericksonian techniques such as metaphor, paradox, double-bind, and confusion.

Although these many efforts to extrapolate and apply the essential ingredients of Erickson's wisdom in particular settings or to identify and examine one or more of his techniques in-depth have been stimulating and useful, they probably are best viewed as effective holding-actions rather than as legitimate strategies for emulating his psychotherapeutic wizardry. They may enable some individuals to act more like members of the "master-therapist" class exemplified by Erickson than would be possible otherwise, but they do not seem to have the potential to transform anyone into a legitimate member of that "master-therapist" class. In fact, rather than representing the paths to such a transformation, these endeavors actually may be symbols or symptoms of a pervasive conceptual perversity which continuously prevents such transformations.

PLATONIC MISDIRECTION

Almost everyone in the Western civilization has the notion embedded deep within their system of fundamental assumptions that correct or enlightened action stems from correct or enlightened thought. Plato originated this orientation with his suggestion that philosophically or rationally derived Truths are the only legitimate basis for right actions and that immersion in discovered Truths will necessarily lead to correct behaviour. Religious Truth soon became another source of guidance and, relatively recently, Scientific Truth has been nominated for that distinction by the positivists. In each case, however, the underlying principle is the same, i.e., that the only conceivable path toward correct action lies in the discovery of a universal secret or special knowledge.

The field of psychotherapy was constructed within a perspective based upon this assumption. Consequently, the primary endeavor of almost all therapists since Freud has been the quest for theoretical truths or empirical truths under the assumption that such knowledge would provide insight which would enable them to do the right thing in the right way at the right time. Failing this, they frequently have turned toward rote imitation of techniques or procedures which have seemed to be the right solution for others. The end result has been either ritualistic repetition of certain acts in the apparent belief that these acts have been magically endowed with special therapeutic powers or consistently ineffective efforts to gain "psychic" insight into and control over a patient's past, present, and future using complex theories, hypothetical constructs and diagnostic categories which have as little basis in fact as astrology.

It is not surprising, therefore, that when confronted by an individual such as Erickson who manifests incredible therapeutic skill, many therapists automatically begin searching for unique truths or magic therapeutic tools. But Erickson refused to facilitate such an analysis of his work. He rejected the use of hypothetical constructs or complex theories of personality, he did not specify the specific stages of therapy and he rarely used exactly the same technique more than once.

Nonetheless, several theories have been proposed to account for his therapeutic success, trends in his style have been formalized into fundamental principles of various forms of therapy and several of his intervention strategies have been endowed with almost religious significance. For example, Erickson sometimes had patients climb Squaw Peak, a mountain near his home. Most of the time, he evidently did so for specific therapeutic reasons unique to each patient. On other occasions, however, he apparently recommended the climb to patients or students simply for the exercise and natural beauty it offered. In any event, Squaw Peak has now become a sacred shrine for some of his followers and mountain climbing has been endowed with a therapeutic significance previously reserved for primal screams and free-association.

Although considerable time, energy, and intelligence has been put into these limitations and analyses, insofar as I am aware no one has yet discovered Erickson's secret for success nor are they likely to do so. The explanation for this failure is quite straightforward, *Erickson simply did not have a secret for us to discover.* Our long-cherished strategy for learning how to do therapy will not work when applied to Erickson because Erickson was not a Platonist in orientation like the rest of us. Instead, he was a pragmatist and until we learn how to approach his work from a pragmatic orientation, we probably will continue to misinterpret or be confused by his works and to overlook or misunderstand his fundamental message.

PRAGMATIC REDIRECTION

Pragmatism is a philosophical orientation recently created as a replacement for the Platonic derivatives which no pervade our thinking (Rorty, 1982). In essence, pragmatism suggests that learning how to be a good human who tends to do the right thing in the right way at the right time is not something to be accomplished by searching for universal truths based upon faith, reason, or science. Pragmatists simply pay careful attention to the way things are and try to make the best of life using their experientially based common sense.

Erickson may not have been a pragmatist in any formal sense of the word, but his constant message to us about how to become effective psychotherapists was thoroughly anti-Platonic and essentially pragmatic. Every effort to generalize his comments into universal truths or basic laws was rebuffed by him and every inquiry regarding the fundamental ingredients of good psychotherapy was responded to with the simple admonition to observe with an open mind.

Erickson's anti-Platonic, "pragmatic" orientation was so different from our usual perspectives that it would be inappropriate and inaccurate to classify his approach as just another form of psychotherapy. His comments regarding the nature of psychotherapy and the process of becoming an effective psychotherapist call for the same kind of revolution in our definition of what we are and what we are all about that was required when modern medicine replaced the witch-doctor. Therapy of all types, including family therapy, takes on new dimensions when viewed from a pragmatic orientation and the requirements for the practice of therapy become noticeably different as well.

ERICKSON'S VIEW

Erickson's definition of psychotherapy in general may be summarized as follows:

> Psychotherapy consists of the skillful utilization of the therapist's unique reservoir of the experientially based learnings and observations to objectively observe the situation and then to create a context or set of experiences which is consistent with and takes advantage of the patient's unique personality, needs,

learnings and motivations in a manner designed to enable and stimulate patients to use their resources to resolve their problems in whatever manner is most appropriate and effective for them.

This admittedly lengthy and somewhat complex summary of Erickson's numerous comments regarding therapy reflects a remarkably pragmatic perspective. In fact, from within a pragmatic perspective this definition, or something like it, is the only conceivable approach available to therapists, including family therapists, hypnotherapists, and individual therapists alike. Any other view of, or approach to, therapy is simply unrealistic or irrational to the pragmatist.

Erickson, however, did not offer us only a redefinition of the nature of psychotherapy and of our role in it. Embedded within this definition is an implication that the quality of our therapeutic actions ultimately will remain a function of the quantity of our "unique reservoir of experientially based learnings and observations' and of our ability to utilize them effectively in each unique situation.

Notice that this definition does not trace therapeutic effectiveness to the quality of the therapist's theoretical insights, hypothetical constructs or magical therapeutic techniques. Rather, this definition traces the quality of an intervention to the quality of the therapist's observations and to the ability to use those observations skillfully. This, in turn, accounts for Erickson's constant admonitions to aspiring therapists to observe and to become flexible in their ability to respond in ways that influence the thoughts, perceptions and behaviours of others.

IMPLICATIONS

There are, no doubt, some lucky individuals who always have observed themselves and others carefully and objectively from a pragmatic perspective and who have practiced using the results of their observations to develop effective covert manipulations of others. I would guess, however, that a majority of therapists are not so lucky. Consequently, it would seem to be necessary for them to make a special effort to acquire the observational skills, observational backgrounds and related interpersonal influence strategies demanded by this form of therapy before they can begin practicing it effectively. Even prior to this endeavor, however, they would have to begin thinking like pragmatists instead of Platonists or else their observations would continue to be distorted or muddled by efforts to interpret them from within some theoretical explanatory system and to attribute significances to behaviours which exist only in their imaginations.

Thus, we cannot rely upon the ineffectual, biased and rigid assumptions, beliefs, observational skills, observational backgrounds and interpersonal influence strategies possessed by ourselves or our students. Erickson's meager reports of the contents of his enormous reservoir of observations and abilities may provide helpful guidance, but they are far from complete. A majority of his comments may be summarized by the simple observation that much of what people do and much of what causes people to do particular things is a function of unconscious patterns of learning, communication and reaction. He left it up to us, for the most part, to notice these unconscious communication and reaction patterns and to learn how to use them to initiate various forms of behaviour or interpersonal interactions.

Family therapists face an especially challenging chore in their efforts to acquire the backgrounds and skill necessary for their work. They must learn to enter a pragmatic orientation in order to observe and practice influencing not only individuals, but also entire families. The complexity of the skills involved in this chore are obvious, and probably cannot be simplified. The fact of the matter is that families present an enormous amount to observe, require an impressive background of observationally based data to comprehend, and demand a familiarity with a huge array of creative covert influence strategies to stimulate them into change or problem resolution. Exotic theories, oversimplied explanations and predesigned interventions may be appealing, but effective family therapy probably will be provided only by those who have taken the time and energy necessary to overcome their traditional biases, to learn how to observe, to acquire a broad background of observations, and to become flexible enough to respond in whatever manner the family seems to need to enable them to alter their dynamics.

Unfortunately, I know of no easy way to shed my ingrained Platonic prejudices, nor do I know how to enable others to do so effectively. The hypnotic state seems to initiate a more literal, pragmatic orientation in most subjects and might prove to be of value in this regard, however additional research would be necessary to support this contention.

In the meantime, the problem of obtaining an open mind or pragmatic orientation would seem to demand the concentrated effort and awareness necessary to overcome much, if not all, of what we have been taught previously. We simply have to learn how to view ourselves and others without the cumbersome collection of theoretical delusions and unwarranted assumptions that pervade the field. I cannot think of a more difficult assignment for anyone over six years old.

Similarly, I know of no simple source of guidance or training in the processes of observation and interpersonal influence. I am in the process of compiling an organized set of exercises and experiences which could serve as a workbook for those interested in improving these generic therapy skills and I would appreciate any suggestions readers might have in this regard. There also have been a large number of Ericksonian training workshops and seminars mentioned in each issue of *The Milton H. Erickson Foundation Newsletter,* some of which probably offer training in such skills.

Ultimately, however, it is obvious that each therapist will have to confront this learning challenge personally on a daily basis. Erickson spent his entire life acquiring the skills and information necessary for therapy and he taught us that we have to be equally willing to pay attention and to work hard every moment of our lives if we hope to master this business called therapy. There are no simple solutions or pat answers and we should be wary of those who promise them to us. We may borrow from others when useful, but we should aspire to the acquisition of the unbiased perspective and interpersonal skills that will enable us to generate our own unique forms of effective intervention. Such is the style of master psychotherapists.

REFERENCES

Rorty, R. *Consequences of pragmatism.* Minneapolis, University of Minnesota Press, 1982.

INTRODUCTION TO CHAPTER 11

In the Fall of 1984, I "discovered" the film "Napoleon" made in 1927 by Abel Gance. The creativity showed by Gance in this film not only awed me but depressed me—I felt my work to be so ordinary. But the black period I spent served as a motivator. I read about Gance and Napoleon, and I felt some hope. The following year I "discovered" another creative genius, Marcel Duchamp, through the books of Henry Martin and Gianfranco Baruchello (See Chapter 1)—Duchamp's life and work was a true inspiration. The following chapter is based upon the adaptation of one of Duchamp's concepts to psychotherapy.

"inframince"

LEA

This drawing is from a photo of Marcel Duchamp. Was he trying to show or give us a visual description of the Infra-thin?
(Drawing by the author)

CHAPTER **11**

INFRA-THIN

An Artist's Perception of Change
Adapted to Psychotherapy

Richard Leva

Artists teach us a great deal about ourselves. From the first drawings of simple animal figures on the walls of caves to modern abstract paintings, artists show us the world as we think it is, as it is, and how it could be. We turn now to an artist whose work can be adapted to a theory of how humans change. Change...such a simple word, but such important implications, especially for psychotherapy.

Through the work of Marcel Duchamp (1887-1968) I have been able to see more clearly what therapy is and how to symbolize the concept of change. Duchamp was one of the seminal minds of the 20th century. Highly regarded as an artist and influential figure during his lifetime, he is seen as even more influential today (Baruchello & Martin, 1983, 1985). Duchamp was discussed in Chapter 1. We now will add to this because his ideas are central to Chapter 11.

In many ways Duchamp's style of living and working resembles Milton Erickson's. Both were mavericks in their fields and delighted in going against the established ways of thinking. Duchamp wanted to bring the mind into art. He wanted to change art from purely "retinal art," where the eye is important in looking at a picture, to art where ideas in the creation challenge the person who looks at it. Along these lines, Erickson was noted for challenging his students with problems and stories. His stories, like Duchamp's paintings, were designed to challenge ordinary ways of thinking and provoke creativity.

Both men also were fond of using language for effect, and both were notorious punsters. Duchamp often attached to his paintings enigmatic titles. His most famous painting on glass is entitled "The Bride Stripped Bare by Her Bachelors, Even." The last word "even" is a little addition which adds much confusion to the title. Erickson would use such words as "perhaps," "still," and "while" which added a time-binding or future orientation to that which preceded it and leaves the meaning of the sentence open-ended. Leaving interpretations open-ended were what both men wanted to do, so that the person looking at the painting or hearing Erickson's story would come to their own conclusions. Toward the end of his life, Duchamp made very clear, albeit to artists, a controversial statement about this viewpoint. Speaking in Houston about the spectators role in art, he said, "The artist is a 'mediumistic being' who does not really know what he is doing or why he is doing it; it is the spectator who through a kind of 'aesthetic osmosis' deciphers and interprets the work's hidden qualities, relates them to the external world and thus completes the creative cycle" (Tomkins, 1965, p. 37).

This idea has implications for psychotherapy also, because as we have pointed out elsewhere, the therapist's words will be interpreted in the context of the client's past history, learnings, and experiences. In this respect like the artist, the therapist cannot know what or why he/she is doing some things. One also could say that therapists are "mediumistic beings"—they create climates for change much as artists do. Certainly, Erickson felt this as he emphasized the client's role in therapy as Duchamp emphasized the role of spectators in art:

> Reliance was placed upon the patient's own thinking and intelligence to make the proper psychological interpretation of her symptom when she became ready for that realization. (Erickson, 1980, Vol. IV, p. 25)

And

Also, properly oriented, hypnotic therapy can give the patient that necessary understanding of his own role in effecting his recovery and thus enlist his own effort and participation in his own cure... (Erickson, 1980, Vol. IV, p. 34)

Too often we as therapists forget that what we say to clients can be interpreted in many different ways. Remember that what the therapist says is not what is important, but rather what the client hears. To see us as mediumistic beings directly focuses upon this crucial concept.

Both men then were interested in change, and both set out to accomplish this through humor, language, shock, and surprise. Both men, in a sense, were artists, and although they were in different fields, they had similar goals.

The Infra-thin:
A Metaphor for Change

But now we come to one of Duchamp's most interesting concepts and one which has great implication for therapy. Duchamp's word for this concept is "inframince," and essentially in English it means infrathin. A literal definition would be "below thinness" or "within thinness."

To begin to understand this concept and use it as concept for change in therapy, we need to go back about sixty years when Duchamp's ideas began to take shape. In a painting context, the Cubists had concerned themselves with how objects were in space and the Futurists were concerned with objects in motion. But according to the Chilean Surrealist, Roberto Matta, (Tomkins, 1965, p. 48) "Duchamp attacked a whole new problem in art and solved it—*to paint the moment of change, change itself.*" In his painting, "Passage from the Virgin to the Bride," Duchamp attempted to show the transition when a person goes from one phase to another. The passage "from a virgin to a bride" is a significant one and a transition that would imply also significant behavior changes. Passages from one state to another are often symbolized by rituals in our society to show their importance (e.g., first communion, Bar Mitzva, taking oaths of office, granting degrees—all these are elaborately staged rituals designed to signify a change from one state to another and along with it behavior change). (See also Chapter 7.)

So we recognize change and transitions as something important, and Duchamp's challenge was to try to paint this important human experience. As psychotherapists, we also are interested in change. Can we also as therapists depict this in some way? Is it necessary to? We cannot ignore transitions and change since they are the heart of psychotherapy.

Change is indeed one of the most important subject matters in psychology and psychotherapy. VonHerder said that "man is never complete his existence lies in becoming" and Gordon Allport, this century's most famous personality theorist, concurred using the word "becoming" as the title of his book from the Yale Terry Lectures (Allport 1955) to show his strong support for the idea that an essential part of personality is its drive towards growth and change.

Maslow's "self actualization" fits here also. Our focus in an earlier chapter on the nature of man was that as counselors and therapists, the main goal of therapy was growth toward self-actualization, and this implies change.

Symbolizing Change Through Duchamp's Infra-thin

Through the artist Duchamp now, we can see how this goal of change and transition can be first symbolized and then achieved. *We have to be more accepting of what is possible, and part of our goal is to communicate this to our clients.* Change and transition do occur, and when they do they occur in what Duchamp called the infra-thin.

Duchamp said,

> The possible is an infra-thin. The possibility of several tubes of color becoming a Seurat is the concrete explanation of the possible as infra-thin. The possible implying the becoming, passage from one to the other takes place in the infra-thin. Possibility, chance and the readymade are connected concepts. They take place in the infra-thin a region beyond time and space that confounds conventional aesthetics. (Adlock, 1983, p. 53)

This first sentence, "The possible is an infra-thin," catches us immediately; it reaffirms our faith in what could be while at the same time making us aware of how tenuous the possible is. We know all things are "possible," but we also know what we think is possible may be difficult to achieve. That the possible is infra-thin carries with it the image of fragility, while at the same time indicating that the change may be imperceptible.

This has important implications for psychotherapy because Duchamp is focusing on the transition, or change from one stage to another. He is calling attention to what could be possible. His use of the word becoming, as Allport does, is a deliberate choice which implies growth rather than recession. Duchamp's analogy of the tubes of paint becoming a Seurat also focuses on the growth aspect and what is possible. It calls attention to what beauty lies in the tubes of paint—it calls attention to what is possible. It is a metaphor for change.

Change Occurs in the Infra-thin

Baruchello and Martin (1983) said that Duchamp always operated in the inframince (infra-thin), and they define this as the world of psychic micro phenomena. *Psychic micro phenomena* can be seen as infinitely thin layers that exist from one moment to another. In this area is where the possibility of change exists. Seen in this way each moment carries with it enormous possibilities. Each moment has then the possibility of change. As with the tubes of paint and the possibility of them becoming a Seurat or a Picasso, each moment is open with unlimited possibilities. When Duchamp as a person operated in the infra-thin, he was allowing himself the possibility of change and transition. He was not bound by past elements as most of us are, and this is reflected in his work which was original and with little or no connection to past schools.

The Infra-thin and
the Unconscious

As shown in Chapter 4, Erickson placed great faith in the unconscious—for him it is a vast storehouse of potentials. Carl Rogers also had a similar view, and this becomes even more evident in his recent writings. In 1985, Rogers appealed for more emphasis on intelligent use of intuition in therapy. Also in 1985 he wrote,

When I am at my best as a group facilitator or a therapist, I discover another characteristic. I find that when I am closest to my inner, intuitive self, when I am somehow in touch with the unknown in me, when perhaps I am in a slightly altered state of consciousness in the relationship, then whatever I do seems full of healing. (p. 565)

Erickson also operated at times in what might be considered a similar state or trance state.

Apparently, the three men were all describing similar phenomena and ways of being in the world. Duchamp operated in the inframince, Rogers in a "slightly altered state close to his intuitive self," and Erickson in a trance state. Moreover, the hypothesis is that what Duchamp called the infra-thin and Rogers the unknown can be taken as examples of unconscious functioning or tapping of internal resources.

No longer are we surprised to read or hear some artist describe the creative process and how similar the descriptions are of how they tap unknown sources of creativity and energy and consciousness is bypassed. For example, the painter Robert Motherwell starts the creative process by doodling, and when his unconscious recognizes a shape, he begins.

Using the unconscious and attempting to use it for creativity is quite common in all forms of art; however, for therapists to do so is unusual. They generally do not focus upon it for themselves as a source of energy and perception as Rogers and Erickson did.

Change and Restructuring

For Erickson clients change as they restructure and resynthesize their beliefs. Effective results occur as the patient goes through the inner process of reassociating his/her experiential life. This idea of restructuring implies a transition from one phase to another, and a helpful process is when we have a notion of where this restructuring takes place. Duchamp gave it to us—it occurs in the infra-thin.

In part, the infra-thin can be used as an analogy of the unconscious where the person can exist. This sentence is made up of infinitely thin moments of change from one moment to another. In this zone the infra-thin is pregnant with possibility for change and restructuring. This idea, that *for change to occur a restructuring and a modification of thinking are necessary,* is a theme running through this book. It is reflected in Araoz's "Metanoia" (Chapter 7) and in Vaihinger's philosophy of "As if" (Chapter 3).

The Infra-thin as
a Zone of Change

If one accepts this analogy of the infra-thin as a zone of change, then the possibilities are endless. As Allport believed, man is always becoming—always in a state of transition; while these transitions may be at the moment imperceptible—they nevertheless occur.

This also implies hope. Since I am in a state of transition and these transitions may not be perceptible, I need not despair. Change is occurring.

In some ways, the figure on the cover of this book can be seen as a visual example of the infra-thin involved in change. The pictures are drawn from photos of Erickson—the right drawing of Erickson when he was in his forties or fifties, and the left one when he was in his late seventies. I chose them to show a transition—the development of the younger therapist to the wise older man. As I usually do, I outlined the features of both pictures and started to work using the stipple method—a series of dots to make up each figure. I work on both figures at the same time. As I usually do when I get to a recognizable stage, I showed it to my wife to see if she could see what I was after. On this occasion she said, "I see, interesting, three faces of a man." Three? I said I hadn't seen the third figure appearing although I had been working on the drawing for over three hours. I left the drawing as is. To me it was more than coincidence. I felt this was not only an example of unconscious recognition but also an example of change in the infra-thin.

A favorite drawing of mine which symbolizes at once the transitional development of a person while still retaining a structure is "I at the Center" by David Oleson, made in the studio of William Huff. The art technique employed is called "parquet deformation" a parquet is a mosaic usually in wood and in these deformations one or more sections of the design are altered (Hofstadter, 1985). The basic "I" symbolizes the personality in the center of the drawing in each quadrant of the drawing. The "I" is present, yet it is quite different and the change sometimes barely perceptible.

Changes as they begin (in the center) are so small that the change is barely seen. This is such a lovely, graphic way of showing what this chapter is trying to say. It visually shows the transition from one stage to another.

Figure 11.1. "The I at the Center." Reproduced by permission from the studio of William S. Huff.

Application of the Infra-thin

Ericksonian and Rogerian therapies lend themselves very well to this philosophy of transitional moments of change. One may even discuss this concept with the client, perhaps as a philosophy. When the therapist is sure the idea of the infra-thin as a transition point is understood then therapy can proceed. However, the client does not necessarily need to understand these ideas consciously. Change is symbolized, but how it occurs is not resolved.

How change occurs may not even be important. Perhaps the best approach would be merely to look at this idea of change not as choice points but that someone chooses to live in the inframince or zone of change.

That is perhaps the important point of this chapter—to choose to live in a zone where growth and change are a moment to moment occurrence; to break with the set ways of operating and look for what is possible.

REFERENCES

Allport, G. (1955). *Becoming.* New Haven: Yale Press.

Adlock, C.E. (1983). Marcel Duchamp's notes from the large glass a N-Dimensional Analysis. Ann Arbor, MI: UMI Research Press.

Baruchello, G., & Martin, H. (1983). *How to imagine.* New Paltz, NY: Documenttext-McPherson.

Baruchello, G., & Martin, H. (1985). *Why Duchamp.* New Paltz, NY: Documenttext-McPherson.

Erickson, M.H. (1980). *The collected papers of Milton H. Erickson, Vol. IV.* E. Rossi (Ed.). New York: Irvington.

Erickson, M.H., & Rossi, E. (1979) *Hypnotherapy an exploratory case book.* New York: Irvington.

Hofstadter, D. (1985). *Metamagical themes.* New York: Basic Books.

Rogers, C. (1985). Reaction to Gunnison's article on the similarities between Erickson and Rogers. *Journal of Counseling and Development,* pp. 565-566.

Tomkins, C. (1965). Not seen and/or less seen. Profile of Marcel Duchamp. *New Yorker,* Feb. 6, pp. 48-91.

SECTION III

TECHNIQUES FOR CHANGE

INTRODUCTION TO SECTION III

TECHNIQUES FOR CHANGE

While we argued in Chapter 1 that adopting Erickson as a partner and developing one's own style is important, nevertheless specific skills and techniques will greatly aid the therapist. Therefore, in this section we draw upon both Ericksonian and Rogerian human communication principles to learn specific skills and techniques.

This section begins with a chapter pointing out further similarities between Erickson and Rogers. We then shift the remaining portion of the book to techniques and counseling theory—concepts which can be utilized in a therapeutic setting for growth and change.

Milton Erickson.
(Drawing by the author)

CHAPTER 12

ROGERS AND ERICKSON SIMILARITIES IN BASIC THEORY

In Chapter 5 Gunnison introduced on a broad scale some of the similarities shown in the philosophies of Rogers and Erickson. In this chapter I expand this and specifically focus on Rogers' six conditions necessary for positive growth, and while doing so also show how Erickson's ideas fit into this overall Rogerian schema.

Carl Rogers' techniques and ideas have been the mainstay of most counseling graduate programs for the past forty years. No other man's ideas have had more of an impact on counseling and psychotherapy in the United States. And what Rogers and his followers have shown to be the necessary ingredients of counseling and psychotherapy are the results of extensive research (Carkhuff, 1969, I, II). While struggling to find a counseling style that worked, Rogers found that those clients of his who improved were often those for whom he had developed a liking. Based upon this observation, subsequent research found that the most important ingredient for positive growth to take place is to be found in the quality of the relationship which develops between the client and the counselor.

ROGERS' SIX ORIGINAL CONCEPTS
FOR THERAPY

Many have described the aspects important to the counseling relationship (Patterson 1974, Ivey & Downing, 1980) but essentially Rogers' six original concepts for effective therapy remain the same. Rogers (1942, 1951) said that for therapy to occur, the following conditions must be present:

1. Two people are in contact.

2. One person, the client, is incongruent, being vulnerable and anxious.

3. The other person, the therapist, is congruent in the relationship.

4. The therapist experiences unconditional positive regard toward the client.

5. The therapist experiences an empathetic understanding of the client's internal frame of reference.

6. The client perceives, at least to a minimal degree, conditions 4 and 5. (Patterson, 1980, p. 486)

Often, in class when I put these six concepts on the board and go over them, students wonder how such a simple set of rules can actually have an effect. When looked at out of the context of therapy and the relationship between two people, the concepts may not appear effective. However, we shall show that Erickson himself adhered to these ideas in practice even though he gave only brief admission that his ideas have some similarity to Rogers (Erickson & Rossi, 1979, p. 51). But let's take each step separately and put them in the proper context because these concepts are the foundation for the techniques that follow along with the meta techniques of Erickson we will utilize later.

1. Two people are in psychological contact.

Rogers continually emphasizes the quality of the relationship necessary for therapy as one in which the participants see each other as people, not as objects. Perhaps he could have used a more specific term than "psychological" to describe this, but in essence he advocates an I-thou relationship rather than an I-object relationship. Often therapists, as scientists, see the client as an object to be studied in a cold detached manner. This is not the "psychological" contact advocated by Rogers.

Did Erickson concur with this? As Havens (1985, p. 30) pointed out, "One of the most fundamental conclusions drawn by Erickson after his years of observation was that every individual is unique."

The following quote shows Erickson's similarity to Rogers—that the client is seen as a person: "And so far as I've found in 50 years, every person is a different individual. I've always met every person as an individual, emphasizing his or her own individual qualities" (Zeig, 1980, p. 220).

2. The first person (the client) is incongruent, vulnerable, and anxious.

People are always experiencing. Daily we are bombarded by thousands of stimuli. To make sense out of the world in an economic way humans use labels to symbolize the vast number of experiences they have. (See Chapters 3 and 7.) From Rogers and Erickson's viewpoint, these experiences always are colored by each individual's own life history and therefore can never be totally accurately represented. All we can hope for is minimal distortion. Now for most of us, our experiences are fairly accurately represented. However, in some cases, a person may begin to deny and distort significant experiences and this may result in feelings of vulnerability and anxiety. Rogers' term for denying and distorting is "incongruence." Imagine two circles, one representing experience, the other representing the person's perception of that experience. When the person is congruent, the symbols used to represent the experience, that is, the person's thoughts about the experience and the experience itself, fit so that graphically the two circles would appear as being one circle. However, when any part of the experience is denied, then one circle appears out of focus and does not fit.

Denying an experience also can occur in therapy. A good example of a distortion and denial occurs in *Three Approaches to Psychotherapy,* which is a therapy demonstration film. Rogers was coming to the end of a very positive thirty minute session with the client Gloria. During this session, Rogers and Gloria both show positive feelings toward each other, and at one point Gloria says how she likes talking to Rogers and wished her father could be like him. Rogers comments that she looks like a pretty nice daughter. Now the sum of this was that the positive feelings are building toward a beneficial experience for the client. The significant dialogue is reproduced.

> **Gloria:** *And again, that's a hopeless situation. I tried working on it, and I feel it's something I have to accept. My father just isn't the type of man I'd dearly like. I'd like somebody more understanding and caring. He cares, but not in the way we can cooperate or communicate.*

> **Rogers:** *You feel that, "I am permanently cheated..."*

> **Gloria:** *That is why I like substitutes. Like I like talking to you and I like men that I can respect. Doctors, and I keep sort of underneath feeling like we are real close, you know, sort of like a substitute father.*

> **Rogers:** *I don't feel that's pretending.*

> **Gloria:** *Well, you are not really my father.*

> **Rogers:** *No. I meant about the real close business.*

> **Gloria:** *Well, see, I sort of feel that's pretending too because I can't expect you to feel very close to me. You don't know me that well.*

> **Rogers:** *All I can know is what I am feeling and that is I feel close to you in this moment.*

What had been a positive therapeutic experience was now being denied and distorted by Gloria. Rogers' genuine feeling toward her was being seen as "pretend." Rogers immediately perceives this distortion and "saves" the experience with his final comment. Erickson often used the technique of "reframing" to help clients resymbolize or to look at their experiences in a positive way. Reframing can be seen as a way of helping the client reduce the distortion which is occurring. Here is an example of reframing I used with a 21-year-old college male who was upset about his parents' divorce and how it was still having effects on him years later. I said to him that it was positive for him to have learned such a valuable lesson at an early age and that it would most likely be a great aid to him as a husband and a father. I reframed what he had been viewing as negative to something that will, in the future, be positive.

As therapists, we do not necessarily need to know "why" humans or particular clients distort their experience. We only need to know where the distortion exists.

Again, did Erickson concur? Erickson was a strong believer that people constructed their own reality as discussed in Chapter 3. The following quotes reflect his position: "As philosophers of old have said, as a man thinketh, he is" (Erickson & Rossi, 1979, p. 262) "and all philosophers say, reality is all in the head" (Zeig, 1980, p. 90).

**3. The second person (the counselor)
is congruent in the relationship.**

When one realizes the rule that denial and distortion, at least to a small degree, is part of everyone's life, then what follows is that counselors are not superhumans or Godlike creatures always accurately symbolizing what is happening to them. What we expect from counselors is that in the relationship, during the therapy hour, they are accurate in their perceptions and distortion is minimal. How else can it be? If I the counselor am perceiving things from my client which are not present, how in any remote sense could I be of help? All therapies (Rogerian, Ericksonian, Gestalt, any others) must advocate accuracy of the perceptions of the counselor. If I see hostility where actually excitement exists, defensiveness where shyness is, anxiety when positive energy is present, how can I be of any help to the client? I will merely be adding to the client's already out-of-kilter perceptions.

While this may appear to be a difficult task to expect of counselors through the experience of working with people, the process evolves and accurate perceptions become the rule rather than the exception.

**4. The therapist experiences unconditional
positive regard toward the client.**

Although largely ignored in the Ericksonian literature, research supports the position that some degree of liking of the client—seeing him/her as a person of worth—is a necessary ingredient in the relationship (Truax & Carkhuff, 1967; Carkhuff, 1969). Rogers uses the term "prizing." As Rogers stated at some point in the relationship, "I want to prize the client."

The liking or prizing does not have to be a deep love. Yet, love would not be too strong a word to use here (although, we should free ourselves from the romantic or sexual aspects of the word with which we usually associate it).

The unconditional aspect of positive regard simply means that no strings are connected to my liking you. The client does not feel bound to act in any particular way for the feelings of respect and liking he/she is receiving from the therapist.

Ericksonian Positive Regard. Even though Erickson wrote very little about the therapeutic concepts of positive regard, he himself is a good example of putting it into practice. In reading many of his case discussions of clients, one is impressed with Erickson's warmth for his clients. Erickson saw his clients in his own home and often members of Erickson's family were about and interacted with the clients. Is a better way possible to show my regard for you than by taking you into my family?

Perhaps because Erickson himself does not discuss this concept directly, his disciples seem to have ignored it. Yet, we cannot overemphasize its importance in the therapeutic relationship. Erickson could not have gotten away with some of his audacious treatment prescriptions if the clients did not feel he liked them.

But this important point has not been ignored by some Ericksonian disciples. Bill O'Hanlon (an Ericksonian therapist, seminar leader, and Editor of the Erickson Foundation Newsletter) was asked at one of his workshops whether there was anything else he would do in an interview while getting the information to make a therapeutic intervention. O'Hanlon answered, "Sure, all the Rogerian stuff—that has to come first."

**5. The therapist experiences an
empathetic understanding of the
client's internal frame of reference.**

Empathy as used by Rogers should not be confused with sympathy. Empathy is an accurate, understanding of the client's world as seen from the inside. In discussing how to create a helping relationship, Rogers said, "Can I step into his private world so completely that I lose all desire to evaluate or judge it? Can I enter it so sensitively that I can move about it freely without trampling on meanings which are precious to him?" (Rogers, 1961, p. 53). This is empathy.

Lopez (1987) said that while both Rogers and Erickson stressed the importance of empathy in the therapeutic relationship, whether their understandings and applications of the construct were similar is debatable. Lopez pointed out that Rogers' empathy construct includes sensing the client's private world as if it were your own, but without losing the "as if" quality (Rogers, 1961, p. 284); while Erickson suggested an "expanded" and more utilitarian view of empathy, one embracing both subjective "private world" experiences and public, symptomatic activity.

Lopez's contrast of Ericksonian and Rogerian empathy are especially helpful, and they give counselors a broader more flexible view of this important construct. According to him, "Erickson's approach challenges one to think more complexly about empathy; is the 'as if' distinction really necessary? Can rapport be more immediately established without it?" (p. 242).

Although misunderstood, empathy is also the cornerstone of Erickson's method, and as with the misunderstandings with Rogers, Erickson had a difficult time convincing his disciples of its importance—especially in hypnotherapy. We will have much more to say about this in Chapters 14 and 15.

The concept of empathy is closely related to what Erickson called rapport, and this again shows the strong similarity between Rogers and Erickson on these important concepts. The concept of rapport is something commonly found in the Ericksonian literature. But essentially rapport, as used by Erickson, is empathy. Erickson and Rossi (1979) called attention to the closeness of the empathetic aspect of Erickson's work with Rogers. In a discussion of the technique of using the client's own vocabulary and frames of reference, Erickson stated, "at this level, our approach might appear similar to the non-directive, client-centered approach of Rogers" (Erickson & Rossi, 1979, p. 51).

Erickson called his method of therapy "the utilization approach." The word utilization was used to call attention to Erickson's idea that the counselor should utilize whatever behaviors the client presented. Had Rogers not been first with his use of the labels "client-centered" and "person-centered therapy," I am sure Erickson would have used them.

Notice how closely the following Erickson paragraph resembles Rogers' idea of the importance of empathy:

> The initial step in the utilization approach, as in most other forms of psychotherapy, is to accept the patients' manifest behavior and to acknowledge their personal frames of reference. This openness and acceptance of the patients' worlds facilitate a corresponding openness and acceptance of the therapist by the patients. (Erickson & Rossi, 1979, p. 53)

And the following quote shows Erickson's realization of the importance of a quality Rogerian-type relationship between the counselor and the client.

> The development of a trance state is an intrapsychic phenomenon, dependent upon internal processes, and the activity of the hypnotist serves only to create a favorable situation. As an analogy an incubator supplies a favorable environment for hatching of eggs but the actual hatching derives from the development of life processes within the egg. (Erickson & Rossi, 1979, p. 54)

If one substitutes "Rogerian counseling" for "trance induction" and "counselor" for "hypnotist" in the above passage, one is struck by the similarity of approaches even in hypnosis.

**6. The client perceives, at least
to a minimal degree, Items 4 and 5**

This is the essence of counseling. That is, concept 6 is really saying that the therapist, after he/she has made accurate perceptions of the client's frame of reference and has developed a positive feeling toward the client, now has to communicate this to the client.

The following quote is the clearest example one can find of Erickson's adherence to this idea:

> The most effective means of focusing and fixing attention in clinical practice is to recognize and acknowledge the patient's current experience. When the therapist correctly labels the patient's on-going here-and-now experience, the patient is usually immediately grateful and open to whatever else the therapist may have to say. (Erickson & Rossi, 1979, p. 5)

Like Rogers, Erickson was saying you first must recognize the client's frame of reference then communicate to him/her that you understand it—this is empathy. When Erickson said the client becomes grateful, we could add that they also feel positive regard and trust. The foundation of Erickson's techniques are basic Rogerian ideas.

NECESSARY AND SUFFICIENT CONDITIONS FOR THERAPY—THE CORE CONDITIONS

What we have been talking about have been referred to elsewhere (Patterson, 1974, pp. 44-59) as the "core conditions" of therapy—these are seen as not only sufficient but necessary conditions for change to take place. Broadly, these core conditions are empathy and positive regard. We say broadly because these can be broken down into sub-categories (e.g., a sub-group of positive regard is acceptance and respect). (See Figure 12.1.) Hereafter, when we refer to the core conditions, we will be referring to them in the broadest sense.

Core Conditions	Subcategories
1. Unconditional Positive Regard	Respect (seeing client as someone of worth) Acceptance (no strings attached) Warmth Prizing the client Genuineness (respect and warmth is real, not insincere)
2. Empathy	Accurate perception of client's feelings, problems Able to understand and perceive client's internal frame of reference

Figure 12.1. Core conditions of therapy. Subcategories of positive regard and empathy.

In the following chapters, we will begin a look at how to implement the core conditions to set up a context amenable to change.

**Rapport and the Core
Conditions—Why They Work:
A Basic Human Need—Understanding**

Humans have basic biological needs (e.g., food and water) but Abraham Maslow pointed out that as humans we also have social and emotional needs that must be met. One of the most important of these, but often overlooked, is the simple need of being understood.

In many cases, just the very fact that someone has feelings which have been heard accurately can be beneficial. The tragic fact in the face of the importance of understanding is that most of us do not make much of an attempt to understand others. Often we are too busy with our own thoughts or we make evaluative comments to ourselves on what has been communicated, ''I don't believe that'' or ''That's dumb'' are just a couple of the ways we evaluate what others have said to us (Rogers, 1961). These evaluations prevent us from understanding. Perhaps our lack of understanding is what exacerbates the problem and makes this need even more intense.

Rogers finds understanding to be helpful to both the client and the counselor:

> To understand is enriching in a double way. I find when I am working with clients in distress, that to understand the bizarre world of a psychotic individual, or to understand and sense the attitudes of a person who feels that life is too tragic to bear, or to understand a man who feels that he is a worthless and inferior individual—each of these understandings somehow enriches me. I learn from these experiences in ways that change me, that make me a different and, I think, a more responsive person. Even more important perhaps, is the fact that my understanding of these individuals permits them to change. It permits them to accept their own fears and bizarre thoughts and tragic feelings and discouragements, as well as their moments of courage and kindness and love and sensitivity. And it is their experience as well as mine that when someone fully understands those feelings, this enables them to accept those feelings in themselves. Then they find both the feelings and themselves changing. Whether it is understanding a woman who feels that very literally she has a hook in her head by which others lead her about, or understanding a man who feels that no one is as lonely, no one is as separated from others as he, I find these understandings to be of value to me. But also, and even more importantly, to be understood has a very positive value to these individuals. (Rogers, 1961, p. 18)

In this passage, Rogers has clearly demonstrated his implementation of the core conditions. When he is accepting the client and the client's problems, no matter how bizarre, Rogers is demonstrating acceptance, positive regard and empathy.

Another way of looking at this is if understanding is not present, then the core conditions are not present, at least part of them are not, and without them therapy will not succeed.

Understanding also results in another essential ingredient: trust.

Understanding Builds Trust

An essential part of the counseling relationship is trust—without it, clients will not communicate essential aspects of themselves which would help them work through their problems.

In our culture, new clients give some amount of trust to their counselors during the first session by virtue of counselors' position of respect via earned degrees. This is usually why clients use a "facade" problem to introduce to counselors when asked why they made the initial appointment. The facade problem, while real, usually is on the surface and underneath lie a myriad of difficulties of much more concern.

My experience has almost invariably been that underneath the presenting problem lie the client's real concerns. Usually approximately twenty minutes of understanding is essential before the deep sharing begins.

When understanding is demonstrated, the client feels, "Here is someone who understands me; and since they are listening to me, they also seem to be interested in me." This kind of thinking results in trust.

ROGERIAN UNDERSTANDING ADDS TO AN ERICKSONIAN APPROACH

Using the Rogerian type of approach with its emphasis on understanding also helps the Ericksonian therapist to avoid making a hasty decision and come in with quick readymade interventions.

Erickson's fast interventions in some cases gives the impression of having to make a decision about what to do almost the moment the client walks into the office. The label of "brief therapy" given by some to the Erickson school adds to this notion. But no substitute exists for patience and building trust through understanding. When the understanding is demonstrated, trust ensues and the therapist will have a much better handle on the client's difficulties.

REFERENCES

Carkhuff, R.R. (1969). *Helping and human relationships, Vol. I and II, practice and research.* New York: Holt, Rinehart and Winston.

Erickson, M.H., & Rossi, E. (1979). *Hypnotherapy an exploratory casebook.* New York: Irvington. (p. 51).

Havens, R.A. (1985). *The wisdom of Milton H. Erickson.* New York: Irvington. (p. 51).

Ivey, A., & Downing, L. (1980). *Counseling and psychotherapy.* Englewood Cliffs, NJ: Prentice-Hall.

Lopez, F.G., (1987). Erickson & Rogers: The differences do make a difference. *Journal of Counseling and Development, 65,* 241-243.

Patterson, C.H. (1974). *Relationship counseling and psychotherapy.* New York: Harper & Row.

Patterson, C.H. (1980). *Theories of counseling and psychotherapy,* 3rd ed. New York: Harper & Row.

Rogers, C.R. (1942). *Counseling and psychotherapy, new concepts in practice.* Boston: Houghton Mifflin.

Rogers, C.R. (1951). *Client centered therapy; its current practice, implications, and theory.* Boston: Houghton Mifflin.

Rogers, C.R. (1961). *On becoming a person.* Boston: Houghton Mifflin.

Truax, C.B., & Carkhuff, R.R. (1967). *Toward effective counseling and psychotherapy.* Chicago: Aldine.

Zeig, J.K. (1980). *A teaching seminar with Milton H. Erickson.* New York: Brunner-Mazel.

CHAPTER 13

BASIC FACILITATIVE SKILLS— TRANCE-ACTIONS

**Comments about Learning
a New Skill**

Counseling, or good human relations, is a skill, and as a skill, it is something that can be acquired. What is needed is understanding and practice. In some ways learning the skills of counseling is like learning any other skill, such as playing the piano or riding a bike. An efficient way to do this is to break the skill down into smaller components and practice each of them until they become a part of you, and then put the components together into a whole and then, of course, more practice.

Counseling skills are acquired this way also, but an additional problem is present. One of the major components of counseling is communication, something which everyone already does, and each of us is quite adept at it, we do it automatically. While we are skillful in communicating, we are probably not using a communication style amenable to counseling. We are so used to exchanging messages (we have been doing it since birth), that it makes it especially hard to focus on our habits and faults, and to try new ways of communicating. We are probably using a method that, while effective for everyday needs, is not effective in helping those with emotional or psychological problems. So another new way of communicating has to be learned. I like to think of learning to counsel people as learning another way of communicating, and I like the idea of having more than one way of communicating in my repetoire.

Perhaps an illustration will accentuate the point. Pick out some skill you have studied which took a while to learn. If you are a musician, use learning to play your instrument as an example. Typing, swimming, and bicycle riding are other good skills to use. Now, imagine if this skill was central to your work, and then someone said that you had to learn the technique a different way as you have a new machine or instrument and the technique you are using will not work. If you play the violin in this example, think of how hard it would be to learn new fingering and bowings and placement of your hand on the bow.

In a sense, as you learn this new way of communicating, you will be confronted with this also. So you feel awkward and mechanical in trying to change something you already do well. But, if you persist, your way of communicating will be improved.

To begin this process, we want to take a very close and rather different viewpoint of the human communication process. We are indebted to the work mainly of Watzlawick, Beavin, and Jackson (1967) for their extraordinary work *Pragmatics of Human Communication* whose ideas contribute to a large part of this chapter.

**Using Trance as a Metaphor
for Communication**

While this book is not directly about hypnosis, a common theme running throughout is the concept that our world is our own creation and a result of how we perceive and put labels on our experiences. The concept of trance as something that influences and guides behavior is appropriate here, as it was in Chapter 3 and as it will be in Chapter 15. (And as we shall see common everyday hypnotic trance that can be found in therapies not necessarily defined as hypnotic.) Now we want to continue with the trance metaphor and apply it to the most fundamental aspect of counseling and psychotherapy—human communication.

The basic unit of human communication—an exchange of information between two people—is usually called a transaction. However, because of all the implications and various ways messages can be used to influence or may be distorted because of personal histories and different perceptions, I like to change the spelling of the word to "trance-actions" to reflect the power that can be contained in human communication transactions.

FUNDAMENTALS OF TRANCE-ACTIONS

Trance-action

A *trance-action* can be defined as any exchange of information between two people, both verbally and non-verbally, which is affected by the context in which it occurs and the cognitive map of the receiver and sender. Remember that each trance-action also contains conscious and unconscious components thereby adding to its complexity. Virtually all behavior that occurs between two individuals can be seen as a trance-action. We begin with a very simple illustration of a single trance-action.

Man: *"Could you tell me the price of this shirt?"*

Clerk: *"It's $28.50."*

The above is a simple single trance-action. The exchange is one of information, and the context permits this kind of exchange and little more. In our analysis of trance-actions we have two major components—the man's question and the clerk's response. But even in this simple trance-action of which we know little of the history and experiences of the participants and a little about the context (a department store), we can glean something about the trance-action. The man does not command the clerk. He uses a permission word: "could." He might have said, "Let me have the price of this shirt" (more of a command) or "Why doesn't this shirt have a price on it?" (a response with criticism).

Notice how a simple question trance-action can generate different interpretations on the part of the receiver.

Wife: *"Do you know what day it is today?"*

Husband: (Defensively) *"No,...should I?"*

For this trance-action we can say that the wife has asked a simple question, but it apparently puts pressure on the husband. The husband is defensive because it appears he may have forgotten an important date (e.g., "Is it our anniversary?" "Is it her birthday?").

Notice that the question may simply be a question—that the wife may simply want to know, "Is this April 4th—I have a doctor's appointment on the 4th."

As these examples show, even simple trance-actions are complex and rich in information. And they become even more complex in the context of the counseling and psychotherapy setting because each participant is more sensitive to what is being communicated.

Let's look at a more complex trance-action between Carl Rogers and the client, Gloria, in the film, "Three Approaches to Psychotherapy":

Gloria: *I know your answer, but what I want you to do is tell me what to do. Tell me whether I should say something to her or not. But I'm afraid you're just going to let me stew.*

Rogers: *No, I don't want to let you stew, but I don't feel it does any good for people to do what others think. They have to decide what's best for themselves.*

In this trance-action, Gloria is making a statement and a command. She is saying "tell me what to do," and she also is trying to influence Rogers to do what she wants by implying this is uncomfortable ("Let me stew."). Rogers' trance-action counters with his own philosophy, "I don't feel it does any good for people to do what others think," and support "No, I don't want to let you stew."

Rogers' trance-action would fit into the category of "advice" since he is actually telling her what to do which is "decide for yourself."

Context of Trance-actions

Situational Context. The context in which a message occurs helps give meaning to the message and contributes to the trance-action. (See Chapter 7.) In the previous example, Rogers and Gloria, although making a film about counselors for educational purposes, are in a situational context which is seen by Gloria and Rogers as a "helping context." One person, the counselor, is seen as the helper, and this context defines what behaviors are permitted by each participant. Gloria also sees this context as one in which she is the person who is there for help.

Rogers helps confirm this situational context by leaning forward and using non-verbals which confirm Gloria's ideas about the situation. The setting also confirms this with chairs being placed facing each other and with close but comfortable proximity (approximately three feet).

Belief Context. Gloria correctly predicts that Rogers is not about to give her advice. Part of her trance-action is based upon the context she finds herself in—talking to a Rogerian counselor whose model she understands does not include telling people what to do.

SOME FUNDAMENTAL RULES
OF TRANCE-ACTIONS

The following are basic to an understanding of trance-actions that take place between clients and counselors and are directly related to the human communication process. An exceptional analysis of human communication is presented by Watzlawick, Beavin, and Jackson (1967), and some of these ideas are adapted to the analysis presented here.

Rule Number 1. Impossibility
of Not Communicating

Is it possible to not communicate?

Usually, when I ask this question in class, some students say, "Sure! It is possible not to say *anything.*" Then when I ask them to demonstrate *not communicating,* they find it hard to do. They immediately sense that if *all behavior* is seen as some form of communication and not just verbal behavior, then to not communicate is impossible. We must see non-verbal behavior as communication, because so many of our verbal messages are qualified by the non-verbal aspect.

During my first year out of graduate school, I attended a workshop for crisis counseling. During one session, the group facilitator asked, "Is it possible to 'not communicate.'" We thought about it and someone then demonstrated by walking out of the room and closing the door behind him. But was this not communicating? I don't believe so. It was surely communicating something. Perhaps the person wanted to stop communication with the group, but that is still a message—it's still a communication. Whenever we have two or more people together, always some message is being exchanged between the two.

Assume you get on an airplane and sit next to someone who has his/her eyes closed. Is this person communicating? Certainly—it's perhaps "I'm tired, and I don't wish to talk with anyone."

Watzlawick et al. (1967) have said that a basic rule is that behavior has no opposite, that is non-behavior does not exist, and if we see communication as behavior then it follows that one cannot not communicate. Whether someone is active or inactive, using words or is silent, messages still are being transmitted.

But you might say, "Well, what if the message I send is not successful? What if it is received differently than I intended?" Certainly this is possible, and in fact happens all the time. This is a separate issue and one with which we are concerned. Yet, it does not change the fundamental point—that communication did take place. People were engaged in a trance-action, but the message one wanted to send was not received.

In fact with some people who are having problems almost all their messages are distorted at some level and this is a major cause of their difficulties. Here is an example:

Wife: *"I see in the paper that the new movie with Meryl Streep is at the Plaza. It's supposed to be very good"* (wife's message is asking indirectly to be taken to the film).

Husband: *"Why don't you see if the Smiths would like to go?"* (The fact that he would go also is unstated, but implied.)

Later during an argument:

Wife: *"You never take me anywhere, even when I ask"* (referring to movies).

Husband: *"You never asked me to take you."*

This example occurs frequently—people do not always communicate fully, and they also assume a great deal which also leads to distortion. An important role of the counselor is to clarify and be an expert communicator.

In summary:

1. All behavior is communication.

2. To not communicate is impossible.

3. All trance-actions follow this rule.

4. Whether the message received was the one communicated or not, a trance-action still occurred.

Rule Number 2. Humans Communicate Verbally and Non-verbally

Humans are the only animals which have evolved an elaborate and complex system of communication which includes verbal and non-verbal forms. Other animals use mostly non-verbal methods. The interaction of the two systems by humans adds to the richness of the communication. For good counseling, an analysis of both is necessary.

Digital and Analogic Communication. At this time, largely because of computer terminology, people have been using the words "digital" and "analog" to refer to verbal and non-verbal forms of communication respectively, and this distinction is a useful one.

An *analog* is the earliest form of communication, and for us it will be used to refer to non-verbal communication. An analog stands for something—a drawing of a cat, for example, is the analog for a four-legged creature with tail, whiskers, and so forth. Words that you read or speak are *digital* forms of communication. The word cat substituted for a drawing of a cat is digital communication. In human development and history, digital communication is the latest developed form of communication.

If you show a picture of a cat to people in various cultures, most would recognize it. If you said or wrote cat in English (digital communicating), people of other languages would not recognize your communication.

However, while analog communication is more universal, cultural differences still exist. Gestures (analog) mean different things in different cultures.

Analogic communication usually takes precedence over digital communication in terms of accuracy. That is, if a person gives two messages, one analogic and one digital, and they contradict each other, the analogic is most likely the valid one. For example, a husband asks a wife if she's angry with him after a spat. And she says "NO!" with a loud voice while she frowns. Obviously the verbal message is inaccurate.

Digital communication has the potential for enormous amounts of messages; words have all sorts of connotations, symbols, and signs. Yet, sometimes words cannot express what we feel. No specific word or phrase will necessarily express what we are thinking and feeling.

Jakobsen in a book by Pomorska and Rudy (1985) pointed to something which we find useful in analyzing our own communication which is that all verbal communications have six factors present if the message is to be operable:

1. addresser (speaker, counselor, or client)

2. addressee (hearer, counselor, or client)

3. code (e.g., language)

4. message

5. context (office, hospital, analogic)

6. contact (psychological connection between speaker and addressee (Pomorska & Rudy, 1985, p. 143)

Since all six factors are present for each message or unit of communication (each trance-action), then messages are always complex. Any change in any one of the six elements can greatly alter the meaning of the communication. Messages received in one context take on different meanings in another. For example, the message, "I like you" in the context of counseling takes on a different meaning than if it is uttered in a new-car salesroom.

Perhaps even more important is the context of the communication system itself. Letters are in the context of words, words in the context of sentences, sentences in the context of paragraphs, and so forth. But verbal communication also lies in the context of analogic communication and each qualifies the other. If a wife asks her husband if he likes her new sweater, and he says yes and then rolls his eyes upward and raises his eyebrows, this greatly alters his verbal message.

Erickson intentionally qualified his verbal messages by varying voice quality or altering his gaze.

**Rule Number 3. All Messages Have
Content and Relationship Information**

The complexities of trance-actions which occur between two people is shown when we look at what Watzlawick et al. (1967) called the "content" and "relationship" aspects of human communication. These become especially important because the quality of the relationship that develops between the client and the counselor affects the outcome of the therapy.

Every communication between two people has two features. One is simply the content which is contained therein. A statement like, "Let's go to the movies" literally taken means "one or more people are invited by one person to go to see a film." The relationship aspect tells you how each person sees himself/herself in the relationship. In this case, if you heard a boy say to a girl, "Let's go to the movies," you would immediately think that they must know each other well enough for him to ask her this.

Control of the Relationship. A basic principle of human communication is that within every communication is a maneuver to control and/or define the relationship. Haley's (1961, p. 7) example helps make this clear: When a boy puts an arm around a girl, he is attempting to define the relationship as one which permits emotional closeness and physical contact. Physical contact is not permitted in our culture with people whom we do not know well. Think how often you have quickly pulled back your leg or arm in a public place when you accidently touched someone. Back to our boy and girl example—the boy has attempted to define the relationship as including amorous behavior. The girl can respond by accepting this (by snuggling closer) or by rejecting it by saying "No." Interestingly, in human communication the following can happen: She can verbally say no, but at the same time snuggle closer. In this sense, no matter what the boy does, she will be in control while he may believe he is. The latter calls attention to another principle of human communication which is listed next.

Humans not only communicate but they communicate about their communication. Haley said, and we already introduced the fact, that this can be done by the *context* in which the communication occurs. For example, a boy's defiance of a mother's command may be quite different depending upon whether the father is around. A command such as "stop" or an "I love you" can be qualified by a "please" or a changing in voice quality or a turning of the head.

When people do communicate, they do more than just pass information from one to another. This communication also imposes behavior, and it also comments on how the information is to be used.

Let's take a simple statement such as, "Please, get me a cup of coffee." Without the context of the statement and to whom it was stated, we can look at only the information or the content which in paraphrase form says to someone that a beverage of coffee is wanted.

If the statement is said to a waiter in a restaurant, the relationship aspect conforms to what is expected. Someone, whose role is a server in a particular setting, is asked to perform a duty. The waiter in this sense serves a subservient role in the relationship.

Let's take this example a bit further. Assume you are sitting next to the person who asks for the coffee, and you have never seen him or the waiter; consequently, you know nothing of their relationship. If you then saw the waiter smile and say to the customer, "Not serving today; too tired from last night" and then saw the waiter walk away and the customer not disturbed by this reaction to his request, you would immediately see the relationship between the two was not strictly waiter-customer but that the relationship permits joking, and therefore goes beyond what is usually allowed.

Another way of understanding the difference between the content and relationship aspects of each trance-action is to look at it from Bateson's "report" and "command" aspects (Watzlawick et al., 1967, p. 51).

The analogy used is the firing of neurons. Let us say we have neurons A, B, C in a chain, and in this sequence A fires, which sets off B, and B's firing sets off C. B's firing has both command and report aspects to it. B's firing is a report to C that A has fired; C then is the content aspect. But B's firing also is a command to C to fire, and this is the relationship aspect.

In human communication, the report and command aspects indicate how the information passed between two people is to be taken. In the waiter-customer example, the waiter was saying that in our relationship joking is permitted; therefore, I am on equal footing with you.

Watzlawick et al. (1967) explained that all statements about relationship contain in them the following elements:

"This is how I see myself in this relationship."

"This is how I see you."

"This is how I see myself seeing you in this relationship."

We also can see the command report-content-relational feature of trance-actions as *meta communication*—that is, all messages have within them messages *about* the communication. Usually, the meta communication in a trance-action is a communication about the relationship.

Going back to our waiter-customer example with the waiter joking with the customer, his meta communication indicated that his definition of the relationship permitted such behavior.

When a salesman is introduced to a customer as "Mr. James Jones " and begins to call the customer "Jim," this is a meta communication which is attempting to put the relationship on a different and hopefully profitable basis.

Rule Number 4. Relationship
Is Always Being Defined

Earlier, we mentioned that all trance-actions included both the content and relationship features. This should give you the clue that communication between two people always involves a struggle in which the relationship is always being defined.

This is not to say that relationships, even pathological ones, are not stable. The norm is that relationships are quite stable, but within that stability, with each transaction, the two communicators are always testing and perhaps even trying to redefine the relationship and what is permitted within it.

Rule Number 5. All Communication
Events Are Punctuated

How a sequence of communicated events is punctuated or viewed as beginning or ending can change perceptual viewpoints considerably.

I remember a cartoon I once saw. In it an experimenter is observing two rats in a Skinner box, and he is getting ready to press the button as soon as the rat pulls the lever so the rat will receive a food pellet. Since he cannot understand rat language, the experimenter doesn't know rat Number 1 is saying to rat Number 2, "I finally got *him* trained—everytime I pull this lever, he gives me some food." I am sure that the experimenter sees it otherwise—"I've gotten the rat trained to pull the lever for food." So each is punctuating the sequence of events differently.

If we see communication as a sequence of stimulus-response events, we must realize that the response also becomes a stimulus for the next response. So my response to your stimulus which is a question also becomes a stimulus for your response which in turn becomes a stimulus and so forth.

An important aspect of communication is to understand how people are punctuating their communications. In counseling, some counselors may say, "I can't work with this client because of his silences." But the client might be saying, "I don't think I'm getting much out of this because there's too much silence because my counselor doesn't give me much to respond to."

Rule Number 6. All Trance-actions
Have Conscious and Unconscious Components

People reading this find that the information about the content part of each trance-action (the exchange of information) to be readily understandable. After all, this is what communication is about, and any high school student could give you a similar description. A large part of the content component of the message is therefore conscious—it's readily available to us. The content is what we know we are talking about.

However, to most reading this, the relationship component of the trance-action is new information. Most people had never realized that a struggle for the definition of the relationship occurs with each trance-action. Therefore, the relationship component is largely unconscious, and it's automatic.

In reading and understanding this material be sure to remember that the term unconscious is used in an entirely different way than was used by Freud. What we mean, by at least one aspect of unconscious, are behaviors that are automatic and not thought of but can become conscious if the person focuses on them. In this sense, we are closer to Freud's idea of preconscious. But the term we use is unimportant as long as the concept is understood that many of our trance-actions are automatic, yet they contain the relationship component.

While all our relationships have certain restrictions and limitations which, in fact, were "arranged" by ourselves, most of us, while we conform to the restrictions, would be hard put to express them.

Hence, we engage in our daily relationships much like a person in trance does without particular consciousness as to what is permitted to take place, yet conforming to these unwritten rules.

Here is an example. In certain offices I walk in and sit down immediately. In others, I wait to be asked to sit. Some offices I walk into without knocking; others, I would not dare to do so. These simple behaviors come about because of how the people who are in these offices and I have "defined" our relationship, and this includes what is permitted and what is not. The simple behavior of knocking or not knocking on the door extends to more complex activity such as whether or not I would invite any of the people in these offices out to dinner.

OUTCOMES OF A TRANCE-ACTION—BERNE'S RULE

This is probably the most important rule for all communication, and it summarizes all that has gone before in this chapter. Berne's Rule (1966, p. 277) takes into account that when people communicate several simultaneous levels of communication are going on at the same time (verbal non-verbal, digital analogic) and that when a discrepancy occurs between the messages (e.g., words say one thing, gestures say another), the outcome will be determined at the psychological level. That is, if my words say I am relaxed but my non-verbals show nervousness and anxiety, people will respond to my nervousness and anxiety. See Chapter 9 for Erickson's use of this principle.

In the following chapters we focus on these principles and use them to create the conditions for effective therapeutic intervention.

In the techniques that follow, try to remember the points made in the section because they will help you to analyze your communications and other's.

Remember that to not communicate is impossible, that we communicate digitally and analogically and these qualify each other. Moreover, people punctuate their communications differently because of different perceptions. Finally, people not only communicate, they communicate about their communication.

ACTIVITIES

1. Look at people's communication in everyday situations.

    a. At a supermarket, how do clerks communicate verbally and non-verbally?

b. How do professionals communicate?

c. How do strangers communicate in various means of public transport?

2. Look at digital (verbal) and analogic (non-verbal) communication closely during two conversations per day.

a. Do the verbal and non-verbal messages go together? Note discrepancies.

b. If discrepancies are present, what do they mean? Which messages (digital or analogic) seem more real?

3. Examine how people qualify verbal messages with context, non-verbals, other verbal messages.

a. Notice how TV commercials use context to qualify messages, e.g., showing men in an outdoor sports scene for beer commercials. Notice how radio commercials use context.

4. Examine at least two situations where you and one other person are punctuating a sequence of communication events in a different way.

5. Content and relational messages. Observe the dialogue in which you engage with a friend. After the dialogue is over, carefully write down one set of trance-actions that you remember especially well. Then try to analyze what is the content featured and what are the relationship features.

6. Relationship information. To help focus on the relationship feature of any trance-action, ask yourself the following questions:

   a. How do I see myself in this relationship (e.g., one down, an equal, a non-equal)?

   b. How do I see him/her seeing me in this relationship?

7. What aspects of "trance" can you find in your own trance-actions with the following:

   a. Strangers

   b. Close friends

   c. Relatives

   d. Service people (e.g., clerk, salesman)

REFERENCES

Berne, E. (1966). *Principles of group treatment*. New York: Oxford Univ. Press.

Haley, J. (1961). *Strategies of psychotherapy*. New York: Grune & Stratton.

Pomorska, K., & Rudy, S. (Eds.) (1985). *Roman Jakobsen: Verbal art, verbal sign, verbal time*. Minneapolis, MN: University of Minnesota Press.

Watzlawick, P., Beavin, J., & Jackson, D. (1967). *Pragmatics of human communication: A Study of interactional patterns, pathologies, and paradoxes*. New York: W. W. Norton.

CHAPTER 14

LAYERS OF COUNSELING: ESTABLISHING THE CORE CONDITIONS

Within this chapter are presented a variety of counseling techniques to be incorporated into your own personal style and within the context of the basic communication rules presented in Chapter 13.

ESTABLISHING A CONTINUUM OF CHANGE

In the previous chapter we introduced the concept of "trance-action" as the basic unit of communication between two people. We also used the trance metaphor to call attention to the fact that in communication each transaction (trance-action) has with it the potential of affecting the receiver of the message in some way, based upon the receiver's own perceptions, history, and experiences.

Listening to an audio tape of a counseling session or reading a verbal transcript of one, we hear a natural flow or stream of responses made by the counselor and the client. The same natural flow occurs in ordinary conversation. We break this stream of interaction into small units or trance-actions so that we can more fully study the various forms of trance-actions we will be utilizing.

If we look at each trance-action separately, we see that a large variety of responses are open to a counselor at any given time. A few large variety of verbal responses which can be utilized includes paraphrases, open-ended questions, close-ended questions, commands, and stories. All have both positive and negative potential in a counseling session depending upon the context and what is taking place at a particular time. Although some techniques implement the *core conditions* (see chapter 12) better than others and some affect change more rapidly, all can be effective when these techniques are incorporated into the counselor's style and used in combination.

Layers of Trance-actions

Because communication occurs in a continuous stream, and each trance-action is not discrete, a helpful procedure is to look at the communication as occurring in layers; each layer being an entity in its own right but having some dependence upon what it followed from and also having an influence on what follows it. That is, each message does not occur in a vacuum. The counselor's response is a result of the client's message in some way, and the counselor's response will have some affect on the client's message.

The large number of responses utilized by a counselor in a counseling session also may be seen as occurring in layers. Each response made can be seen as a very thin layer, and each layer builds upon another to create a continuum of change. No formula or particular order is used. The sequence depends upon experience and preference, and of course, should be spontaneous. Yet, we can organize the techniques in a way that shows which are more instrumental in building the foundation (or core) layers and those which are more productive after the core layers are set.

Basic Trance-actions
Implementing the Core Conditions

Our philosophy is that in order to utilize the meta (advanced) techniques, foundation layers must occur first. Establishing these core conditions is best implemented by the judicious use of questions which obtain information, paraphrase, summarization, and reflection of feeling. These, although not exclusively, focus on the conscious part of the client and give him/her the opportunity to let down defenses and be more open and receptive as counseling progresses. While still utilizing these basic techniques, the meta techniques (indirect associative focusing, implication, open-ended suggestions, linguistic causality, self-reference, and response amplification) can be introduced. These are called meta techniques because they are advanced in that they are introduced after rapport has been established, and they seem to be effective with parts of the person perhaps not well understood and referred to as the unconscious.

Building Rapport

Later, we shall demonstrate more fully a basic technique used by Rogerian and Ericksonian counselors to amplify the client's ongoing experience. However, in this chapter we introduce four essential techniques to establish rapport—the paraphrase, reflection of feelings, questions, and non-verbal listening.

PARAPHRASE

Paraphrases are preferred responses from a Rogerian point of view. They are preferred because they force the counselor to pay very close attention to the verbal portion of the client's message and to determine the essence of the verbal message—in other words, the counselor must listen. The paraphrase is then accomplished by putting the message in his/her own words and repeating it back to the client.

Paraphrases are preferred also from an Ericksonian point of view. Erickson used a version of the paraphrase (the simple restatement) on many occasions. Erickson also said that gaining rapport was important, and this was accomplished by using the client's own language.

The following list summarizes some of the paraphrases most important functions from both the Rogerian and Ericksonian viewpoints.

Paraphrase Functions:

Rogers

1. Demonstrates to client he/she has been heard.

2. Helps build rapport.

3. Helps therapist understand client.

4. Increases trust, therefore, client is willing to give more information and feels free to continue.

5. Increases feelings of self-worth for the client.

6. Checks out the accuracy of the counselor's perceptions.

Erickson

1. Helps build rapport by using the client's own words.

2. Establishes a "yes set."

If you have a series of paraphrases which are accurate, you will find that the client gets into a "habit" of responding yes to them; and thereafter a positive set or "yes set" is established.

A Method of Using Paraphrase

To do paraphrasing, we need to pay close attention to the client's verbal messages. Now, we could use simple restatements, but it's best to try to use different words while still keeping the client's verbal message intact.

The following is an example of the simple restatement paraphrases utilized by Erickson:

B: *I just want to know what it feels like.*

E: *You want to know what it feels like. Do you think you are in a trance right now?*

B: *I am afraid not.*

E: *You are afraid not. Now, I am going to touch you on the head.*

B: *I still feel my heart is beating too fast.*

E: *You still feel your heart is beating too fast.*

B: *I want to slow that heart down.*

E: *You want to slow that heart down.*

B: *My circulation is too fast.*

E: *Your circulation is too fast. And what else?*

(From *Life Reframing in Hypnosis.* Rossi, E.L., & Ryan, M., 1985, p. 88)

Erickson used exact or literal paraphrases in the above example, and this is a useful way to start—that is, simply repeating what the client has said—as this has the effect of demonstrating to clients that they have been heard.

However, my preference is to use other words than the client's without distorting the basic message. This becomes easy to do if we think in terms of "sensing verbs." That is, verbs that deal with the senses of touch, vision, hearing, taste, and smell. People usually communicate utilizing one of these senses. With vision, for example, they might say, "I see what you mean" or "I'm looking for an answer" or "It's not clear."

Formula. To do a paraphrase then is a simple matter if one uses the following formula:

1. Pay close attention to the client's verbal messages.

2. Select a verbal message you wish to paraphrase.

3. Identify the sense verb the client is using (e.g., CL: "I don't *feel* I know what I want, what I want to do").

4. Change the sensing verb and repeat it back to the client. "You can't get in *touch* with what you want to do."

Later, as this skill becomes spontaneous, paraphrase can be longer perhaps even a summary, and the words changed can go beyond simple changes of sense verbs.

Paraphrasing is a useful tool, and it can be used often. An interesting note is that in ordinary conversation it is seldom used. Check this out. Pay attention to a conversation you have with someone. Note how seldom paraphrase is used. Use paraphrases also in ordinary conversation, and note how much more information it generates.

In addition, paraphrases are useful in that they help provide a check on the accuracy of the counselor's response. If your paraphrase is wrong, the client is given an opportunity for clarification.

Two examples of paraphrasing follow:

First example

Cl. *I think I'm too bored with my life as it is and thinking of this constantly is making one more confused about what to do.*

Co. *It's puzzling you, life is not interesting but what can I do?*

Second example

Cl. *That's why I like substitute mothers. That's why I like talking to a social worker like you. So I can look like I have a close relationship with someone.*

Co. *Are you saying it's pretend?*

Forms of a Paraphrase

Paraphrase can be made as a direct statement or can be in the form of a question. Paraphrasing in question form is done merely to give the client the opportunity to correct the counselor if he/she has misinterpreted what the client said. In this sense, a paraphrase in question form is more tentative, but it is still a paraphrase. Any response we make can be in any number of forms. In some cases, a paraphrase or some other response may be put in question form but may be done so only to be tentative and give the client the opportunity for clarification.

Paraphrase Tells the Clients
They Have Been Heard

Paraphrasing also satisfies the basic human need of understanding. All people have the need to be understood—this fact is the foundation of counseling.

Listening is the most fundamental skill of any counseling model. How can you help someone if you don't know what they have said. On the other side of the coin, one of the most fundamental needs of all people is to be heard. Most times, when we observe communication between people, we find that understanding is severely lacking.

If you simply say, "Yeah, I understand" or "Yeah, I hear you," I have an idea that I may have been heard, but I cannot be certain. An accurate paraphrase takes out the guesswork. If the paraphrase is accurate, the clients know they have been heard.

Most people recognize the verbals and non-verbals which indicate that they are not being heard,and most of us experience this non-listening many times in our ordinary conversation.

Yet, the need to be understood and heard is still there, and when this is demonstrated, it makes the communication more effective.

When the client gives a particular message, the counselor could nod his/her head and give other non-verbal cues to continue. The counselor could also say "Um-hum," "Yes," or "Yes, I hear you," and these are acceptable responses. But, unless the client hears at least some of his/her messages repeated back, the client will not really know if he/she is understood or being listened to. This is where paraphrase is particularly effective.

REFLECTION OF FEELING

Presently, we find ourselves in an age often called the "Age of Reason." High value is placed on our intellect and the rational parts of our being. For high functioning in our society, a computer-like brain is required to manipulate codes and to decode countless numbers of symbols. Modern living requires reading papers, books, formulas, assignments, listening to instructors' lectures, and so forth.

Most of this kind of processing has been shown to take place (for most right-handed people) on the left side of the brain which is the site of language and is considered to be the rational part of the person.

While we have reached a very sophisticated level of symbol manipulation, this has not come without a cost. Because the rational part of ourselves is so heavily stressed, the other still human part of existence has been pushed back into the recesses. This part I refer to, of course, is the feeling part of personality.

To continue to respond rationally almost exclusively is similar to responding as if our head was cut off at the neck and that we only respond to and manipulate the symbols that impinge on us daily while cutting ourselves off from any feeling.

Moreover, ours is not a culture which permits expression of feeling to begin with, and with modern technology and fast changing of society, we have become more alienated from our own inner voices and feelings than at any other time.

Children are brought up to control feelings. Whereas in the past only boys were taught not to cry; now girls, with the feminist movement in full flower rightfully demanding equal status, are being taught also to not express fear, anxiety, and in general to keep the lid on.

Need to Identify Feeling

Yet, feelings (pleasant and unpleasant, high points and low points) are part of the human experience. Feelings are what make us human and also make our experiences rich in different colors. This point is made very well by the therapist in the film "Ordinary People." His client is a teenager who attempted suicide and now is wanting desperately to control his feelings. At one point, he finally allows himself to feel unhappiness and anger, and the therapist's message is that in order to feel happy, one also must allow oneself to feel the depressed moments.

People do have feelings, and these feelings can become buried and yet they can interfere with our decisions and lives. We can try to push them out of existence, but they remain with us and they build. We don't feel quite right, but we don't know why. This is also the incongruence that Rogers talks about.

A major role then of the counselor is to help clients identify feelings that they have but are consciously unaware of. When this is accomplished, two important counseling processes are put in motion: first, and most important, communicating an awareness of someone's feeling state is an empathetic response (Rogers' concept No. 5 for effective therapy—see Chapter 12) and empathy communicates understanding and this generates trust. This in itself is therapeutic. Second, by identification of unconscious feelings the client becomes aware of and explores trouble spots.

Let me give an example of how feelings can go unrecognized and unresolved but have an effect. The client was a 21-year-old college male whose father had died one year earlier. The student was barely passing his courses. He had little direction and because he and his father had been close, he was still grieving the death of his father. One year of grieving is going beyond what would be considered a normal "period of mourning." After a few sessions, a feeling of anger toward the father was revealed—not a rational anger, because the love was still there, but a feeling of "How could you leave me and mom and the rest of the kids when we needed you." Since the death was unexpected, these now identified feelings had a sort of logic to them. Now in the open, they could be seen for what they were and without feelings of guilt, and a final resolution with the father and a goodbye could now take place.

Identifying Feelings

Whereas the paraphrase can be seen to be made up of strictly verbal material, feeling responses are mostly identified through non-verbal or analogic observations. Feelings are generally shown through posture, eye movement, facial expression, and vocal tone. And non-verbal messages are generally more "truthful" than verbal messages. For example, a loud "No!" in response to the question, "Are you angry?" betrays the literal verbal message.

To identify feelings then requires paying close attention to the client's non-verbals.

Formula. The following formula can be utilized to identify and make feeling responses:

1. Pay close attention to non-verbals.

    a. Look at posture—is it relaxed or tense?

    b. Eye contact—is it direct or does client look away? Do eye contact breaks occur? If so, when? Do they occur with certain subject matter for example?

    c. Voice quality—what is tone like? Is it relaxed or tense?

2. Label the feeling you have identified (e.g., sad, happy, depressed, tense, anxious, nervous, out of sorts, angry).

3. Put the feeling word in a sentence (e.g., "You seem to be angry." "I get the feeling you're not happy."). While it is not necessary to include a reason for your observation, this is a good variation: That is, "you seem to be angry with the way your Father is trying to help you."

4. Say the sentence to the client.

With this formula, be certain you have used a feeling word. Perhaps because we are so unaccustomed to expressing feelings, we have a hard time labeling our own or someone else's feelings. As a result we often take the easy route and use such evaluative non-descript words such as "good" and "bad." While our feelings and emotions are in actuality rich, we usually stick to "feeling good" or "feeling bad." Avoid these.

**Differences between Paraphrase
and Feeling Responses**

While paraphrase and reflection of feeling can be thought of as being exclusive of each other as a way of learning the skills, in reality, however, an overlap often occurs as most counseling skills do.

One useful way to illustrate the separateness of the skills while still showing the overlap is to use the grid developed by Richard Vaughn of the Foote, Cave, and Belding Advertising Corporation (Edwards, 1985, p. 109). Using the grid (See Figure 14.1) we can see that paraphrase lies in the upper lefthand quadrant and feeling responses in the upper righthand quadrant.

Involvement	Think (Conscious)	Feel (Unconscious)
	Paraphrase	**Reflection of Feeling**
High	Dealing with words ideas, the rational part of the person	Dealing with aspects of client's emotions, and feelings of which they are unaware
	Digital communication	May deal with stated feelings but genuine feeling responses are those identified by counselor of which client is unaware
Low	No emphasis on unstated emotion	Focus on digital communication
	No focus on non-verbal behavior	Little focus on words, ideas

Figure 14.1. Grid Utilizing Thinking and Feeling as Aspects of Counselor Responses.

Paraphrase deals mostly with words and therefore is most appropriately seen as occurring in the thinking area. So to do a paraphrase, high involvement in thinking is necessary. Also this grid (the left side of the grid) is useful to identify more exclusively the domain of conscious behavior with feeling falling more in the unconscious area.

While clients are aware of many of their feelings, as we stated earlier, they also are blind to others, and these unconscious feelings are the ones which cause problems. The effective counselor is the one who can use both aspects of the grid: using paraphrases to communicate understanding (high involvement in the thinking, verbal area) and paying attention to the non-verbals to pick up feelings of which the client is unaware (high involvement in non-verbal, unconscious feeling states).

QUESTIONS

Rogerian Use of Questions

In a strict Rogerian sense, questions are seldom used except to obtain new information. This will become especially clear when we see from the Eriksonian view how questions can be used to direct, suggest, and influence.

Rogerian questions usually ask for new information. Hidden implications embedded in Rogerian questions are avoided, although as we shall see, this can be tricky. Rogers seldom asked questions that vary from the types that ask for new information ("How many children have you?") or what the client's feelings or thoughts were ("What would you like to do?").

In order to bring this section into more clear focus, it is best to begin with a distinction between open and close-ended questions.

Close-Ended Questions. Close-ended questions can be answered either by a statement of fact or a yes or no.

Examples:

How old are you?

Are you married?

Do you have children?

Do you go to school?

Are you here to talk to me?

Close-ended questions are seldom used in counseling and therapy because they have a tendency to reduce the session into an interrogation. In the beginning stages of therapy, the counselor is trying to establish understanding and the core conditions. Close-ended questions usually do not facilitate this process because they reflect the counselor's, rather than the client's, thinking.

The following is an example where the close-ended question actually detracts from the counseling process:

Cl: *And it's not that I don't enjoy school or that I'm not putting in enough time, because I am. I study at least two hours every night. It's just that I can't seem to bring my average up in those two courses.*

Co: *Have you talked to the instructors of those courses?*

This close-ended question could be seen as advice (it has a suggestion embedded in it), but it also ignores the client's message of confusion.

Rule. In the initial session or sessions of therapy the counselor's main goal is to establish understanding and the core conditions, therefore close-ended questions should seldom be used.

Open-Ended Questions. An open-ended question encourages the client to say more than yes or no or a statement of fact. Usually open-ended questions begin with such openings as what, who, where, could, would, or why.

Many times we begin a question with could, such as "Could you tell me what happened next?" Now in this case the counselor is clearly asking the client for more information than a simple yes or no answer. However, the client may respond with a "no" answer if he/she either does not want to communicate or just doesn't know.

For our purpose, however, we will label this an open-ended question because the counselor's intention was not one of discouraging talk but of encouraging the client to give an open-ended answer. When we use "could" or "would", we are simply giving the client permission to refuse. In this sense, we are being polite.

What, Where, How, and Why Questions. "What," "where," and "how" usually are good opening leads for open-ended questions. Although exceptions do occur, "what" and "where" questions usually are answered with facts while "how" questions often obtain answers that reveal feelings.

"Why" questions have their own client response pattern. Although "why" is used frequently in ordinary conversation, it is seldom used by counselors because it can engender defensiveness in the client. Because we want our clients to be open and free, we want to avoid making any response that might encourage defensiveness.

Questions such as "Why did you do that?" "Why are you going to school?" and "Why did you buy that?" may on the surface seem in - noccuous, but they ask the client to defend or state an answer to what he/she has done, and this has the seed of defensiveness.

Questions Which Help Build Rapport. Some direct statements can be used to seek new information but remain neutral and are relatively free of hidden directives and implications. These are grammatical statements such as "Please explain further" or "Tell me more about that." These are commands, but they only direct the client to continue explaining or to go into more detail for the most part. While they may be seen as directive because they ask the client to continue to focus in a particular area, they are free of hidden advice and usually free of setting off unwanted mental associations.

Many times I wish the client to continue in a certain area. I may need more information but do not wish to influence or give advice, so I simply say "Go ahead, could you talk more about that." A good example of the use of this device, to obtain more information without influencing the client, is shown in intelligence testing. While giving an intelligence test, examiners must make certain that they do not give cues to the testee while still giving them a chance to answer fully. Many times testees will give a partially correct answer, and the examiner must use questions which do not contain hints about the correct answer. For example, to the question,

"What should you do if you find an envelope in the street that is sealed and addressed and has a stamp?" If the testee says "Pick it up and read the address," the examiner cannot say, "Would you take it anywhere?" which gives the suggestion of responsible action. Questions such as, "Tell me more about that," allows a more complete answer without giving suggestions.

Ericksonian Use of Questions

In order to implement the core conditions, the counselor would be well advised to proceed mainly with the Rogerian use of paraphrasing, and reflection of feeling. Nevertheless, Erickson's use of questions is introduced here by way of contrast and to show how easily questions can be used in an indirect way to give advice and influence. Sternberg (Erickson & Rossi, 1979, p. 18) quoted research in memory studies which indicated that when the human brain is questioned it conducts an exhaustive search throughout its entire memory system on an unconscious level. Erickson's intuitive recognition of this unconscious search and activation of mental processes which lies beyond consciousness was at the heart of his indirect approach. He knew that by asking what appeared to be an innocuous question, he could get mental processes activated, and that the client might incorporate or utilize the suggestion embedded within the question.

Questions then can be a useful way of initiating an unconscious search which may ultimately benefit the client. However, an important procedure at this point is to distinguish the Ericksonian method of questioning from the Rogerian. Although we can never be fully neutral in our use of questions, we underline that Rogers' method attempts merely to seek new information. While no one would deny that even an innocuous question such as "How old are you?" can initiate unconscious search, in the Rogerian method questions such as these are not designed for this purpose.

The following forms of questions fit the Ericksonian model. By recognizing these forms with their potential to influence, initiate, and guide behavior, they also give us a check on what we may be doing without intention.

Directive Questions. Any question that has a suggestion embedded in it which did not originate with the client can be considered a directive question. In some therapeutic models, this would be considered advice.

Here are some examples from counseling interviews. Note that in ordinary conversation these appear to be questions. Yet, embedded within them each has a suggestion which the client could consider to be a possible course of action the counselor wishes them to take. The embedded suggestion is given in parenthesis:

1. Have you thought about dropping the course?
   (Drop the course.)

2. Did you talk to your teacher?
   (Talk to the teacher)

3. Did you consider going to another physician?
   (See another physician.)

4. Don't you see how that is not what you really want to do?
   (Don't do that.)

5. Are you going to take the course now?
   (Take the course now.) (Could be—Don't take the course now—depending upon voice inflection.)

As we have shown earlier, communication takes place in a context. In the context of counseling, implication takes on additional power because the counselor or therapist is seen as someone who is an expert. When this is added to the perception that people go to counseling for answers, then we have a fabric which adds to the possibility that many messages will be seen as implying a directive to the client. In this framework, the question "Have you thought about divorce?" which may have been intended as simply obtaining information becomes in the client's perception as "The counselor thinks I should get a divorce." Moreover these implications usually take place outside of the client's awareness.

How does one get information and avoid implication? Simply by asking questions that are open-ended and do not contain specific suggestions. With someone who is having marital problems, the questions could be: "Could we explore what you have been doing?" "What have your most recent thoughts been?" "What do you wish you could do?" While all of these have the implication that something should be done, none have specific suggestions.

In summary, questions are useful to obtain information, but a distinction needs to be made between a Rogerian use of questions which is neutral and an Ericksonian use of questions which may have the intention of setting off in the client associations which result in implication and suggestions for behavior.

NON-VERBAL LISTENING

Listening non-verbally can be seen as communicating to the other person's unconscious that they are being heard. How often have you been in a conversation and the other person non-verbally (looks away, poor eye contact, fidgety) gave you the impression that you were not being listened to? We have internal monitors or sensors which give us these cues, and we may change what we are saying because of the cues we are getting. Seldom do we ever hear someone say, "Hey, you're not listening to me!"

To communicate listening non-verbally, use the following as guidelines:

1. Relaxed posture. Leaning forward in our culture communicates listening. However, you need to use the posture that is comfortable for you.

2. Good eye contact. Not staring, but maintaining contact with the other person's eyes.

3. Absence of distractions and being fidgety.

   a. Avoid looking at watch

   b. Drumming pencil

   c. Taking notes

ACTIVITIES

1. Practice each of the techniques described in this chapter.

    a. Try paraphrasing in ordinary conversation and notice the effect it has.

    b. Try asking exclusively open-ended questions or close-ended questions.

    c. Notice suggestions (advice) embedded within many close-ended and open-ended questions.

    d. Notice non-verbal aspects of listening in various situations, e.g., notice how people stop conversations non-verbally by "pulling away." What other clues give away a person who is not listening but is nodding his/her head as if not listening?

2. Make a list of feeling words. Use these feeling words to describe behaviors observed.

3. Observe differences between verbal and non-verbal behavior in everyday interactions.

REFERENCES

Edwards, B. (1985). *Drawing on the artist within.* New York: Simon & Schuster.

Erickson, M., & Rossi, E. (1979). *Hypnotherapy: An exploratory casebook.* New York: Irvington.

Rossi, E.L., & Ryan, M. (1985). *From life reframing in hypnosis.* New York: Irvington.

CHAPTER 15

HIDDEN HYPNOTIC COMMUNICATION IN ROGERIAN THERAPY—META TECHNIQUES

One of Erickson's major contributions to the field of psychotherapy and the communication process between the client and the counselor was his observations of the power of words and how they influence people in ways that may be outside of awareness. Even careful counselors can influence clients in ways that lie outside of the conscious awareness of either party. Interestingly, this kind of subtle influencing can occur more frequently with Rogerian or person-centered counselors, who usually adhere to a non-advice-giving approach, because of the climate generated by the Rogerian style. We will focus more intently on how to use these *hypnotic* moments in Chapter 16. For now we stress that the context of counseling itself provides a setting which encourages the receipt of advice and that language can influence and affect attitudes and behavior. We call this hypnotic because usually the effect lies outside of conscious awareness. A study of how language can influence thus serves two purposes:

1. It helps focus on how our seemingly innocuous communications can influence.

2. It provides a rationale for selecting communications which are open-ended so the client can select his/her own "solution."

In a seminal article written in 1976 (see Chapter 9), Erickson and Rossi detail Erickson's theory of how trance is induced and suggestions are utilized by the client. Since this process is important to all counseling (as we shall show) a detailed explanation and its relationship to counseling follows. In this chapter, we combine the work of Erickson and Rossi, Bandler and Grinder, and we focus on three techniques: indirect associative focusing, implication, and open-ended suggestion.

ERICKSON'S MULTILEVEL COMMUNICATION

To understand Erickson's multilevel communication process and its implication for theory in general, one must first explore Erickson's use of "context theory" in human communication. His idea, supported in research (Jenkins, 1974), is that when messages are understood, the general context of the message is what establishes meaning rather than the individual or structural units. For example, in any given message (oral or written) which someone wishes to communicate, the choice of which sentences and words are used are endless and arbitrary, almost any number could be utilized. Overall, the general meaning of the sentence is registered in consciousness. The individual structural units (words and letters) that make up the words are obscured and "forgotten."

To make this point one only has to listen to a newscast or read a passage and focus on each structural unit rather than to listen for the overall message. When the focus is turned to the individual pieces that make up the message, it becomes apparent that all that is retained is a few words or letters while the message itself is lost.

Thus two levels of communication are in each communication: (1) the overall or general message that registers in consciousness, and (2) the individual structural units (e.g., words and letters) which register in the unconscious. That the individual units are processed unconsciously is supported by the fact that individual units have to be understood at some level in order for the message to be decoded. For more information on unconscious processing, see Chapter 4.

Individual words used for a particular message may have individual associations that can be reorganized in the unconscious and result in an additional meaning or feeling depending upon the listener's associations with these words. This point can be illustrated with a personal experience.

For a period of time, I had been spending three mornings each week using weights in the weight room at the college where I teach. I had not done one exercise but was familiar with it by way of watching others do it. It was done in the corner of the room and was called "corner row" where a bar with weights on it is lifted toward the exerciser's chest as in a rowing motion. A sign caught my eye for about four mornings which I read without even registering much of a conscious meaning. However I received a pleasant feeling every time I read it while doing my exercises. The sign read: *Do Not Use Bar In Corner To Do Corner Row.*

At least four separate mornings I read this with its accompanying pleasant feeling without any conscious awareness. I did observe something was happening. Then it occurred to me that "corn" and "corn row" are individual units of this sentence and have their own meaning. I don't know why but for some reason the image of corn and rows of corn is a pleasant visual to me.

Ericksonian Language

Because Erickson knew the subtle way words can affect people, his use of language was exquisite—it was precise and muscular without any fat. I once spent a morning in Phoenix at the Erickson Foundation watching Erickson on a videotape doing therapy. He was in a group session, and in addition to the usual interactions with members of the group, he was telling stories. After more than two and one-half hours of viewing the video, it suddenly occurred to me that Erickson's language had been so precise I could not recall a stammer, a stutter, a "you know" or an "uh." In reviewing other tapes, I kept this in mind and tried to look for the common errors in speech we all make, but few, if any, were present.

Erickson knew what he wanted to say—but he also knew the many different ways and meanings each of his words and sentences could be taken by the client. He knew each client's history was different, and because of this any interpretation of words also would be different.

Thus, Erickson "invented" the indirect and multilevel methods of communication. He knew when people communicated they did so on the basis of multiple levels. The different levels go beyond the usual dichotomy of verbal and non-verbal communication (digital, analogic) and extend the verbal into such categories as implication, linguistic causality, and indirect associative focusing.

These linguistic methods have vast implication for therapy because they occur naturally in all people's language. What made Erickson so effective was that he carefully studied these linguistic methods and used them to affect change in his clients. Since these linguistic devices do influence, an important procedure is to recognize them and know how and what effects they can have—otherwise, the influencing occurs without the therapist's awareness. This is doubly important for a Rogerian therapist who may want to abstain from influencing.

The most important process which cuts across all other linguistic processing is indirect associative focusing—hence, we present an extensive discussion of it.

INDIRECT ASSOCIATIVE FOCUSING

At some point during dinner, I can usually tell which direction the conversation will go. If my seventeen-year-old daughter starts talking about one of her friends, my ten-year-old son will usually follow with a story about his friends. If Tracy talks about school subjects, Anthony usually follows with a story about something that happened to him in school.

You have probably had similar experiences. Introduce a topic—the movie you saw last evening—and invariably, whomever you are talking to will begin to talk about the movie they saw recently.

Many other examples could be given, but the experience is usually the same: topics introduced by one person spark, *indirectly, associations* linked to that topic by other people listening to the first person.

Erickson used to say if you want to get your client to talk about his mother, then talk about *your* mother. Technically, what is happening in these situations is an automatic sequence of mental activity. In human communication, words and phrases said by one person result in personal associations of these words or phrases in another person. Knowledge of this mechanism, called *indirect associative focusing* by Erickson, can greatly aid the counselor. Many examples can be presented. Erickson said:

> I can get anyone of you to think about your school by saying "University of Wisconsin." I can tell you I was born in the Sierra Nevada Mountains, and all of you will know where you were born. You think about that. I speak about my sisters, and you think about yours if you have some—or think about not having sisters. We respond to the spoken word in terms of our own learnings. Therapists ought to keep that in mind. (Zeig, 1980, p. 70)

> If I want you to talk about your family, the easiest approach and the one least likely to arouse resistance is for me to first talk about my family. (Erickson & Rossi, 1979, p. 386)

What occurs in human communication is a sequence of events in which messages are interpreted and understood by directly relating them to the message receiver's ongoing experiences.

Making Sense Out of Messages

People must make sense out of messages almost every minute of every day. In order to do this, one must continually call on past experiences to help make sense out of the messages. With language, the process of analyzing words and paragraphs takes place at a subconscious level.

Bandler and Grinder, (1975a, 1975b) pointed out that in everyday communication, we use a set of language processing strategies which help us to make sense out of the words and sentences people use.

Each sentence in natural language has a *surface structure* (the way the sentence sounds) and a *deep structure* (referring to the actual meaning). For example, in the sentence, *"The door was broken,"* the surface structure is the representation of the actual sounds made or the letters making up the words that are written. More important for our example, is the deep structure which the person recovers to make sense out of the message. In this case the deep structure reveals "someone, in the past, broke a door with something."

What is important to notice is that not all parts of the deep structure occur on the surface. For example, "Someone broke the door and with something..." does not appear in the surface structure but does appear in the deep structure.

Technically in language schools this is called "transderivational search." However, we shall use "indirect associative focusing" to refer to this process which more readily describes what happens when messages are exchanged in counseling.

The sequence of events goes as follows:

1. The person hears a well-formed sentence. (This is the surface structure.)

2. The person understands the meaning of the sentence at a deep level, but the meaning has no relevance to him/her.

3. The person activates a search for additional deep structures which are relevant to his/her ongoing experiences.

The whole process of recognition, sorting, and selection of words takes a fraction of a second. Emanual Donchin of the University of Illinois, a leading researcher in the field of cognitive psychology has done a great many studies using the evoked potential, a sophisticated brain wave measure, to track the timing of the mind's operation. "In our research we find the mind recognizes a word within the first 150 milliseconds of seeing it. But nothing shows up in awareness as the subject reports it for another 150 milliseconds or so, if it shows up at all" (Goleman, 1985).

Using Personal Background As a Helper

Indirect associative focusing shows us that when a person hears a message (especially a general one without a specific reference) at an unconscious level, the person exchanges the general reference to a specific and personal one. This message is then analyzed against a background which is most relevant to the individual's personal experience.

Therefore, if you start talking about your mother, your school, or your girlfriend, then I make an unconscious search from my personal experience which exchanges your mother for my mother, your school for my school, and your girlfriend for my girlfriend. These exchanges then help me to make sense out of your message. Humans need a common reference point so that they are talking the same language.

Think how difficult it would be if we did not have these common reference points. For each concept, idea, or thing that was introduced by one person of which the other person did not have prior knowledge the first person would have to go into a very long explanation. An example of this is the explanation you have just read of indirect associative focusing—something practically all reading this were unaware of until now. Hence the long explanation.

When someone does introduce a topic or concept with which I am familiar, I begin to recall my own experiences that I have had with that event. This does give us a common ground, and it probably will help stimulate and elaborate the conversation. That is, you start talking about your semester's experiences in a biology class with a good instructor, and I help the conversation along by talking about my experiences in a biology class with a bad instructor, or perhaps if I did not take biology, I may begin to talk about other courses I have taken or perhaps about other good instructors.

Therefore, indirect associative focusing is a method of introducing a particular topic without directly doing so. In a sense, a natural sequence of events is set in motion and the client starts "naturally" talking about something. When a topic is introduced this way, it helps to avoid all the particular negative interferences that occur when the counselor asks directly a seemingly innocuous question which can set off many unwanted associations. For example, a client is talking about financial problems and the difficulty he has making ends meet. This is the first meeting, and the counselor merely wants to find out what solutions have been tried. At one point, if the counselor asks, "And your wife, does she work?" in the context of counseling, all sorts of associations can be set off. The client may see this as a suggestion. The counselor is hinting, "If my wife works, we could solve these financial problems." Or he thinks "I need help—I can't do it on my own." A far better approach in this situation would be to bypass these conscious associations and use indirect associative focusing.

In an oblique way, the counselor might say, "Financial problems for families are quite common these days and equally common are the variety of ways they have attempted to solve them." This will set off the associations of all the solutions that this client (and his family) have tried without directly asking the client to discuss this and without giving suggestions.

Erickson also believed that most clients' resistance resided in the conscious part of their personalities. Many times clients may resist answering questions about specific things. One way to avoid conscious resistance but still obtain information is to utilize indirect associative focusing. Rather than ask directly, try using sentences about other clients or personal references which will indirectly focus the client's attention in the area where you seek information.

Indirect Associative Focusing as a Hindrance to Empathy

My experiences, no matter how similar they are to yours, can never be exactly like yours. My experiences with mother and therefore my concept of mother and feelings toward mother are unique to me. And while our experiences help to give us a common ground to perhaps talk about mother, our reactions and experiences probably are very different. My mother may have been loving but strict; yours may have been aloof but loose with rules. Because of just this small difference, if I try to understand your feelings toward your mother by looking through only my experiences, I will be making an error.

Therefore, as counselors we need to be aware that any personal associations of what the client tells us gives us a background—something to relate to. But to understand them, we need to try to free ourselves of personal associations which can be a hindrance.

IMPLICATION

Psychological linguistic implication is quite common in ordinary language, and our discussion of it can begin there.

Interestingly often we respond to psychological implications in everyday interactions. When we answer the phone caller's question of, "Is Mary there?" with "Just a minute, I'll get her," we are responding to the implication that the caller wants to talk to her. Why else would they call and ask? Often too lazy to get coffee myself, I'll say to my wife, "Is there any coffee left?" This implies, of course, that I want some coffee. Otherwise, again, why would I ask. These are fairly simple conventions. However, implication can be used negatively and make people defensive. "Why" questions usually fit the second category. A simple, "Why did you do that?" with different inflections can have all sorts of meanings. It could be heard as "That was a stupid thing to do!" or "You shouldn't have done that!"

Remember that with psychological implication it is the person's own associations which are being stimulated (usually at an unconscious level), the speaker is only providing a stimulus. And perhaps more importantly because of this, *everything* we say has implications. The therapist must be alert to this to realize that all his/her messages can be taken in ways that may not have been intended. So, to begin a study of implication, we examine in what other ways our messages may be received.

Questions which seem innocuous on the surface can usually have far-reaching implications.

An illustration of what appears to be an innocuous question but which is in fact something which influences a person's response is shown in the following experiment by Barber, Dalal, and Calverly (1968). When subjects were asked, "Did you experience the hypnotic state as basically *similar* to the waking state?", 83% of the subjects reported they did. However, when asked, "Did you experience the hypnotic state as basically *different* from the waking state?", 72% responded they did. The first question has embedded within it the suggestion that the hypnotic state is similar to the waking state, and subjects respond accordingly. In question two, the alternate situation is given, and subjects again take the suggestion. We can add that people's experiences can be altered, especially when they do not have personal references to fall back upon. In this example, most people had not had hypnotic experiences, so when questioned, they took the cue from the experimenter. For our purposes, any question which has new information in it will not be considered a question but will be analyzed as possibly altering or adding to the client's conscious or unconscious experience.

Questions with Implication

Erickson pointed out that what the therapist says is not what is important but what the client hears. The words used in any sentence have the function of setting off all sorts of personal associations in the client. Questions, although they may appear to be a linguistic device which would be less vulnerable to triggering many different associations, actually can encourage this. Questions seem so innocent. They always seem only to be seeking new information, but they usually have the seeds for the growth of many different associations.

Contrast a question, for example, with a paraphrase. A paraphrase (assuming it's accurate) simply repeats back what the client has said. For example:

CL. *I need help with this decision. There are too many things to consider, and it's confusing.*

CO. *You're confused about this, and you need help.*

In this example, little else can be associated by the client than what they have in fact said themselves.

But what if instead the counselor asked the following question: "This is confusing, and is this similar to how you felt a year ago when you started drinking heavily?"

This is far more than an innocent question, and it has to set off many different associations. Unconsciously, the client is processing the following: "Does the counselor think I am going to start drinking? Do I drink when I need help? Do I drink when I am confused? Is there a pattern to my drinking?"

The following are questions which go well beyond seeking new information and all contain hidden implications which are usually processed outside the client's awareness. The hidden implication is given in parenthesis after the question.

1. Isn't that what you used to do as a child?
(I'm acting like a child; I shouldn't do that; it's childlike.)

2. Didn't you see her before, and it didn't help?
(It won't help if I see her again.)

3. Aren't you happy about what happened to him?
   (I should be happy about it.)

   Contrast the above with, "How did you feel about what happened to him?" (This is a "true" question, and it's neutral.)

4. Were you angry when he said that?
   (I should feel anger about what he said.)

   See Chapter 14 for more examples of questions with hidden messages in them.

Positive Implication

Recognition of the power of implication is especially important for counselors in order to avoid giving advice and suggestions because of inexperience. However, implication can be used positively and still within a Rogerian philosophy when it is used to stimulate the client's own inner resources and creative processes.

A basic version of implication takes the form of the if-then sentences. As with almost all the linguistic devices explained in this book, the human mind accepts as fact things that are associated with each other in a sentence if one part of the sentence is true even though logically no connection is present. The conjunction "and" is a useful device, and it serves as a good example of this phenomena.

Often in a session if I detect the client is nervous, I might say something like, "You're becoming more relaxed as you sit in the chair and talk to me." Usually, the reaction is an immediate dropping of the shoulders and the client sits back in the chair. In this sentence, I have given two statements of fact (sitting and talking) and joined them with a desired behavior (relaxation).

The if-then statement works in a similar way—"If you listen to my questions, you will help yourself to find solutions." In this statement, the client's own inner resources are mobilized by a simple if-then implication: if you listen to the questions, you will begin to find solutions. While this may or may not be true, it is a positive implication which the client accepts.

Why such ready acceptance?—probably because the mind works logically and does not sense that it does not necessarily follow that listening to questions will result in solutions. Erickson believed that such statements bypassed conscious awareness where he believed much resistance to change and habitual patterns of behavior existed.

In summary, questions are used to obtain information, but a distinction needs to be made between a Rogerian use of questions which is neutral and an Ericksonian use of questions which may have the intention of setting off in the client associations which result in implication and suggestions for behavior.

OPEN-ENDED SUGGESTIONS

The cornerstone of the Rogerian approach is that people have within them the necessary resources to help themselves. Erickson's beliefs were compatible with this view. He felt that the therapist's role was mainly to help the client tap his/her inner resources.

Clients Have the Resources to Help Themselves

Originally, Carl Rogers' therapy was called "client-centered therapy" to call attention to the fact that the therapy was for the client. While we may think such a distinction now to be unnecessary, at the time therapy seemed more an attempt to fit the client into some category or theory or to shape him/her to be something other than he/she was. While some are still guilty of this, the humanistic person-centered view, with its focus on client's needs and personal growth, is widely accepted.

Later, the term "non-directive" was applied to Rogers' therapy. The non-directive label was utilized to focus on the idea that clients have the resources to help themselves and should be given the opportunity to do so rather than be given quick readymade answers in the form of advice. This is still an important concept, especially for those who are drawn to Erickson's therapy because it is a therapy which lends itself easily to falling into the error of quick solutions.

While Erickson was more apt to give advice, he still adhered to the idea that clients had the resources to help themselves. He called his model

"The Utilization Approach" to focus upon this idea. The therapist helps clients find and utilize what skills they already have. He also has called his approach "indirect" because he knew that what the therapist says is not what is important but rather what the client hears. The words of the therapist, or of anyone for that matter, function only as a stimulus which set off many associations in the client's conscious awareness and unconscious. The basis of this is explained in the section on indirect associative focusing (the personal associations stimulated are based upon the client's history and experiences).

While Rogerians strongly try not to influence the client, they must be well aware of the fact that they have no control of what the clients hear, and many of their seemingly neutral remarks, as we have shown from an Ericksonian framework, can be taken as influencing or even as advice.

Both Rogers and Erickson felt that providing the right climate was the key to unlocking the hidden resources which lie in the unconscious and the unconscious is a vast storehouse of resources.

One way to tap this storehouse is to utilize open-ended suggestions. Open-ended suggestions allow the person to use their own resources and to use whatever resources are available at that time. Because the suggestions are open-ended, the choice is the client's, and if the client is successful, then he/she will receive the credit, not the therapist.

Open-ended suggestions can be utilized with or without trance. In trance, Erickson felt that the open-ended suggestion was more likely to be acted upon by the unconscious.

The following are examples of Erickson's open-ended suggestions:

1. We all have potentials we are unaware of and we usually don't know how they will be expressed.

2. You can find yourself ranging into the past, the present, or the future as your unconscious selects the most appropriate means of dealing with that. (Erickson and Rossi, 1979, p. 26)

Open-ended suggestion Number 1 is also a "truism" and like many of these techniques, it makes use of implication. Notice how open-ended both suggestions are. The possibilities are endless and to what the outcome could be. Because of the unlimited responses and the fact that no direction is given by the therapist, open-ended suggestions fit very well into Rogerian thinking. Notice however that the use of the word suggestion does imply some direction is given but this usually is a suggestion to use one's potential but no specific instructions are given.

The following are some open-ended suggestions which fit the Rogerian model:

1. The fact you are here shows how interested you are in exploring all the different ways you can help yourself.

2. The unconscious has unlimited potential and you wonder how your's is going to be expressed.

3. Which direction out of the hundreds possible will our session take today?

ACTIVITIES

Activities in Indirect Associative Focusing

1. Notice how indirect associative focusing occurs in everyday conversation.

    a. Introduce a topic without introducing it (e.g., talk indirectly about film, television, a relative, illness and see how the people you are with indirectly associate).

2. Use indirect associative focusing with clients.

    a. Instead of asking direct questions, help the client to focus by indirectly introducing the topic. For example if you want to find out about educational preferences—talk about *your* educational career.

Activities in Implication

1. Negative Implication

    a. Listen to people in ordinary conversation. Memorize three or four statements they make. Analyze the implications of the speaker's communication to the listener.

    b. Write ten questions which counselors may use, and determine what possible courses of behavior or thought the client might feel was implied in the questions.

    CO: *Should we begin our session today by talking about your father?* (Implication: talk about father; father is important.)

2. Positive Implication

    a. Write ten if-then sentences which take on positive implications.

    CO: *If you continue to talk, then your feelings will become clearer.*

3. Tape record some of your sessions with clients. Study selections of these tapes for your and the client's statements for implication. Divide the statement into the conscious implication possibilities and unconscious implications.

Activities in Open-ended Suggestion

1. Make a list of open-ended suggestions which deal with the following topics:

a. School   f. Smoking
b. Family   g. Eating
c. Bringing up children h. Anger
d. Drugs   i. Pain
e. Drinking   j. Working

(e.g., open-ended suggestion for overeating: "You will eat as much as you are willing to cover the next few time periods").

REFERENCES

Bandler, R., & Grinder, J. (1975a). *The structure of magic, I.* Palo Alto, CA: Science and Behavior Books.

Bandler, R., & Grinder, J. (1975b). *Patterns of the hypnotic techniques of Milton H. Erickson, M.D., I.* Cupertino, CA: Meta Publications.

Barber, T., Dalal, A., & Claverly, D. (1968). The subjective reports of hypnotic subjects, 18. *The American Journal of Clinical Hypnosis,* 74-88.

Erickson, M.H., & Rossi, E. (1979). *Hypnotherapy an Exploratory Carebook.* New York: Irvington.

Goleman, D. (1985). Insights into self deception. *N.Y. Times Magazine.* May 12, pp. 36-43.

Jenkins, J.J. (1974). Remember that old theory of memory? Well forget it. *American Psychologist, 29,* 785-795.

Zeig, J.K (Ed.). (1980). *A teaching seminar with Milton H. Erickson.* New York: Brunner/Mazel.

CHAPTER 16

IDENTIFYING AND UTILIZING TRANCE CONDITIONS IN ROGERIAN THERAPY*

Influence of Rapport

Erickson said that "trance is a special state that intensifies the therapeutic relationship and focuses the patient's attention on a few inner realities" (Erickson & Rossi, 1976, p. 19). However, my observations show also that the therapeutic relationship is a special state that intensifies trance.

---

*A version of this chapter was presented as a short course at the 3rd International Congress of Ericksonian Approaches to Hypnosis and Psychotherapy, Phoenix, Arizona, December 7, 1986.

That trance can intensify the therapeutic relationship, that special state unlike all other human interactions, is an important observation. But in this chapter we also show that the therapeutic relationship can be observed as a special state that encourages trance and focuses the patient on a few inner realities.

Trance Elements in Non-hypnotic Therapies

Lankton and Lankton (1983) were among the first to recognize that trance elements can be generated in therapies that have not been defined as hypnotic in nature. They wrote:

> We speculate that all effective therapies, hypnosis or otherwise, involve the same elements of indirect suggestion and hypnotic trance phenomena. This psychological level of communication directs the framework of trance phenomena and ultimately the understanding and experiences conveyed. We expect that this situation is true with all or nearly all "normal" communication. (p. 241)

Now by "effective therapies" they can only be referring to the common elements or core conditions found to cut across all effective therapies. These are the elements of trust, warmth, genuineness, acceptance, respect, and positive regard. It has been shown that these elements (referred to as the *core conditions*) are common to all effective therapies. Note that these elements are most characteristically Rogerian or person-centered counseling rather than those used by cognitive behavior oriented counselors/therapists who tend to direct attention toward specific changes in behaviors and/or cognitions (except of course in cases when they use generalization and relaxation imagery) (Gunnison & Renick, 1985).

Core Conditions and Trance Development

Person-centered (Rogerian) oriented counselors place high emphasis on the relationship and on understanding how the client perceives the self and the world. As the relationship becomes more therapeutic, clients perceive counselors as genuine, caring, and so forth. In other words, the core conditions are present and a strong connection develops (Gunnison & Renick, 1985). According to Erickson: "Actually the development of a trance state is an intrapsychic phenomenon dependent upon internal processes and the activity of the hypnotist serves to create a favorable situation'' (Erickson, 1980, p. 151).

Erickson also described trance state as having many kinds of connections and depicted hypnosis as colored by "rapport." Rapport is really Erickson's word for empathy, and Erickson was aware of the importance of the presence of the core conditions to induce hypnosis (Erickson, Rossi, & Rossi, 1976, pp. 58-59). He felt that the best means of focusing attention was to recognize and acknowledge the patient's current ongoing experience—the here and now. He felt, as did Rogers, that when the therapist labeled the experience the patient was grateful and open to whatever else the therapist had to say. Acknowledging the client's reality made them more open and receptive.

However, an important point here is that at this level of building rapport, Erickson used the client's own vocabulary and a form of paraphrase which is a prominent Rogerian technique. Erickson felt that at this level his approach was similar to Rogers' client-centered approach (Erickson & Rossi, 1979, p. 51).

We repeat the following quote from Chapter 12 which clearly demonstrates Erickson's recognition of the use of empathy in therapy and hypnosis:

> The most effective means of focusing and fixing attention in clinical practice is to recognize and acknowledge the patient's current experience. When the therapist correctly labels the patient's ongoing, here and now experience, the patient usually is immediately grateful and open to whatever the therapist may have to say. (Erickson & Rossi, 1979, p. 5)

Importance of Trust in All Therapies and Hypnosis

Not surprisingly, we find elements of trance in Rogerian therapy when we realize that the important element of trust is a necessary ingredient for all therapy. Later in this chapter, we shall cite dialogue in one of Rogers' own counseling sessions which clearly demonstrates the development and use of momentary trance. Hypnosis simply will not occur if the client does not trust the hypnotist. What Erickson taught us was that to hypnotize someone you must be in tune with their internal feelings and frames of reference and feed their feelings and thoughts back to them. When this feedback is accurate, they of course feel understood and trust develops. As a consequence of this they are more likely to allow some control to go to the therapist and to experience a trance state. Trust is the cornerstone of Rogerian therapy and trust is developed through empathy and identifying the client's internal frame of reference. Individual differences aside, Rogers and Erickson advocate the same thing: build trust by observing the client, identify frames of reference, and then feed this back to the client. Rogers calls this empathy; Erickson, rapport.

Erickson's Use of the
Paraphrase to Induce Trance

The following example shows the use of paraphrase by Erickson to build trust when beginning an induction (excerpted from *Healing in Hypnosis,* Rossi, Ryan, & Sharp, 1983, pp. 144-146):

E. (to subject on stage) Now I really don't know anything about you, your hypnotic history or what you have learned.

E. Now you have never seen me induce a trance. How do you think I go about it?

S. I don't know.

E. You really don't know. Do you suppose there is any important thing to do about inducing a trance: (paraphrase and question with implications gets information on what client expects).

S. Well, maybe a light touch to my hand or arm.

E. So you think there should be physical contact. (paraphrase) Now one of the things that we all learn from childhood is that it is possible to communicate by a nod of the head, by turning the head from side to side. Do you recognize that you may be in a light trance, and just let your hand slowly touch your face and take a deep breath and go much more deeply into a trance. That's right, close your eyes. (S's eyes flutter.)

E. Now why don't you open your eyes and rouse up.

S. I don't know.

E. You really don't know, do you, in what way did I touch your elbow differently? (paraphrase with question)

S. I just felt I should open my eyes.

E. You felt you should open your eyes. Now why did your arm go up (paraphrase) (pause) you have no answer. Are you awake right now?

S. I think so.

E. You think you are, you're sure about that? (paraphrase)

S. Yes.

The paraphrasing in this dialogue has acknowledged the client's experiences and in so doing builds trust and rapport while the follow-up questions were comments on the experience that lead the client.

Indirect Patterns of Communication and Trance

Recognizing that influential trance moments occur becomes important as we realize that while some of the communication patterns in therapy are direct and specific, many are indirect, ambiguous, and open to various interpretations. As we showed in Chapter 15, even careful counselors may influence clients in ways that are outside the awareness of either party (Gunnison & Renick, 1985). Therefore, an important responsibility for all counselors is to be aware of what trance is. We begin with a definition of trance and follow with ways to utilize it.

Common Everyday Trance

In addition to interpersonal situations which actually encourage the development of trance, trance behavior is also a common thing, and it occurs daily in everyone. Reading a book or watching T.V. and becoming absorbed by the characters or involvement in a sports activity and losing track of time are just a few of the examples of what Erickson referred to as common ordinary trance. People exhibit trancelike behavior when they enter an elevator and stare at the numbers. I often have seen students during a lecture get a faraway look in their eyes. Before studying Erickson, I thought the students were simply not paying attention. Now I see this as a form of common everyday trance usually stimulated by something in the lecture or the room.

Rossi (1982), in an interesting article, speculated that trance occurs for each of us periodically through each 24-hour cycle because of the ultradian cycles which occur every 90 minutes or so and during which our bodies slow down and we go through a natural rest period. Rossi speculated that Erickson knew of these periods and often waited for them to occur before he began trancework. Since the body will naturally go into a trance, all one has to do is observe the signs and then just guide and amplify them.

Therefore, we have in addition to those times when the core conditions result in momentary trance the phenomenon of naturally occurring trance during the 24-hour cycle, and this of course can happen during the therapy hour.

Definition of Therapeutic Trance

Trance used to be conceptualized as a blank state during which an individual was easily programmed. But now the realization is that this blank state idea is misleading. Individuals retain their own personalities during trance. Hypnosis has been defined in many ways and for our purposes the following seems the best:

> Therapeutic trance is a period during which the limitations of one's habitual frames of reference are temporarily altered so that one can be receptive to more adequate modes of functioning. While the experience of trance is highly variable, the overall dynamics of therapeutic trance and suggestion could be outlined as a 5-stage process: (1) fixation of attention (2) depotentiating habitual frameworks (3) unconscious search (4) unconscious processes (5) therapeutic response. (Erickson & Rossi, 1979, p. 14)

Erickson also considered hypnotic trance to be a state of heightened internally concentrated awareness that had its less specialized correlate in the form of common everyday trance which most people experience intermittently as a matter of course throughout the normal daily shift in consciousness. He saw hypnosis as a state of consciousness in which ideas are better communicated and exchanged in a manner superior to normal waking state consciousness. Moments of receptivity can occur during a formally induced trance or during common everyday trance as attention is fixed and absorbed in a matter of great interest. Therefore, trance can be an invaluable therapeutic aid. However, in order to use trance, you must recognize it.

Recognizing Signs of Trance

Many visible signs of trance exist and learning to recognize them and the variety of them is essential. Erickson often pointed out that to do hypnosis, you have to recognize what it is. In Figure 16.1 (adapted from Erickson & Rossi, 1979; Rossi, 1982) is summarized the most common trance indicators and behavioral changes that can occur in trance.

A study of these signs and recognition of them as they occur alerts the therapist that a therapeutic (trance) moment is occurring. The therapist also can use the information to increase the response or reflect empathy.

PHYSIOLOGICAL

Altered heart rate
Altered blood pressure
Slowed pulse (acute observation of veins in neck)
Breathing change (respiration slows, breathing becomes
    shallow)
Swallowing
Lack of startle response

MOTOR BEHAVIOR

Comfort, sitting in a relaxed position
Blinking (slows)
Eye Contact—defocused (or in response attentiveness
    may engage therapist)
Reorientation of body after trance (change in seating
    position)
Body movement slow, economy of movement
Facial features smooth and relaxed
Vocal change—voice quiet, slows
Eyes (dilate, blinking, closure)
Reflexes slowed

COGNITIVE BEHAVIOR

Loss of sense of time (client has sense of time
    moving quickly or it slows)
Autonomous inner experience, engaged in inner search
Literalism (word phrases taken literally, consciousness
    is engaged)
Amnesia

Figure 16.1. Common Indicators of Trance (Adapted from Erickson &
Rossi, 1979, p. 11, and Rossi, 1982, p. 24).

Response Attentiveness

For the beginner, the easiest way to begin to recognize and utilize momentary trance behavior is to look for what Erickson and Rossi (1979) described as response attentiveness, where the client is showing very close attention to the therapist.

Response attentiveness is recognized when the client shows the following:

1. focused eye contact

2. open and receptive body language

3. attitude of interest and expectation

4. quietness of body (catalepsy)

5. acceptance of suggestions (Rossi, 1982)

Utilization of Momentary Trance—Amplification

During these moments—many times ignored even by the experienced therapist—the client may be engaged in an internal search, and unconscious processing may be occurring. (See Chapter 13 and 14.) Alert to these moments the therapist can utilize them by only slight alteration of his/her existing style. Even if the therapy has not been defined as hypnotic, one could amplify what seems to be occurring.

Even in ordinary conversation one can note those momentary pauses when the other person is quietly looking off into the distance or staring at something as he/she reflects inwardly. This usually indicates internal search and unconscious processing. Rather than ignoring these moments or even intruding upon them when these moments occur, the alert therapist can use them as choice points in therapy to enhance the trance and to build upon his/her hypnotic skills. One could simply be quiet and observe the behaviors, and this may be the choice on some occasions depending upon the situation. However, one could facilitate the inner search by saying "That's right, continue as you are."

As clients become used to these moments through the therapist's use of them, the experiences will lengthen.

The following dialogue from the Carl Rogers section of *Three Approaches to Psychotherapy* clearly shows the client, Gloria, entering what might be considered momentary trance. In addition, we also will analyze Rogers' communications which enhanced this process.

Examples of Hidden Hypnotic Communication
and Momentary Trance from
Three Approaches to Psychotherapy (Carl Rogers)

Client had been talking about feelings and what she would like to do.

1. **Gloria:** "But, I don't know where to go, I don't begin to know where to go. I thought that I had pretty much worked over most of my guilt but now that most of this is coming up I feel disappointed in myself. I really am, I like it when I feel whatever I do, even if it's against my morals, or my upbringing that I can still feel good about me. And now I don't...like there's a girl at work who sort of mothers me and I think she thinks I'm all sweet and I sure don't want to show my ornery side with her...I want to be sweet and it's hard for me to...(Gloria stops in mid-sentence, pauses). This all seems so new again and it's so disappointing."

2. **Rogers:** "Yeah, it's...I hear the disappointing...that here a lot of these things that you thought you worked through...and now the guilt and the feeling that only a part of you is acceptable to anyone else." (Only a part of you is acceptable in a conscious-unconscious dichotomy.)

3. **Gloria:** "Yeah...." (listening intently, eyes defocused)

4. **Rogers:** (Looking directly at Gloria, monitoring her non-verbals) "That keeps coming out..." (This sentence is stretched as he watches her. His communication changes as he sees her drift into momentary trance.)

5. **Gloria:** (Silence. Eyes lower to her right. Ten seconds of silence....)

6. **Rogers:** (Still focusing intently on Gloria) "I guess I do catch the real deep puzzlement that you feel as to what the hell she has to do with what I can do."

7. **Gloria:** "Yes, and you know what I can find Doctor, is that everything that I start to do...impulse that seems natural, to go on a date or tell Pam...I'm comfortable until I think how I was affected as a child, and the minute that comes up then I am all haywire. Like I want to be a good mother so bad and I feel like I am but then there's those little exceptions...."

Later

8. **Gloria:** (Continuing to talk about her sexual relations) "Still I think it's wrong unless you're in love with a man, but my body doesn't seem to agree."

9. **Rogers:** (Eyes focused directly on Gloria) "Sounds like a triangle to me doesn't it...." (Gloria's head tilts, eyes focused directly on Rogers) "You feel that I or other therapists say it's all right, it's natural enough, go ahead, and I guess you feel your body lines up on that side of the picture but something in you says, but I don't like it that way, not unless it's really right."

10. **Gloria:** "Right." (Eyes down. Rogers is looking directly at her. 18 seconds. Gloria takes a deep breath, shoulders rise and fall with it.) "I have a hopeless feeling."

11. **Rogers:** (Shakes head.) "Uh huh."

12. **Gloria:** "I mean there are all the things I feel myself." (Reorients body, arms open up. She shifts body position.) "And I say, o.k., now what?" (Looks down and to the right.)

13. **Rogers:** "And you feel...it is a conflict and it's just insolvable and therefore it's hopeless and you look to me and I don't give you any help and what is it you wish I would say to you?"

14. **Gloria:** "I wish you would say, 'take a risk.'"

To make our analysis of this dialogue easier, we have numbered each of Rogers' and Gloria's responses.

Rogers' first communication in the sequence (No. 2) on the surface seemingly merely acknowledges Gloria's feeling (disappointment) but he also adds a powerful message, "only part of you is acceptable to anyone else." This message has two features: implication and a personality split or dichotomy.

"Only part of you is acceptable" on the one hand sounds as if a negative part may exist but on the other hand it also implies a positive part that is acceptable. By dividing the personality (part of you), he also splits it and this indicates a conscious and unconscious dichotomy.

Notice in No. 3 that Gloria is beginning what could be considered momentary trance. Her eyes are defocused and she is listening intently.

No. 4 shows how intuitively Rogers monitors this shift to trance and he changes his voice inflection and lengthens his words to meet the new conditions Gloria is presenting.

In No. 6 Rogers' use of the words "deep puzzlement" continues the unconscious metaphor begun in No. 2. And the metaphor continues in No. 9, "but something in you says...."

In No. 10 Gloria's eyes go down. There is a full 18 seconds of silence—a very long time in one-on-one communication. She is clearly in internal search and momentary trance.

Her deep breathing and body reorientation are indicators that then she was in momentary trance. No. 12 gives additional cues that she was in trance as she shifts body position.

Watch for similar moments in your own sessions. We now turn to how to specifically use these moments.

Working Trance into Rogerian Therapy

At some point during the initial session I like to say the following to my clients,

> "Part of what we will be doing here is that you will be talking and I'll be listening. At some points I'll tell you what I hear (developing core conditions by use of paraphrase and reflection of feelings). Sometimes what I tell you I hear may be different than what you think you have told me. When this occurs, sometimes we will clarify. Sometimes I'll try to help you to amplify what you have said and perhaps even experience the thoughts and feelings more fully. I may do this in a number of ways. I may ask you to close your eyes and go with the feeling or I may give you cues to help you relax and help you access parts of you that you may not be aware of (conscious/unconscious dichotomy)."

Some variation of this paragraph is used with most clients. Whether the situation is defined as hypnosis or not depends upon each client and what their particular belief system is about hypnosis.

In order to work in momentary trance, I use the following variation of Araoz's (1983) method:

1. Carefully observe client's language and non-verbals. Look for significant words, problems, patterns.

2. Develop core conditions through extensive use of paraphrase and reflection of feeling:

   a. Paraphrase; use the client's language. (See Chapter 13.)

   b. Reflection of feeling, note non-verbals, look for discrepancies. (See Chapter 13.)

3. Make sure you have several pieces of information about the client that can be utilized to develop trance (e.g., interest, abilities, behaviors). Avoid any ritualized and mechanical frame of hypnotic induction. I believe my own development in the use of hypnosis in therapy was at first hindered by becoming dependent on a "formula" technique learned for research purposes.

4. When momentary trance is recognized, amplify.

   a. Avoid standardized induction. Vary your technique with each client.

   b. Use what client is giving you during amplification (breathing, swallowing, words to amplify). For example, if the client's breathing is slow and regular, a simple but effective comment would be: "Your breathing is slow and regular." Another comment would be to observe inhales and exhales and time your comments to when these occur, or just before they are to occur (e.g., "You exhale, and with each exhale you are becoming more relaxed."). In this way you are tapping into the client's system and ongoing experience and connecting it to a desired behavior: becoming relaxed. Earlier, we used the term congruence to reflect when a person is in touch with his/her experience. Congruence also can refer to the counselor being in tune with the client's experience.

c. If appropriate, and you know what you want to accomplish, give suggestions for personal growth.

5. Discuss the experience with the client.

I almost never begin trancework until the session is well into the hour—if I need more time, I use it. Seldom do I feel crowded for time so that I cannot use this approach. Erickson would not stick to a prescribed hour format—probably for the reason of adapting the trancework to when the client was ready, even though this might mean over an hour later. This is also made easier by scheduling clients two hours apart.

ACTIVITIES

1. Look for common everyday trance in ordinary situations such as elevators, bus stations, restaurants.

2. Notice everyday trance moments in ordinary conversations. Think of ways to encourage everyday trance moments when they occur.

REFERENCES

Araoz, D. (1985). *The new hypnosis.* New York: Brunner/Mazel.

Erickson, M. (1980). *The collected papers of Milton H. Erickson,* Vol. I, E. Rossi (Ed.). New York: Irvington Publishers.

Erickson, M., & Rossi, E. (1979). *Hypnotherapy: An exploratory casebook.* New York: Irvington Publishers.

Erickson, M., Rossi, E., & Rossi, S. (1976). *Hypnotic realities.* New York: Irvington Publishers.

Gunnison, H., & Renick, T.F. (1985). Hidden hypnotic patterns: Implications for counseling and supervision. *Counselor Education and Supervision, 25,*1, September, pp. 5-11.

Lankton, S., & Lankton, C. (1983). *The answer within: A clinical framework of Ericksonian hypnotherapy.* New York: Brunner/Mazel.

Rogers, C. (1969). *3 approaches to psychotherapy.* Orange, CA: Psychological Films, Inc.

Rossi, E., Ryan, M., & Sharp, F. (1983). *Healing in hypnosis.* New York: Irvington.

Rossi, E.L. (July, 1982). Hypnosis and ultradian cycles: A new state('s) theory of hypnosis? *American Journal of Clinical Hypnosis,* Vol. 25, Number *1,* 21-32.

CHAPTER 17

THE USE OF SELF-REFERENCE IN ERICKSONIAN THERAPY

In this chapter we introduce a new idea: self-reference or self-reflexivity. Introducing this concept and embedding it in the context of Rogerian-Ericksonian therapy forces us to review and analyze in a new light the concepts discussed in earlier chapters. We hope this approach will help tie some things together. While others have talked about self-reflexivity in a therapeutic context (Frankl, 1963; Watzlawick, 1974), to my knowledge no one has specifically adapted it as a therapeutic technique.

Self-Reference

Self-reference in fields other than therapy is not new, and the concept may appear under the name of *self-reflexivity*. But essentially they are referring to the same thing: the ability of an object, a formula, a sentence or a thing to curl back and reflect upon itself. When this does occur, the result can be simply amusing, or it can result in chaos, or it may cause creativity and spawn new levels of awareness. We, of course, are interested in therapy so we will focus on the creative aspect as well as the usefulness of self-reference as an indirect approach to therapy.

I first became interested in the possible use of self-reference as a therapeutic device after reading about it in Douglas Hofstader's "Metamagical Themas" and seeing the similarity of it in Erickson's work. As we shall see, Erickson used self-reference as a device many times when he used the unconscious/conscious dichotomy. But first we need a thorough discussion of self-reference and how it occurs out of the therapeutic context. Hofstader (1985) defined self-reference this way: "Many systems have the capability to represent or refer to themselves somehow, to designate themselves (or elements of themselves) within the system of their own symbolism. Whenever this happens, it is an instance of self-reference" (p. 7). His extensive and amusing articles about self-reference are educational, and many of the examples used here come from his fertile mind, and the reader is referred to this work. The easiest way to introduce self-reference is to look at some playful sentences.

Self-Referential Sentences

The most famous self-referential sentence is the Epimendes' paradox: "All Cretans are liars." Since Epimendes was a Cretan, how is one to take the sentence? If all Cretans are liars, then the sentence is a lie. Therefore, since Epimendes is a Cretan, then the sentence is false. If it is false, then all Cretans are not liars, so therefore it is true. And so on. Another way of looking at the Epimendes' paradox is the statement, "This sentence is false." The perplexity of these sentences is contained in the element of self-reference—the statement is referring to itself.

What is one to do with the following sentences?

1. Do not read me.

2. Do not read this sentence.

3. Disobey this command.

These three sentences all have the effect of causing a certain uneasiness when they are read. While they are easily understood, they all have a sort of backlash effect when the reader pauses and tries to figure out the perplexity. The pause caused by the perplexity is one of the things that makes self-reference useful in therapy. Remember, Erickson liked to distract the conscious part of the person, and he did so with many devices such as puns to shock and surprise and fixate attention. Like a pun, the self-reflexive sentences serve the same purpose—they shock and surprise. When one is confronted with sentences such as "Do not read me," surprise ensues and attention has been fixated. The peculiarity comes about because we assume, and this takes place unconsciously, that what we say about something should not be part of that something (Varela, 1984). This will be important later when we use self-reference as a therapy tool. But probably more important than the use of self-reference to shock and surprise is the use of it as a model to understand how humans symbolize themselves. We turn our attention to this now.

Self-Reference in Humans

Note that self-reference is a common occurrence, it happens when people say "I" or "me" or when a TV station does a story about television (Hofstader, 1985). With this in mind, we can see that language and humans have ways of referring to themselves or symbolizing themselves.

The fact that humans can symbolize themselves and make self-references is both a reason for the creation of difficulties within a person and also the means by which they can help themselves out of difficulties. Isn't it my own self-doubts that stop me from progressing? Isn't it how I see myself, how I really think I am, that results in depression? On the other hand, isn't it the times when I'm pleased with what I have done that give me great pleasure? Man is indeed a creature of self-reference. In fact, to think of the world of humans where self-reference does not play a part is hard to do.

Another way of looking at self-reference is to realize that in our experience we are both subject and object at the same time. Our perceptions are always perceptions of perceptions (Varela, 1984). Our descriptions are always descriptions of descriptions. We are at once both cognitive and experiential beings, and whatever we experience we cannot step out of the experience and view it—we are both subject and object.

This is an important but perplexing point. Modern Constructionist philosophy (dealt with extensively in Chapter 3) is an extension of this. In that chapter we made the point that reality can never be known, that we *invent* our reality by putting our stamp or interpretation upon it. We can now accept this more readily when we see that we can never step outside our experience—we are always part of it. We can never objectively look at ourselves, because we are the object being looked at. As we shall see this fact has vast implications for the therapist as well as the client.

Before we look at the implication of self-reference in therapy, let me present a few more examples of the occurrence of self-reference in ordinary situations.

Self-Reference in Art

Currently, self-reference is a device utilized in literature, film, and drawings. One is referred to the exquisite engravings of Maurice Escher—many are based on self-reference. In one picture, two hands are seen, each is being drawn by the other. A seemingly impossible situation but a good reference to our own experience of being both the creator and participant of our own experiences.

The popular film, *Back to the Future,* with the actor Michael J. Fox makes use of self-reference in an unusual way: a person goes backwards in time to alter *his future*—an impossible situation made possible by the device of self reference. In the film, Fox, by the way of a time machine is transported backwards in time some 20 years, and in the past he meets his parents before they are married. As it turns out, his interventions into his parents lives in the past results in their marriage and ultimately his birth. Hence we have a person who creates his own life.

John Fowles' novel and subsequent film, *The French Lieutenant's Woman,* are good examples of the current use of self-reference in literature, but they also show how the use of self-reference can result in a newer higher level of creation. The film contains two developing stories, each containing similar and interconnecting elements enabling the viewer to create a third or meta-level story. This latter concept introduces the idea that a self-reference device or technique can be used much as Erickson did to enable clients to come up with their own solution or higher level of creation.

Indirect Self-Reference

Indirect self-reference occurs when the circularity or self-reference is not readily apparent. It is used as a way of giving messages indirectly so that the receiver is unaware of what is happening. As we shall see, indirect self-reference fits a therapeutic model and, in fact, was used often by Erickson because he felt that therapy should be one step removed from the client's awareness.

A good example of this in television advertising is a series of ads to promote Channel 11, WPIX of New York City. The subject of each of these ads is a fictional Channel 11 worker, Henry Tillman, who has been given the job of coming up with a symbol for the TV station which all New Yorkers will recognize. The symbol actually is the twin Trade Towers (present in every one of the ads) which, of course, resembles the number 11. The story of every ad is Henry's search for the ideal symbol. However in the ads he is oblivious to the World Trade Tower idea as a symbol. In each ad, the symbol appears but eludes Henry as his view is blocked, or he is just impervious to his surroundings. One ad, an elaborate dream sequence, shows the Twin Towers and promotes all the programming available on Channel 11 (Yankee Baseball, movies, etc.), but Henry wakes up and the dream is forgotten.

The viewer sees the ads as entertainment (and they are skillfully done), but the ads are ads nonetheless. By virtue of indirect self-reference, everything the station wants to advertise is stated in the ads, but it is done in an indirect fashion. Messages of this type bypass conscious awareness and fall in the unconscious, and this makes them particularly powerful as methods of change.

Creating Newer Levels of Awareness

Remember that Erickson felt that to bypass conscious awareness with all its resistance was necessary in order to help people. But perhaps more important is the idea that this bypassing results in newer levels of awareness which occur in the unconscious at first.

This was wonderfully illustrated by a student of mine. He had been in therapy and now was taking a counseling course from me. In one of his papers referring to his own experience in therapy, he made the following observation which illustrates not only the self-reference position but also how change and higher levels of awareness occur outside of consciousness:

"The final point I'd like to touch upon is his (Rogers) idea of easy alteration (of behavior). There were numerous times when it wasn't until after the event occurred that I realized I had acted differently than before. I never did..still don't..know how those changes came about, but they were some of the most satisfying parts of my therapy. When I tried to *consciously* change my behavior, I couldn't; and it was very frustrating. It is important that therapists recognize this too."

These personal observations illustrate very well how we grow and change without immediate awareness, but as self-referential beings we manage to step out of our experience at a later date and observe the changes we have made.

Before illustrating some specific self-referential therapeutic techniques, let's summarize what we have been trying to communicate:

1. Self-reference is something that occurs quite readily in ordinary life.

2. Humans, because they use symbolic language and think, use self-reference quite often.

3. Self-reference is an illustration of how we are both subject and object of our experiences at the same time.

4. Because self-reference can be confusing and perplexing as in this sentence, "Do not read me," it can be adapted to distract the conscious part of the person. Therefore, messages can be given indirectly when they are embedded in a self-referential context.

5. The most important part of the results of self-reflexivity is the creation of a new higher level of awareness.

Let's now look at some self-referential techniques.

Conscious-Unconscious Dichotomy as Self-Reference

Erickson often used the conscious-unconscious dichotomy in therapy. In addition to statements like "your unconscious knows more than you do," he would say things like, "I had long forgotten that, but my unconscious remembers" (Erickson, Rossi, & Rossi, 1976, p. 288).

He also said, "Now, the unconscious mind is a vast storehouse of memories—your learnings. It has to be a storehouse because you cannot keep consciously in mind all the things you know" (Zeig, 1980, p. 173).

These sentences and others like them were used by Erickson so he could create a dichotomy. The dichotomy then would allow him to bypass consciousness and its resistances. These sentences create confusion because they are self-referential and dichotomous—they refer to the person but at the same time the message is, "I'm not really talking to you. I'm talking to your unconscious." But yet that's still part of me. So it's me. What is hard to handle is that what we say about something should not be part of that something.

Erickson's self-referential statements and stories enabled him to say things to clients with the appearance as if he wasn't saying them. For example, he said, "You don't even have to listen to my voice because your unconscious will hear it" (Erickson, Rossi, & Rossi, 1976, p. 89). The dichotomy (conscious-unconscious) enables him to separate, but still refer to, the person; and he in essence can talk to the person without talking to him/her or say things without saying them.

Take the following sentence Erickson was fond of using, "Your unconscious knows much more about you than you do" (Erickson & Lustig, 1975). This is a variant of self-reference in that it says I both know more and less at the same time. Confusing? Yes, perhaps consciously. And if this was said to us, we probably would pause and try to figure it out. No matter whether we are conscious of its meaning or not, it will still have the effect Erickson wanted. Indirectly, he is saying, you have potential—trust yourself.

Variation of Self-Reference:
Saying Things Without Saying Them

An interesting self-referential phrase that usually gets positive responses is to start out by saying, "I know this is stupid, but..." and to follow the but with the message you want to give such as "I know this is stupid, but have you tried not talking to her when she comes home late?" The "I know this is stupid" acts as a magnet for any negative thoughts or feelings the client may have about the message. After all, you have just said it's stupid. However, the "but" then negates the prior phrase, and the message is then received in a more positive context. For example, I was working with a professional racquetball player to help him improve his athletic performance. He was particularly vulnerable to other people's negative suggestions. On one occasion a player, older and ranked higher, had told him that he was playing well, but the fact that he was playing in a small college town with few good players would hold him back. At one point, I said, "You know this may sound dumb, but I wonder if Tom is saying that to psych you, since you told me he likes to use psych tricks to keep him one up." "No, that's not dumb, I think I see what you mean" was the reply. We then went on and amplified what the implications of such remarks did to his own thinking.

Had I just said, "He's saying that to psych you" would have sounded expert and may have resulted in resistance.

Erickson's Use of Stories
as Self-Reference Strategy

The essence of the indirect approach is that its interventions are always one step removed from the conscious awareness of the client. That is, the prescription or idea for change is never directly told to the client but is given nonetheless in some form and is understood by the unconscious while remaining outside of conscious awareness.

Stories lend themselves very well to this format, and Erickson's use of them was extensive. Stories fall in the self-referential category because stories can have stories within them which refer to themselves and lead to unconscious processes and ultimately resulting in a higher level of thinking and/or solutions.

Stories also can be constructed in a self-referential style which would insure their being one step removed from the client's awareness. For example, the following story can be used by a therapist with clients who may be having difficulty going into a trance. I have amended the story from one of Erickson's. In this way the story actually is a story about a story and is therefore once removed:

> Milton Erickson who was a master hypnotist once had a subject who was having difficulty experiencing deep trance. He gave her the suggestion that she could "learn to go into a trance."
>
> He told her about the experience he knew of a hypnosis subject in another city. A professor had been working with her on some hypnotic experimentation

and he told Erickson, "We tried and tried to have her go into a deep trance and she simply can't."

So the experimenter had the subject essentially make believe she was going into a trance. this is what he said to her: "I told her to open her eyes and just be able to see my hand. Then I told her that her peripheral vision would close down and down until it was limited to my hand. And there were four other sensory areas. And pretty soon she felt something, she could only see my hand, without the desk, or me, or the chair then I told her to come out and go into her light trance. She repeatedly simulated trance until it actually became real." (Rosen, 1982, p. 85)

Erickson's subject listened to that story. She simulated deep trance until it became real.

This story can be used in any number of ways to help clients achieve trance. It is especially effective when it is embedded in an interaction which has seemingly no reference to whether the client will experience trance or not.

Self-Reference as Meta Communication

Self-reference also can be seen as meta communication because what is occurring is communication about what I am communicating. Doing so has the appearance of putting a different frame around what the message is. Nevertheless, the message is still being heard.

This is why the conscious-unconscious dichotomy is useful and can be used to explain if the message has an effect. That is, consciousness is distracted because of the unusual and confusing way the message is presented. Consciousness is rigid and logical and because of this can be easily distracted. But, according to Erickson's theory, the unconscious can make all sorts of associations with messages, and it can act on such a message. (See Chapter 4.)

The following hypnotic induction is based upon self-reference. It is designed to give cues for hypnosis which will be embedded in a seemingly understandable but confusing self-referential style. Some variation of the following is used after rapport has been established and the client shows signs of response attentiveness and/or trance readiness with comments where appropriate. Also the sentences, while almost all exclusively self-referential, are altered to fit what behaviors the client is showing.

Self-Referential Induction

1. What I am saying now will remind you of hypnosis and all the things you associate with it. (Asks client to think of hypnosis without saying to do so specifically.)

2. I am going to say a number of sentences and paragraphs and they will be heard all or in part by you. Now it's not necessary for me to tell you what these sentences mean because at least part of you will know. (Conscious-unconscious dichotomy)

3. For example, it's not necessary for me to say that the last sentence was about part of you knowing and that was referring to your unconscious because you already know that your unconscious mind can be listening to one thing while your conscious mind is listening to something else. (Saying something without saying it.)

4. Now the next sentences I am going to say are going to be about hypnosis and how people respond to it. (Self-referential)

5. For example, these sentences tell that while people become deeply relaxed, breathing becomes slow and regular. No matter how relaxed they become, they can always hear my voice. (Self-referential)

6. The next sentence is about eyes and how peoples' eyes close as they become more and more relaxed. (Self-referential—command for eye closure)

7. Although you know what each sentence means, I am telling your conscious mind so your unconscious mind can listen to what it wants to. For example, the next sentence is about hearing noises outside the room and that you can let the noises wash through. You will continue to relax. (Conscious-unconscious dichotomy)

8. This sentence tells you how you are listening to my voice and feeling the chair against your buttocks while you are becoming more and more relaxed. (Self-referential-linguistic

causality) And it goes without saying that as you breathe slow and regular as you are doing you are feeling a pleasant state of relaxation. (Saying something without saying it—linguistic causality)

9. Now as you continue to relax I could tell you that your eyes are blinking and now are closing and I would be referring to something that your unconscious knows and perhaps your conscious knows. This last sentence was about your eyes as they have closed. (Observes eyes—blinking, closing)

10. Now all the sentences I have used have served as a paragraph recognizable by your conscious mind if it was written. And now I am starting a new paragraph about something which occurred in your childhood. It is about how hard it was to learn the alphabet—the i or is it a j, where to cross the t, the w is an upside down m; which way does the d go, or is it a b?

These sentences and this paragraph are about the learning which you now take for granted. This sentence tells you that all these abilities are in your unconscious. Will you let these sentences be absorbed by your unconscious so your unconscious can do its work? Will your conscious mind recognize that the unconscious is a vast storehouse of learning? (Deepening and regression techniques)

The therapist can continue doing these lines to the desired state and once achieved can continue to use self-referential statements for trancework and reorientation.

I have focused mainly on self-reference from an Ericksonian perspective, because as a therapeutic device it fits into an Ericksonian format. For example, I can easily see how self-reference could be listed in a chart or table listing devices used by Erickson to distract consciousness. It would fit in somewhere between jokes, puns, and stories.

But we would be selling the whole idea of self-reference far short if we saw it only as a device and forgot that it is an important human phenomenon. When we see it in this context, as a way humans think, that they can think about themselves as both subject and object at the same time, we also can see how this self-reflexivity is an important way to look at Rogerian person-centered therapy.

Self-Reference and Client Incongruence

In an earlier chapter we presented Rogers' Six Concepts for Therapy. The second one stated that clients come to counseling because they are incongruent. That is, they are denying and distorting their experiences and as a result are feeling vulnerable and anxious.

Another way of looking at this concept of incongruence is to put it in the context of self-reference. As a being that has the capacity to look at itself a human can easily distort experiences at some point either when the experience is happening or afterwards. While this knowledge alone will not necessarily alter behavior, the important point is that clients recognize this perplexing characteristic of themselves.

Perhaps most importantly is that from a Rogerian perspective, self-reference also gives us a new way of looking at the *immediacy* of the therapeutic relationship, a topic we have left for the closing chapter of this book.

ACTIVITIES

1. To understand the concept of self-reference more fully, write a series of self-referential sentences.

   Examples:

   a. If Milton Erickson had written this sentence, this book would have a better chance of selling itself.

   b. If this sentence isn't about self-reference, then it isn't in this section.

2. Look for examples of self-reference in everyday conversation.

3. Find examples of self-reference in literature, television, ads, film.

4. Notice how people say things by not saying them.

REFERENCES

Erickson, M., & Lustig, H.S. (1975). *Verbatim transcript of the artistry of Milton Erickson, M.D.* (2 parts).

Erickson, M., Rossi, E., & Rossi, S. (1976). *Hypnotic realities.* New York: Irvington.

Frankl, V. (1963). *Man's search for meaning.* New York: Washington Square Press.

Hofstader, D. (1985). *Metamagical themas.* New York: Basic Books.

Rosen, S. (1982). *My voice will go with you: The teaching tales of Milton Erickson.* New York: Norton.

Varela, F. (1984). The creative circle: Sketches on the natural history of circularity. In P. Watzlawick (Ed.), *The invented reality,* 304-323. New York: W.W. Norton.

Watzlawick, P. (1974). *Change.* New York: W.W. Norton.

Zeig, J. (1980). *A teaching seminar with Milton H. Erickson.* New York: Brunner/Mazel.

CHAPTER 18

SELF-REFERENCE AND THE IMMEDIACY OF THE THERAPEUTIC RELATIONSHIP

I'd like to close this book on therapy by relating the concept of self-reference to the *immediacy of the therapeutic relationship* and also to two other concepts introduced in the beginning chapter—those of personal reality orientations (cognitive maps) and the relationship between two people as being its own reality.

A point often forgotten even by experienced therapists is that for all the devices, techniques, and cleverness that are brought to bear in therapy, the quality of the relationship that develops between the client and the counselor is what truly dictates the effectiveness. Without a quality relationship (one built on trust and respect), even the most accurate and clever interventions will be ineffective. Thus, these necessary Rogerian conditions must underlie any Ericksonian intervention. Therefore, from time to time the effective counselor monitors the relationship he/she has with the client—often this has been called *immediacy* of the therapeutic relationship. However, when this is done, immediacy is clearly an aspect of self-reference, and when it is viewed in that context, new insights and dimensions of this important concept spring forth.

Self-Reference and Immediacy

According to Patterson (1974), immediacy refers to the current interaction of the therapist and the client in the relationship. He went on to say that the clients' behavior and functioning in the therapeutic situation is important because it is significant and indicative of their functioning in other relationships outside the therapeutic situation. Therefore, clients learn how they are relating to others in the therapeutic situation, and if they learn new and better ways of relating, this will generalize to other situations. This will take place more readily if the counselor focuses on the *immediacy* of the situation. That is, from time to time the counselor must reflect and comment upon the current interaction that is occurring between himself/herself and the client. This is clearly an act of self-reference. Because it is, it presents unique problems.

Self-Reference, Cognitive Maps, and Relationship as Reality

In Chapter 3, we talked about two important aspects of human thinking. First, that as human beings we invent our own reality—we make some sense out of the world in our own way. Cognitive maps are what guide us, as some people say. Some also have cautioned us that in dealing with perceptions to remember that the map is not the territory. However, if a person acts a particular way because of his/her map, shouldn't we say the map *is* the territory?

Secondly, we also said that as humans our own invented reality falls apart as soon as another human is introduced—then the reality is in the relationship. Two people are interacting, and they are doing so in a unique way. Their relationship and what takes place are unlike any other, and this is a reality. What takes place in this reality has been recognized under certain conditions to be therapeutic.

If we look at immediacy as falling in the self-reference category, we can more readily see why it presents the therapist with a powerful technique but also one which is difficult to learn. It is powerful because it comments on the reality of what is happening right then and the client learns a new more accurate perception of reality—a different one than the distorted one he/she has brought to therapy. Because the therapist is also *part* of that something that he/she is observing, to step out of the situation and observe it may be difficult.

Like an Escher etching, the enigma of therapy lies in its self-referential quality. The therapist cannot totally step outside of the picture and look at it; he/she is always a part of it, but being a part of it is the only way growth and change are possible.

REFERENCES

Patterson, C.H. (1974). *Relationship counseling and psychotherapy.* New York: Harper and Row.

INDEX

INDEX

E

Edwards, B. 225, 232
Ego 20
Eliot, T.S. 100, 112
Emotional bridge 128-9
Empathic understanding 192-4
Empathy
  figure 195
  hindrance 240
Entropy
  definition 66-7
Epictetus 40
Erickson, M.H. v, vi, vii, 1, 3, 11
  17, 28, 31, 39, 42, 47, 55, 58, 64,
  65, 66, 67, 68, 71, 72, 73, 137,
  141, 144, 157, 159, 162, 164, 176,
  177, 183, 188, 191, 193, 195, 198,
  229, 232, 245, 248, 251, 254, 255,
  256, 262, 262, 268, 269, 275
  as myth 9-17
  biography 2-3
  climiate 67-9
  communication abilities 64
  creative thinking 13-4
  goals 71-2
  growth 70-1
  life story 11-2
  myth 10-2
  parallels with Rogers 63-73
  pictorial drawing 7, 186
  popularity 9-10
  similarities to Rogers 63-73
  theory 67
  trust 57
  uniqueness 63-73
Evans, R.I. 64, 66, 67, 72
Experience 23

F

Failure 138-9
Family therapy 172
Feeling
  formula 223-4
  identify 222-3
  reflection of 221-6

Feeling responses
  differences from paraphrases
    224-6
Fezler, W.D. 120, 134
Fisch, R. 93, 102, 112, 113
Fixation
  table 160-1
Focus
  indirect associate 236-40
Formula
  paraphrase 219-20
Fowles, J. 266
Fox, M.J. 266
Frames of reference
  break 139-40
  internal 192-4
  shifting 138-9
Frankl, V. 25, 26-7, 31, 263, 275
  freedom 26-7
Freedom 23, 24-5
  choice 25
  Frankl, V. 26-7
  personal 25
Freud, S. 1, 20, 45, 48
  view of the unconscious 21
Freudians 19
Fromm, E. 25, 31
Functions
  biological 46-7
  unconscious 46-7
Fundamentals
  trance-action 201-3

G

Gance, A. 174
Gemeinschafts gefuhl 30
Genuineness
  figure 195
Gilligan, S.G. 66, 72
Gloria 190, 202-3, 257-9
Goal
  counseling 19-31
Goleman, D. 238, 248
Gombrich, E.H. 33, 40, 42, 81, 84
Gordon, D. 71, 72, 131, 134
Gregory, R.I. 33, 40, 42

ABOUT
THE
AUTHOR

Richard A. Leva, Ph.D.

Dr. Leva was born in 1936 in Schenectady, New York, where he resided until 1963. He received his B.A. from the State University of New York at Albany; his Masters degree from Alfred University, Alfred, New York; and his Ph.D. from the University of Utah in Salt Lake City. He is an Associate Professor of Psychology at the State University of New York-College at Fredonia, Fredonia, New York, and also Director of The Milton H. Erickson Institute of Western New York.

Richard enjoys creating ink drawings (some of which are included in this book), has been a runner for his own enjoyment since 1970 logging over 10,000 miles, is an amateur cook, has been a St. Louis Cardinal Baseball fan since 1946 and is a baseball card collector. He finds great pleasure in listening to music, plays the piano and the guitar by ear, and enjoys world traveling. He is one of the charter members of CIAO (Chautauqua Italo-American Organization), a newly created group dedicated to studying and preserving the Italian heritage and Italian American experience.

Dr. Leva lives in Dunkirk, New York with his wife, Judy, and their two children, Tracy who is seventeen and Anthony who is ten.

About the Author   295